Motorcycle Journeys Through the
Alps & Beyond

Adventures through the Alps, Corsica, the Pyrenees, and Picos de Europa

Fourth Edition

John Hermann

Whitehorse Press
Center Conway, New Hampshire

Whitehorse Press books are also available at
discounts in bulk quantity for sales and
promotional use. For details about special sales or
for a catalog of motorcycling books, videos, and
gear write to the publisher:
  Whitehorse Press
  107 East Conway Road
  Center Conway, New Hampshire 03813
  Phone: 603-356-6556 or 800-531-1133
  E-mail: CustomerService@WhitehorsePress.com
  Internet: www.WhitehorsePress.com

ISBN 978-1-884313-70-7

5 4 3 2

Printed in China ·

WARNING!
Alpine roads and scenery and culture are known
to cause Alpinitis, a disease that creates an almost
uncontrollable urge to return. There is no cure.
The only relief is more Alpine riding, which
results in reinfection.

Dedication

All these roads have been discovered and enjoyed and played on and replayed on with such a wondrous company of friends as any person could hope for.

To ride the roads again, or to write of riding them, or to read of riding them, is to recall those good friends with whom they've been shared. Indelibly etched on my mind with each hairpin, each view, each culinary delight, is the memory of good friends who were there with me. To them, with the hope that they too remember, I would like to dedicate this book.

Until we ride again in the Alps.

This Triumph rider from New York met the "King of the Alps" atop Passo Falzarego. He found the pass using this book.

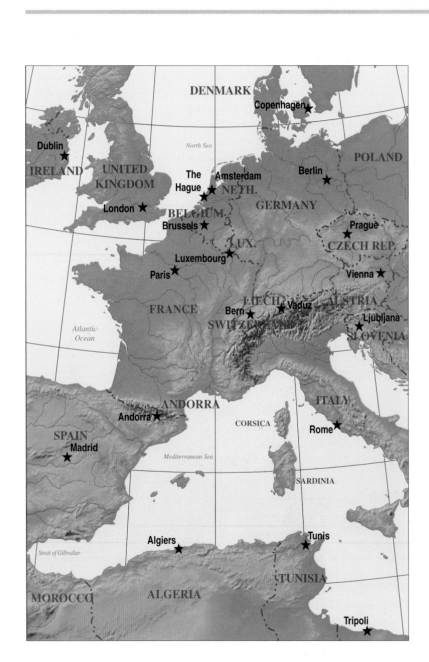

Contents

APPENDICES

Foreword

I've been working very hard since the last edition of this book. Would you believe I've had to spend two trips a year riding into every nook and cranny of the Alps. Terrible work. Everywhere I find riders using the book. Things in the Alps do keep changing. New roads, new passes, new tunnels, new connections, new hotels, and new trips. All here. A motorcycle is a wonderful magic carpet. With it I can explore little gnarly twisting mountain roads and then hop on the autobahn at 100 mph.

Here are my basic rules:

    I. Freude am fahren. Have a good time.

    II. Go where places are good.

    III. Go now.

    IV. Most roads are better shared.

Don't put it off any longer. Head for the Alps.

The author on Austria's Grossglockner Hochalpenstrasse in front of a sign, similar to the one the Grossglockner company sent to his home in California.

Worth a Special Journey

That French outfit, Michelin, produces guide books, red books, green books, maps, as well as lots of other stuff. They have a three star rating system for wonders of all kinds as well as for restaurants. One star advises stopping if you are passing by. Two stars mark spots worth a detour. Three stars: well, three stars are worth a special journey. The Alps are worth a special journey. Or many.

The Alps arc across Europe from Austria to the Mediterranean, cutting off Italy's boot from the rest of the continent. How to get across them? Ancients hacked through gorges and hung roads on mountainsides, finally reaching a pass into the next valley. They must have agonized over which pass to risk, how to carry supplies for a long journey, how to trade with natives, how to defend against bad guys. Ultimately, roads were built for wars and trade. Lots of roads.

Near the Italian-French border, by Nice and Monaco, the Alps leave a rugged coastline and disappear into the Mediterranean. Then they seem to pop up out of the sea again making the mountainous island of Corsica full of roads. Worth a ferry ride.

Now, all those roads make a motorcycle play ground. Spectacular roads. One after another. Scenic overload. Worth a special journey indeed.

Herein one star marks roads much more exciting than average. Two stars mark roads worth that special journey.

BESIDES ROADS

The south slopes of the Alps speak Italian, drink cappuccino, eat pasta at ristorantes and ice cream at gelaterias. They drive Fiats and Ducatis with skill on an amazing maze of mountain roads. They call a road over the mountain a "passo."

The westerly slopes speak French, drink vin, eat French fries and French bread and glace at restaurants with French doors, and drive Citroens and Renaults (say wren oh) over some of the highest roads in the Alps. They call a road over the mountain a "col."

The north and east slopes of the Alps speak German, be they Austrian, Swiss, or Bavarian. They drink beer, eat Wiener Schnitzel (breaded cutlet), Eis (say ice) at Gasthofs. They drive BMWs and Mercedes very seriously on spectacular roads. They call a road over the mountain a "pass."

Be they cols or passos or passes, they all have names and unique personalities: Passo Sella, Col du Galibier, Grimsel Pass, so call it "the Sella," or "the Galibier," or "the Grimsel." Check out each one.

At the Alps' core is Switzerland. That's what we call it in English. For the German speakers who live there, it's Die Schweiz. The French who live there call it Suisse, and the Italian speakers call it Svizzera, while Swiss stamps call it Helvetia. In any language, it's motorcycle central.

When the snow melts, Swiss put away their skis and get out their bikes. Motorcycling is so popular that German-speaking Swiss have a special word for it, "Toff," pronounced "tough." Technically, there are two dots over the "o" in Toff called an umlaut. Not in this book. A Toffler, of course, is a biker. A Gasthaus may have a sign, TOFFTREFTPUNKT, meaning a motorcycle meeting place. Tiny Switzerland even has its own motorcycle press, *Moto Sport Scuweiz*, and *Toff*.

At the very center of the Alps, in Switzerland, is a small village with no traffic but with wonderful roads in every direction: Andermatt. Commercial traffic goes under Andermatt in the long St. Gotthard tunnel.

Most Americans will enter the Alps from international airports at Zurich, Munchen, Frankfurt, or Milano. Andermatt is almost as close to Milano's airport (Mal Pensa) as Milano is. It's an easy ride from Munchen or Zurich.

So why not start there there with roads almost designed and reserved for motorcycle riding with no traffic, at Andermatt? Then ride all the wonderful roads westerly toward the Mediterranean, and then all the roads south toward Italy, and then all the roads to the east? That's what this book does until every road in the Alps is covered with a trip from a base camp, starting with Andermatt.

While you're getting started, here's some good stuff to know.

MONEY
Money is good to have. Almost all countries in the Alps use the Euro. But Swiss use the Swiss Franc. ATM machines will dispense local currency, and all machines will work in English. Credit cards charge in local currency. It all comes back to your bank in dollars.

TOLLS
Autobahns in Germany are free. Autobahns (including some with only two lanes) in Austria and Switzerland require a vignette displayed on the vehicle. Austrian vignettes are available for short periods of time. Autobahns and autoroutes and autostrade in Switzerland require annual vignettes. They are available at most gas stations and auto club offices. Many autoroutes in France and autostrade (plural for autostrada) in Italy are toll. Usually one takes a ticket upon entering, and that ticket is used to calculate the charge upon exiting. At toll plazas it's probably best to use a lane with a human toll taker.

Many toll roads have reduced rates for motorcycles, listed here from west to east across the Alps; Mt. Blanc tunnel France-Italy, 21.10 Euro; Great St. Bernard tunnel Switzerland-Italy, 11 Euro; St. Gotthard and San Bernadino tunnels in Switzerland are free with the vignette; Arlberg tunnel east and west in Austria, 8.50 Euro; Timmelsjoch, Austria, 10 Euro; Brenner Pass in Austria, 8 Euro; Felbertauern tunnel, Austria, 8 Euro; Grossglockner, Austria, 18 Euro; Tauern Autobahn, Austria, 9.50 Euro; Karawanken tunnel, Austira-Slovenia; 7.50 Euro.

Some mountain roads in addition to those above are privately maintained and have tolls.

MAPS AND PLACE NAMES

Europe and the Alps are pretty well covered by GPS. Good maps help, too. Sometimes they don't all agree. You still have to know where you want to go. Every route here has been personally checked on the ground. Names here are local, so it's Wien not Vienna and Lac Leman, not Lake Geneva.

AUTO CLUBS

Some European auto clubs have excellent Europe-wide roadside service for motorcycles. They also sell insurance at reasonable prices for foreign registered bikes. Try the German club, ADAC, which claims to have 1.5 million motorcycle members. AAA membership will **not** qualify for roadside service.

HOTELS

In the Alps, hotels have discovered that motorcyclists are good business. Hotels advertise in motorcycle publications and band together to promote business with bikers. Check www.alpen-motorradhotels.com; www.moho.info; www.trentinoinmoto.com; www.motourrad.com; www.motor-bike-hotels.com.

In addition, gasoline companies and auto clubs put out maps highlighting motorcycle roads and motorcycle friendly hotels. American style motels are not very common.

Best Western has hotels all over Europe including the Alps. No cookie cutters, they're all different, easy to access and make reservations on the internet. A variety of hotels are mentioned in the text for each chapter. Each has a web site.

Time to ride.

Around Andermatt

Andermatt

Draw a straight line across the Alps from Milano, Italy, to Zurich, Switzerland. Right in the middle of that line, in the very middle of the Alps, is Andermatt, Switzerland.

Imagine you and your bike in Andermatt, in the mountain canton called Uri. There are four major Alpine trips over some of the highest passes through some of the most spectacular country in the Alps starting right in Andermatt. Uncluttered by cities, these trips are good in any order, in any direction.

The village of Andermatt, at 1,450 meters, is almost as high as Zermatt. Zermatt has the Matterhorn and hoards of tourists. But Zermatt doesn't have any roads. Andermatt does.

For centuries, Andermatt was the crossroads of the Alps: Italy to the south, France to the west, Germany to the north, Austria to the east. Now, thanks to one of the longest highway tunnels in the world, tour buses and trucks, everybody with fear of heights, and anyone with urgent business, all go through the mountain instead of through Andermatt. Andermatt is for Alpinists and motorcyclists. That's what this book is about—where the crowds don't go but motorcycles do.

The main road through Andermatt was recently repaved in authentic cobblestones with smooth slippery granite slabs for carriage wheels and motorcycles.

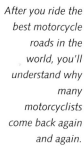

After you ride the best motorcycle roads in the world, you'll understand why many motorcyclists come back again and again.

Park by the cafe of the Hotel Monopol-Metropol in Andermatt. You're on the inside corner of one of the best sweeper roads in the world, the Oberalp Pass. It starts right there at the hotel. The first sweep goes around the hotel. The road continues, arc after arc of smooth asphalt, never straightening out, up the face of the mountain.

In mid-summer, it's light until after 10 p.m., and bikes come from the great cities in the valleys to ride the Oberalp in the evening. The pass is worth several passes. (Mind the decreasing radius in the tunnel, coming down.)

Looking down from the sweepers of the Oberalp, you can see Andermatt huddled in a corner of its mountain-ringed valley, some modern buildings, some shingled chalets, some log buildings, with a Baroque church tower above all. The cobblestone main street has smooth granite slabs for wagon wheels. The street looks ancient, but was brand new in the 1980s.

A hypotenuse bypass leads across the valley from the granite Kaserne (military base) toward the St. Gotthard Pass. A cable car goes from the west side of the village up on Gemsstock Mountain, 1,500 meters above the town. The cog railway weaving around the Oberalp road leads down to a train station in Andermatt, where it meets two other cog lines. This is the land of the Glacier Express train between Zermatt and St. Moritz.

Andermatt has restaurants, gas stations, banks, shops, and the Post, Switzerland's post office, telephone exchange, and bus station. You can dial anywhere in the world from the Post and pay when the call is completed. Just remember that the east coast is six hours behind the Alps, and the west coast nine hours. So 6 p.m. in Andermatt is noon in New York and 9 a.m. in California. All the Alps have daylight saving time. They just start and end on different dates than ours in the U.S. and even than other countries in Europe.

The Post is where all those yellow buses park, the public buses that deliberately motor into every cranny of Switzerland, sometimes towing a baggage trailer and tootling their three-note horn. The horn is supposed to send all other traffic scrambling to get out of the way. Most importantly, the Post sells freeway stickers, called "vignettes," that all vehicles must have to drive on a Swiss freeway, including many tunnels and many two-lane roads that have limited access. Swiss vignettes are annual. The vignette does not substitute for tolls, and there are a couple of toll roads in Switzerland. (Austria also requires a vignette to use the autobahn, although Austria has short term ones, good for a week or a month).

Andermatt's travel bureau is: Verkehrsburo; CH-6490 Andermatt, Switzerland. (In Euro addresses the ZIP comes before the town. In this instance, 6490 is the ZIP, CH is the code for Switzerland.) 41 887-1454; www.andermatt.ch; e-mail: info@andermatt.ch. (Note: The telephone country code for Switzerland is 41 and the area code for Andermatt is also 41. So, calling Andermatt from another country dial two "41s".)

A sampling of the many hotels in Andermatt includes:

The Hotel Monopol-Metropol, on the corner where the Oberalp begins, is a building with an international flavor and a kitchen that blends Swiss and French cooking.

The Drei Konige Hotel (three kings, as in "We Three Kings of Orient Are") is located in the crook of the cobblestone street through Andermatt, right beside a rushing mountain torrent. It's traditional Swiss. The German author, Goethe, stayed at the Drei Konige in the 18th century. It's been updated since.

The Sporthotel Sonne (sun) is a multi-story log building in the village center, with a door that opens directly onto the cobblestone street. It's much more modern than it looks, with a cozy dining room and a garage for motorcycles.

In Switzerland, those proposing to build a new building must erect a scaffolding to show the actual size and shape proposed. Then those concerned can see what view might be affected, and what shadow cast. Such was the case for the Alpenhotel Schlussel in Andermatt. The scaffolding was up for years. But now, there's a brand new hotel.

Find postal and e-mail addresses along with telephone and fax numbers for these hotels in the Appendices.

In any language, Swiss money is called a Franc. Traveler's checks and money can be changed at a bank or at any Swiss train station.

German is the working language of Andermatt, but most locals can speak some English. The waitress may be a Norwegian who spent her last holiday in San Francisco, while the clerk in the sport shop very likely can discuss slopes at Aspen.

One evening, visitors in Andermatt heard band music. Rushing to the balcony, they observed a military band coming down the cobblestone street with a very deliberate drum major. European bands march much slower than American bands at football games. Tum . . . tum . . . tum . . . tum. But this band was in strange uniforms . . . greenish: It was a Russian Army band, in Andermatt, Switzerland, commemorating the 200th anniversary of a battle between the Russian army and Napoleon in the Schollenen Gorge just north of town. Come back in 2099 for another concert.

Approaching Andermatt from the Furka and St. Gotthard, the highway sign clearly illustrates the hypotenuse that by-passes the village.

The bull with a ring in its nose on the yellow flag of canton Uri, the red and white flag of Switzerland, and the bear flag of Andermatt mark the Oberalp Pass intersection in Andermatt.

Besides the Oberalp Pass heading east, three roads lead out of Andermatt. West across the valley beyond Andermatt, the Furka Pass snakes up the mountain. Compared to the Oberalp, it's narrow and tight and irregular. Working up the mountain south is the St. Gotthard Pass. To the north an unbelievable road squeezes down through a gorge called the Schollenen, made by the Reuss River.

Information on road conditions in English can be obtained from Swiss Auto Clubs: ACS (Automobilclub Schweiz); Bern, 31 312-1515; TCS (Touring Club Swisse); Geneve; 22 735-8000; www.tcs.ch.

Trip 1 Furka, Grimsel, Susten

Distance   *About 120 kilometers from Andermatt*

Terrain   *Steep twisting climbs into glacier worlds, three steep twisting descents, plus the narrow Schollenen gorge, mostly modern highway, some tunnels*

Highlights   *Rhone Glacier, Aareschlucht water storm, favorite motorcycle cafes, Sherlock Holmes site, Devil's Bridge and stone, autobahn tunnel entrance, ★Furka Pass (2,431 meters), ★Grimsel Pass (2,165 meters), and ★Susten Pass (2,224 meters), the Schollenen Gorge, Oberaare road, Goscheneralp road, Gen Tal road*

At 2,431 meters, the Furka Pass is one of the higher roads in the Alps. Just a few kilometers from Andermatt, up among glacial peaks and rushing water, it's easy to feel civilization is very far away.

From the Susten Pass road, bikes head up the military road to the base of Steingletscher. Traverses of the Susten Pass in the distance lead to its summit, up right.

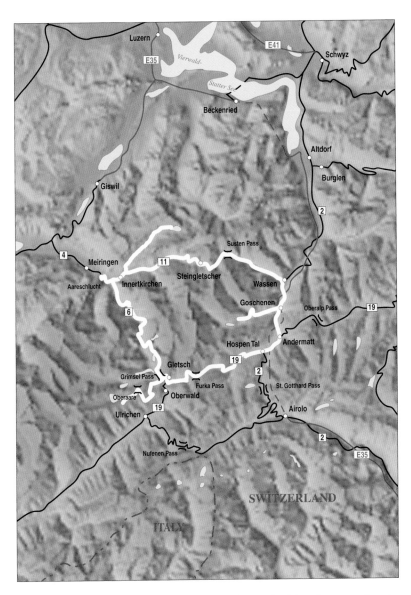

West from Andermatt the road follows the Furka-Oberalp cog train, the route of the Glacier Express, through Hospen Tal, a village with a stone watch tower, and where the St. Gotthard Pass road turns up and south. The cog train and the Furka road continue on west across the valley to Realp where the train enters a tunnel under the pass. (So the Glacier Express folk never see the pass or its glaciers. They ride the train through the tunnel in the dark. When the pass is closed, cars and bikes have to take the train, too.)

Starting up the Furka Pass toward the tiny village of Gletsch, the mighty retaining walls holding the traverses of Grimsel Pass tower overhead. Although this picture is of the Grimsel, the road in the foreground is below Gletsch.

Across the top, on the west side there's a parking lot on the south side of the road. From it there's a magnificent view of the Rhone Valley, called the Goms, and the mass of the Rhone Glacier, and the cantilevered hairpins of the Furka road down below, and the zig zags of the Grimsel Pass road climbing the far mountain, and the lake at the top of the Grimsel, and the peaks beyond, and . . .

Climb down below the edge of the parking lot. Look closely. The lot is atop a gun emplacement that commands the whole scene. It's so well camouflaged that it defies detection just a few feet away.

The westerly side of the Furka is mostly new alignment. Then at one hairpin, you're face to face with the Rhone Glacier. Drive right up to the base of the ice, source of the Rhone River. Water melting from this glacier runs to the Mediterranean at Marseille, France. (Back at Andermatt, all the water was running to the Rhine and the North Sea.) At the glacier there's a parking lot terraced on the edge of the mountain, with an outdoor cafe that's popular with bikers.

Restrooms are down under the parking lot. A tunnel carved into the glacier permits a walk into the blue world inside.

It's only 31 kilometers from Andermatt, across the Furka Pass and past the Rhone Glacier, down to Gletsch, where the Grimsel Pass road intersects and heads up and north. Gletsch is just a couple of stone buildings at the tree line.

Once some American bikers got trapped at Gletsch by avalanches and mud slides on the pass roads. The Grimsel was closed. The Furka was closed. The Goms road west was closed. The stone hotel building had no electricity. But the cog train was running back and forth through the Furka train tunnel. So, the bikers went down below Gletsch to Oberwald and put their bikes on a flat car. They sat on the bikes through 25 minutes of dark tunnel and debarked at Realp over by Andermatt.

The traversing road up the Grimsel from Gletsch leads to hairpins supported by walls of massive stones and offering great views of the Rhone Glacier.

Several restaurants around the lake at the top of the Grimsel (don't ask the lake's name) are popular with motorcyclists. The one farthest north, Hotel Alpenrosli, has a large parking area marked for motorcycles only. It's often full of bikes, while the riders enjoy the sunny restaurant terrace.

Those grey buildings down there are Gletsch, all of it, seen here from the last couple of hairpins on the Furka Pass. Between the buildings is the turn to start up the Grimsel Pass road, seen on the hill above the village.

Just west of the Hotel Alpenrosli (to the left, facing the hotel) is a tiny short road you have to try if it's open—the Oberaare. It looks like a driveway with a traffic light. About ten kilometers long, it snakes up high above the top of the Grimsel Pass and then down to a lake, the Oberaare See. Views are awesome . . . glaciers, snow-capped peaks, icy white lakes, and the ribbon of the Grimsel Pass road winding down north. Traffic is one way at a time, controlled by the traffic light at each end of the road.

It's only 37 kilometers north from Gletsch, across the Grimsel, past the Hotel Alpenrosli, down past dams and lakes and hydroelectric plants and through several tunnels, one of which has a decreasing radius curve, into forests and through meadows to Innertkirchen, where the Susten Pass road heads east. This is countryside known in song and story as the Berner (Bernese) Oberland, canton Bern, the valley of the Aare River. Just a few kilometers below Innertkirchen, the Aare goes through a very narrow gorge called a *Schlucht,* as in *Aareschlucht.* It's a spectacular display of enormous volumes of frothing water. There's a parking lot on a hairpin where a wooden catwalk leads into the water storm.

Just below the Schlucht is the base of the Reichenbach Waterfall, the great cascade where Arthur Conan Doyle had Sherlock Holmes fall to his death in a fight with the villain Moriarty. A marker at the base of the falls says it happened on May 4, 1891. It must be so, because the monument was erected by "The Norwegian Explorers of Minnesota!" The marker is in the parking lot of a

From the Oberalp Pass the whole village of Andermatt can be seen, the whole thing, nestled in the corner of its high mountain valley. The Reuss River is at left, along with the last, lower sweepers of the Oberalp. To the right is the Glacier Express train station, and the hypotenuse road that takes through traffic toward St. Gotthard Pass. In the distance, the Furka Pass road.

The Devil's Bridge

By the freeway entrance to the long tunnel is a giant rock with the flag of canton Uri on it: gold, with a black bull's head with a ring in its nose and a red tongue hanging out. The big rock was moved aside at great expense during freeway construction because:

Long ago, the villagers failed to get a bridge across the gorge. The devil offered to build it in exchange for the soul of the first to cross the bridge. But the villagers fooled the devil by sending a goat across the bridge first. Enraged, the devil hoisted the huge rock to smash the bridge, only to drop the rock when a villager made the sign of the cross.

The rock's still there to prove it. Pictures of the **Teufelbrucke (Devil's Bridge)** abound around Andermatt.   ■

"Klinik." There's a statue of the great detective in the nearby village of Meiringen. (Meiringen and the roads of the Berner Oberland are in the next chapter, Trips 5, 6, 7, and 8.)

Just four kilometers up the Susten Pass road from Innertkirchen there's a dead-end valley to explore, north up the Gen Tal. The turn north seems insignificant, into the woods. Climb out of the woods into high meadows, and come face to face with a toll gate. Past the toll gate, the road climbs steadily about ten kilometers through meadows to 1,835 meters to the Engstlen See where there are a couple of pleasantly sited restaurants.

On the west side of the Susten Pass, a couple of hairpins before the summit, is Hotel-Restaurant Steingletscher named after the glacier on the peaks to the south. Explore the dead-end military road that starts beside the hotel and works its way up to the base of the glacier. Narrow, but mostly good asphalt. Usually there are troops around, sometimes firing artillery. If there's a gate down across the entrance to the road, it may be necessary to buy a ticket at the hotel.

Hotel Steingletscher can arrange accommodations at a Gasthaus way up above the top of the pass. Access to it from the top of the pass is a steep road that passes in front of the restaurant there.

The climb up the Susten Pass from Innertkirchen goes from meadows back up to the land of glaciers. The parking lot at the top of the Susten Pass, surrounded by glaciers, is another favorite motorcycle gathering place. The restaurant has a view terrace from which there's free access to the restrooms below (Euro restrooms are usually marked "WC").

The road on east is a tunnel. Sit on the terrace and try to identify the bikes coming from the east by their exhaust note magnified in the tunnel.

It's 53 kilometers across the Susten Pass from Innertkirchen on the west to Wassen on the east. The east side, east of the tunnel, after a couple of hairpins, is delightful, open sweepers until the final tight curves and tunnels down into Wassen. From the curves, if you can take your eyes off the road, there are views of one of the major engineering feats of the Alps, the four-lane freeway in the gorge of the Reuss River. It connects Zurich with Italy through the St. Gotthard tunnel. The gorge is so narrow and steep that the road is either on a bridge or in a tunnel. Here it's called an autobahn, and it leads to the tunnel under Andermatt, once the longest vehicle tunnel in the world. The tunnel daylights as an autostrada in Airolo (see Trip 2).

It's only a couple of kilometers south, up the Schollenen gorge from Wassen to Goschenen, where the freeway enters the long tunnel, and where the really steep part of the gorge begins. The main line of the railroad goes in a tunnel, too, leaving only a cog line to grind on up to Andermatt alongside the hairpins of the gorge road. (There's a fun dead-end road westerly from Goschenen to a high Alpine dam and lake called Goscheneralp. There's a restaurant at the dam.)

The old Devil's Bridge, the Teufelbrucke, in the Schollenen Gorge affords the best view of the Russian Monument carved in a nearby granite cliff. It commemorates a battle in 1799 when a Russian Army was temporarily trapped here by Napoleon.

Switzerland, like many Alpine countries, has signs addressed to motorcyclists. This one is on Grimsel Pass.

The climb up the gorge toward Andermatt goes right by the Devil's Bridge and another bridge of Roman origin. And there's a spot in the gorge that will be forever Russian. A turn-off near the Devil's Bridge leads down to an enormous carving in the mountainside with script in Cyrillic. Seems it commemorates the Russian army. Defeated by Napoleon on the plains, it retreated south and was trapped in the gorge.

The monument's named after the Russian general, Suworow. Turn into the monument parking lot and continue on down the old gravel road over the old Teufelbrucke. (The road is closed to cars.) The best view of the monument is from this road. (For other Russian monuments in the Alps, see Trip 69, Filzmoos and Tauern Passes, and Trip 74, Three Country Loop.)

A final short tunnel opens out onto the high Andermatt valley. The main road is the hypotenuse bearing right toward the St. Gotthard and Furka Passes. A mini interchange leads into the village, past the vast stone Kaserne, home to much of Switzerland's citizen army. In the village, soldiers patrol around and occasionally roar by in rubber-treaded tanks, or astride an army Condor motorcycle, assembled in Switzerland with a Ducati engine.

Remember the DB-1 Bimota that was on the cover of every bike magazine once? There it was, parked in Andermatt. Tiny, beautiful. Tracked down, the owner allowed as how it had indeed cost a bundle of Swiss Francs. "You could have bought a Harley for that!" The owner reached into a pocket and pulled out a card. He was a Harley dealer.

Trip 2 St. Gotthard, Nufenen, Furka

Distance *About 110 kilometers from Andermatt*
Terrain *Three steep twisting climbs and descents, mostly modern highways*
Highlights *St. Gotthard Museum, a favorite motorcycle cafe,*
concrete-roofed sweepers, in and out of Italian-speaking, cappuccino land,
St. Gotthard Pass (2,108 meters), ★Nufenen Pass (2,478 meters), ★Furka
Pass (2,431 meters)

It's a good sweeping ride up the St. Gotthard to the top, where all of a sudden, it's no longer the St. Gotthard, but the San Gottardo. The south slopes of the Alps speak Italian, eat pasta, and drink cappuccino, even in Switzerland. The old-time hospice at the pass summit has been turned into a museum of the historic attempts to conquer the pass, including the history of the Devil's Bridge. Water here runs to the Po River in Italy, and thence to the Adriatic. A monument out front commemorates aviators' attempts to conquer the pass. Crossing the Alps in early planes was a major undertaking.

Bikes charge out of a hairpin on the Furka Pass that's been modernized by extending it on stilts over space. That's more of the Furka continuing on the left down to the village of Gletsch. The Grimsel climbs the far slope. Finsteraarhorn dominates the horizon.

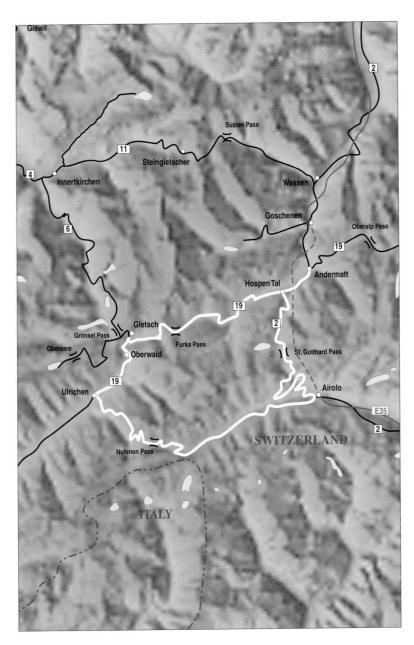

Behind the museum there's a an old cobblestone road down to the south. It's known in Alpine lore as the Tremola, and many feel the urge to try its many rough and convoluted hairpins. Sometimes it's closed to through traffic. The best views of it are from the newer, main road.

The main road down the southern slope of the San Gottardo starts in kilometer-long, covered concrete sheds designed to protect motorists from avalanches. The sheds are open on one side and the road surface is good at highway speed. About halfway down there's a view spot cafe, and lower, some military fortifications. A couple of hairpins are built out in space on stilts.

One of the longest vehicle tunnels in the world, the one that enters the mountain as an autobahn at Goschenen on the north side of Andermatt, comes out on the south slopes of the pass at Airolo as an autostrada, having passed under all these good roads. By following the signs for Passo della Novena (that's what the Nufenen is called in Italian) it's possible to avoid getting involved in the tunnel traffic at Airolo. The Nufenen, a newly laid out road and one of the highest in Switzerland, climbs west out of Airolo.

Often photographed are the three flags flying at the top of the Nufenen, the Swiss flag flanked by those of the two cantons connected by the pass, Ticino and Wallis. Behind the flags, way across the Goms valley, are the peaks of the Berner Oberland, including the Jungfrau. The most prominent as viewed from the Nufenen is the Finsteraarhorn at 4,274 meters.

The cafeteria at the top of the pass is popular with bikers, because the northerly descent, way down into the Goms at Ulrichen, is a wonderful piece of road: good pavement, steep, and full of predictable hairpins.

The monument commemorates the first flights by aviators over the St. Gotthard Pass.

Often photographed are the three flags flying at the top of the Nufenen Pass, the flags of the two cantons united by the pass, Ticino and Wallis, with the flag of Switzerland in the center. The restaurant is just a cafeteria, but its parking lot is a favorite bike stop.

Ulrichen is down in meadowlands, so it's a real climb from it back up and east to Gletsch where the Furka and Grimsel meet. The road passes some military airstrips and the railroad loading ramps at Oberwald, where cars and motorcycles can be driven right onto the train for a tunnel ride under the Furka Pass back to Andermatt. Should you choose this method, just ride onto a flat car and take a seat in a passenger compartment, or maybe sit on your bike. Switzerland claims to be planning a steam cog train using the old abandoned tracks over the pass.

Climbing up to Gletsch from Oberwald the awesome switchbacks of the Grimsel Pass are straight overhead. They've been rebuilt in recent years. There's lots of concrete behind those huge stones.

The parking lot of the Rhone Glacier revealed a bunch of bikes, including a YB-1 Bimota. The rider turned out to be a dentist from Disentis, over the Oberalp beyond Andermatt. "Your English sure is good." "Oh, I teach part time at the University of Illinois!"

Trip 3 Oberalp, Lukmanier, St. Gotthard

Distance *About 154 kilometers*
Terrain *Three climbs and descents, plus a valley run*
Highlights *Oberalp Pass (2,044 meters) and the world's best sweepers, less-traveled Lukmanier Pass (1,914 meters), St. Gotthard Pass (2,108 meters), a taste of Romansch culture, deeper into Italian-speaking Switzerland*

Sweep up the Oberalp from Andermatt into canton Graubunden (sometimes called Grisons in English), where buildings are usually stucco with arches and deep set windows and stenciled decoration. The official language is Romansch. Nobody speaks it, but they print signs in it. The working language remains German. (Elementary school children in many parts of Graubunden are taught in Romansch.)

Across the Oberalp, at a pretty good-sized town called Disentis-Muster, the Lukmanier Pass road heads south. Disentis is famous for a big monastery

There's often motorcycle traffic on the east side of the Oberalp Pass.

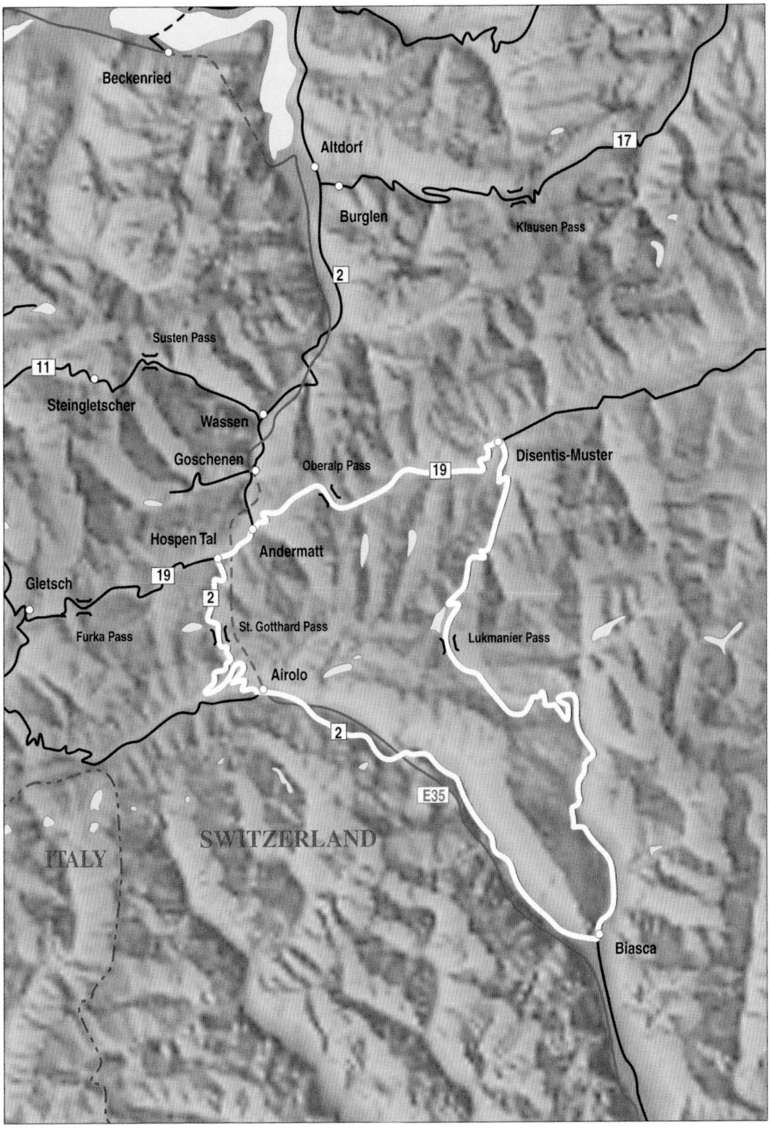

Beckenried

Altdorf

17

Burglen

Klausen Pass

2

Susten Pass

11

Steingletscher

Wassen

Goschenen

Oberalp Pass

19

Disentis-Muster

Hospen Tal

Andermatt

Gletsch

19

Furka Pass

2

St. Gotthard Pass

Lukmanier Pass

Airolo

2

E35

SWITZERLAND

ITALY

Biasca

church visible just above the town. To visit it, you have to park below on the main road and hike up. The interior is sort of Spanish baroque. To head for the Lukmanier, take a sharp right in the middle of the town down across the Vorderrhein River. The sign for the pass in Romansch will be CUOLM LUCMAGN. As soon as you cross the pass, the signs will be in Italian, and the pass will be called Passo del Lucomagno. The pass road is modern all the way to Biasca. There's a functional restaurant at the top of the pass.

A pleasant stop might be the Hotel Olivone and Post, about 18 kilometers down the Ticino (south) side.

The Passo del Lucomagno meets the San Gottardo Autostrada at a town called Biasca.

Biasca is in one of those major valleys that cut deep into the Alps, the Valle Leventina. It's the best route from the great cities of Italy to Zurich, via the long St. Gotthard tunnel. So a lot of traffic is heading for the St. Gotthard (called *San Gottardo* here), and since it's about 35 kilometers north, the autostrada may be the viable route to get there. Just be sure to exit the autostrada at Airolo, or you'll be treated to at least 20 minutes of tunnel behind a diesel-belching bus or truck, all the way to Goschenen.

On the climb up the St. Gotthard from Airolo there are a couple of tight sweepers on stilts out over the valley, with big metal expansion joints that are slippery when wet. A turnout has a little restaurant with a fine view of the can-of-worms interchange squeezed into the valley down in Airolo where the autostrada, the tunnel, the Nufenen Pass and the St. Gotthard Pass roads all meet.

A Kawasaki pulled into the restaurant at the top of the Lukmanier once. The rider was all in white—white leathers, white boots, white gloves. He allowed he worked for Swiss-air. "How do you keep it white?" "Oh, that's my wife's job!"

On long summer evenings, bikers come from the great cities of Europe, not to mention the rest of the world, just to ride the sweepers of the Oberalp Pass above Andermatt.

The Schollenen gorge, with the old road below, and the current road above, is marked by a painting of the devil on the granite.

Often called the Tremola, the old cobblestone road snakes up the south slope of the St. Gotthard (San Gottardo) toward Andermatt. It's been replaced by a sweeping modern road from which this picture was taken, which, in turn, has been replaced with one of the (ugh!) longest vehicle tunnels in the world.

Trip 4 Klausen, Pragel, the 'eggs'

Distance *About 200 kilometers from Andermatt*
Terrain *Tight climbs and descents on narrow, less-traveled roads*
Highlights *William Tell country, a historic highway on lakeshore, Klausen Pass (1,948 meters), Switzerland's little-known ★Pragel Pass (1,550 meters), Ibergeregg (1,406 meters), Sattelegg (1,190 meters), Etzel (950 meters)*

Dash north down the Schollenen Gorge from Andermatt and hop on that Alpine masterpiece, the autobahn, down toward Luzern. In a couple of minutes, you'll be in Altdorf almost at sea level, at least the level of Lake Luzern. Klausen Pass climbs east from Altdorf.

The lake that we call Lake Luzern the Swiss call by the tongue twister Vierwaldstatter See (four forest state sea) after the four cantons of William Tell's day. And we call the country "Switzerland" after Schwyz, one of the four forest cantons.

There's a helpful and well-stocked Kawasaki-Yamaha shop called Gisler Motos at Shattdorf, on the main road just south of Altdorf.

Climbing out of Altdorf on the Klausen, the next village is Burglen, Tell's home, where there's a small statue of Tell.

About halfway up the Klausen from Altdorf on the inside of a 180, there's an attractive hotel and restaurant called Hotel Posthaus Urigen. It's handsomely decorated inside and out and advertises itself as a motorcycle meeting place.

East of the Klausen summit, still in canton Uri, the road crosses a high, mountain-ringed valley called Urnerboden. It's open range populated by cows. Thousands of cows. Signs beg vehicles to stay off the pastures. It's also desirable to dodge cows and cow pies.

The bottom, on the northeast side of the Klausen, is in canton Glarus, with a capital city of the same name. Once down, the road passes through village after village, each with a 50 kilometer per hour speed limit. Recently, Glarus had a cantonal meeting, one of those very Swiss affairs, an open forum, and everyone debated spending millions of francs to build a more modern road around the villages. The new road was voted down. So we're stuck with the slow route through the villages.

Down below the Klausen in the town of Glarus, the road to the Pragel Pass intersects, but the pass is so small and remote that there's no sign for it. Watch for a sign pointing to the left, west, to Klon Tal or Klon Taler See (*Tal* added to a German word means valley).

It's possible to head down out to the high mountains by riding through Glarus to the main east-west autobahn along Walen See. Or, a scenic way is to turn right in the center of Nafels, seven kilometers down stream from Glarus.

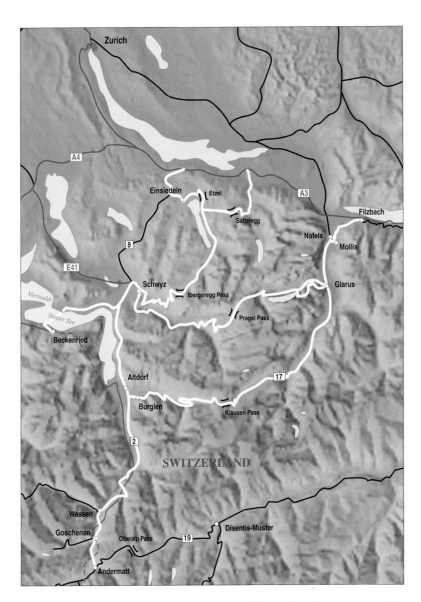

Through the village of Mollis, the road climbs pleasantly to the mountain edge above the lake. At Filzbach there are several hotel-restaurants with fine views down across the autobahn and lake to the mountains beyond. In thirteen more kilometers, the road merges back down with the autobahn.

The road from Glarus up the Klon Tal forks as it starts out of town. The left tine, southerly, is narrow, through the woods up over a summit called Schwammhohe, then back to join the other road at the Klon Taler See.

The right tine is two lanes as far as the lake, Klon Taler See, where there's a modern terrace restaurant and hotel called Hotel Rhodannenberg. The rest of the road over the pass is one paved lane and has a feel like maybe nobody's ever been there. But a long period with no oncoming traffic doesn't mean there isn't a logging truck around the next corner. The asphalt is smooth but has a significant lip on each edge. It follows the lake for several kilometers, where there are triangular warning signs advising drivers to look out for frogs. Across the lake are sheer vertical cliffs of almost a thousand meters. Spectacular. Looks like Lake Louise at Banff in Canada.

Signs along the road with lengthy passages in German say that this part of the road is not open to traffic on weekends. The same signs greet the rider coming from the other direction across the pass at Muota Tal, the valley on the other side. Muota Tal leads down to Schwyz, the town the country's named after. (Heading for the Pragel from Schwyz, follow the signs to Muota Tal, as there are none for the pass.)

At Ibach, next to Schwyz, the main road passes the Victorinox factory, one of the "original Swiss Army Knife" factories. Showrooms have everything for sale. Moto-Center Schwyz is north of the Victorinox factory about 2 kilometers. From Schwyz, the main road back toward Altdorf and Andermatt is called the Axenstrasse because it was carved by ax from the steep cliffs around Lake Luzern, Vierwaldstatter See.

Until recently, the Axenstrasse, hanging on the east side of the Vierwaldstatter See, was the only way around the lake toward the St. Gotthard. Now, there's a four-lane autobahn tunnel through the cliffs on the other side of the lake, where before there was no road of any kind. (Following the lake in the opposite direction, actually west, from Schwyz, there's a ferry across the lake to Beckenried and connections with the roads of the Berner Oberland, Trip 6. There's a good hotel at the ferry landing across the lake.)

A lesser pass, the Ibergeregg, 1,406 meters and heading northeasterly, starts in the middle of Schwyz, by the church. The view over Vierwaldstatter See from the restaurant at the top is great. Little-trafficked and heavily forested, the Ibergeregg comes down by a couple of lakes and a huge pilgrimage church at Einsiedeln, not far from Zurich. The church is of modest historic or artistic interest, but it is big.

Short of Einsiedeln, a one-lane road (with a few meters unpaved) crosses a handsome covered bridge and snakes over a woodsy ridge called Etzel coming down out of the forest to the town of Pfaffikon and to the congestion of Zuricher See.

An even less challenging pass called Sattelegg, 1,130 meters, loops east from the north end of Ibergeregg back toward Zurich See and civilization. Sattelegg has a pleasant restaurant, but an unpleasantly low speed limit.

West of Andermatt

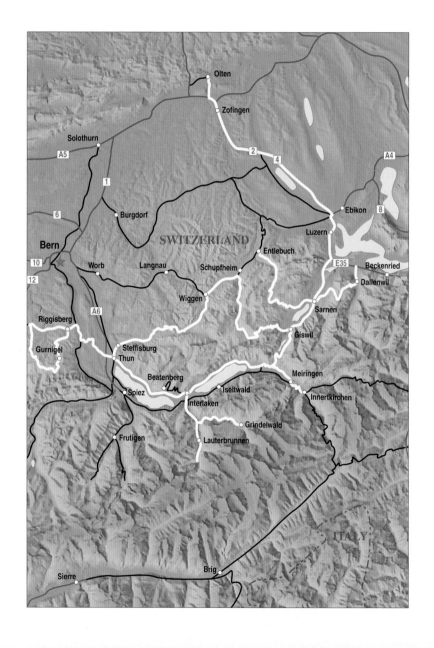

The Berner Oberland

West of Andermatt, west of the Furka and the Grimsel and the Susten, downstream from the Aareschlucht, in the valley of the Aare River, is the town of Interlaken. It's in canton Bern, in the area called the Berner Oberland, the high mountain country south of Switzerland's capital, Bern.

Interlaken is between two lakes made by the Aare River, the Brienzer See to the east and the Thuner See, to the west. It has been host to every guided tour that hits Switzerland. It's the jumping-off place for cog train rides up the Jungfrau Mountain. It's also a great place to buy a Swiss army knife or a watch from Bucherer or a cup of genuine English tea. On one cross street into the old part of town, there's a hardware store (Eisenwaren) with everything from hand tools to Swiss cowbells. The saving grace of this tourist trap town is the public parking in front of most of the shops, and the good riding in the nearby mountains.

From Brunig Pass, there are glimpses of green fields and Lungernsee.

The area is crawling with hotels. There are big ones and little ones, expensive and cheap, in the bigger towns, on lakes, and hanging on the mountainside above little villages.

The island village of Iseltwald, one potential home base, hugs the cliffs on the south shore of Brienzer See. To get there, take the autobahn around the south shore of the lake and take the exit (ausfahrt) onto Iseltwald.

A choice hotel right on the lake where the lake steamer stops is the Strand Hotel. Upon exiting the freeway onto Iseltwald, there's a parking lot for tourists. The road into the village is marked with the international DO NOT ENTER sign. But the little white sign underneath reads to the effect of, UNLESS YOU HAVE BUSINESS. So ride on in and have some business.

Another village with hotels, restaurants, and rooms for rent is Beatenberg, on the cliff hundreds of meters above the north shore of the Thuner See. Follow signs from the north side of Interlaken. From the whole village, there are sweeping views of Thuner See below and the Berner Oberland Mountains beyond, including the Jungfrau. Beatenberg is a good place to catch Alpenglow, the almost hot pink glow of snow covered mountains in the rising or setting sun.

On the opposite shore of Brienzer See from Iseltwald is an outdoor museum called Ballenberg with a collection of farmhouses from all parts of Switzerland. They're furnished and have costumed people working in and around them. There are two entrances (and exits), a lower one near the town of Brienz, and a higher one about halfway up the Brunig Pass. Park and walk in.

Riders grab choice seats on the deck of the Gasthof Gabelspitz atop the Schallenberger in order to keep track of bikes coming and going below.

Moto-Center Thun sports a cafe in front, and huge sales floors of bikes and accessories, with a fine repair facility as well. Bike rentals are available.

A steam cog train climbs from Brienz to a mountaintop restaurant called Rothorn.

On the north bank of the Aare River in Interlaken is Hotel Goldey.

The City Hotel is small and modern with underground parking just off the main drag in Interlaken, behind the post office and across a little plaza from the hardware store.

Right on the main drag in Interlaken is Hotel Krebs with a cafe overlooking the street, but with rooms and parking on the quiet backside.

West of Interlaken, on the south shore of the Thuner See at Faulen See, is the Strand Hotel Seeblick.

Down at the far end of the Thuner See is the town Thun. The Aare River, draining the lakes, rushes through the town below a castle from the Middle Ages. On an island in the river is a Best Western Hotel called Freienhof. There are restaurants and shops along the river banks, and other hotels in the old square facing the old Rathaus (city hall). On through Thun is Moto-Center Thun with bike sales and rentals and service.

Trip 5 Switzerland's Yosemite

Distance *About 60 kilometers round trip from Interlaken*
Terrain *Curving valley roads*
Highlights *Spectacular cliffs, waterfalls, and glaciered mountains*

There's a dead-end valley 12 kilometers south of Interlaken so breathtakingly beautiful, such a joy to behold, that it's worth a detour. It's called Lauterbrunnen, valley of the waterfalls. The valley is narrower than Yosemite, and has at least as many waterfalls, one inside the mountain, called Trummelbach. Trummelbach has a sort-of incline elevator that takes visitors inside the mountain almost to the top. Winding and narrow stairs lead to viewing platforms of the water storm inside the mountain, and then back down to the bottom. Take at least your rain suit jacket. It's possible to stay in the valley. Two hotels are the Schutzen and the Jungfrau. The latter has a good indoor pool.

In Lauterbrunnen, the valley of waterfalls, you can stay right near the base of Staubach falls at the Jungfrau Hotel.

A cable car from Lauterbrunnen goes up to the top of the Schilthorn Mountain to what is reportedly the highest revolving restaurant in the world. You may have seen it in a James Bond film.

The road to Lauterbrunnen intersects with a road into the next valley east. It leads in just a few kilometers to the village of Grindelwald. Grindelwald is pretty touristy, but it's at the base of the Eiger, the mountain face that Clint Eastwood played on in the movie, *The Eiger Sanction.* It's handy to know that the Eiger, another word for "devil," is separated from the Jungfrau Mountain, "the maiden," by a mountain called "Monk."

There are several villages with hotels above Lauterbrunnen and Grindelwald accessible only by cog train or cable car.

There are plenty of hotels in Grindelwald.

A cog train crosses the mountain connecting Grindelwald and Lauterbrunen, stopping at Kleine Sheideg (2,061 meters) the base of the vertical face of the Eiger. From there, another cog train circles inside the Eiger to daylight at Jungfrau Joch (3,454 meters).

Trip 6 North of Interlaken

Distance *About 180 kilometers from Interlaken via Glaubenberg Pass, plus about 40 via Acherli Pass*

Terrain *Sweeping and twisting through meadows and forests on five lower passes, some narrow, tight stuff*

Highlights *Bucolic motorcycle favorite roads, a couple of motorcycle cafes, mostly off tourist routes, Schallenberg (1,167 meters), ★Glaubenbuelen Pass (1,611 meters), ★Glaubenberg Pass (1,643 meters), Brunig Pass (1,008 meters), ★Acherli Pass (1,458 meters)*

This loop offers pleasant, bucolic, often challenging, but not exotic riding off the main tourist routes. Alpine guidebooks don't mention these roads.

Thun, at the westerly end of the Thuner See, is crowned by an impressive castle.

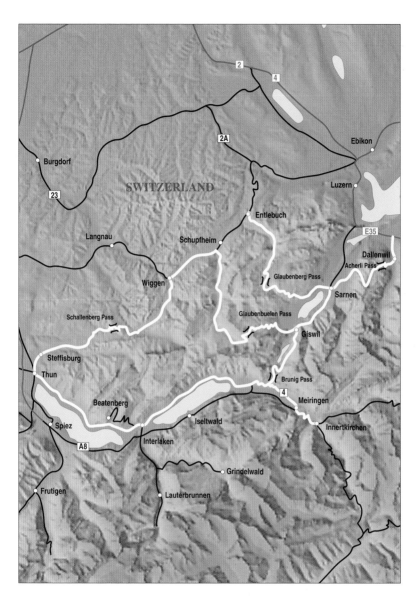

The Schallenberg road starts climbing from the town of Thun, at the west end of the Thuner See, the westerly of the two lakes that bracket Interlaken. From the north side of Thun, signs direct you first to Steffisburg, then to Schallenberg. (The English ear doesn't distinguish between "burg" and "berg," but technically the former is a fortified town and the latter is a mountain.) From the autobahn, take the Steffisburg exit, which seems convoluted. Just follow the signs. At last, the road exits on a street, with signs to Schallenberg to the right.

A block beyond the Schallenberg sign is one of the largest motorcycle shops in Europe, Moto-Center Thun. It's on the main road, but the entrance is a left turn before you get to it. The place is huge and attractive with Hondas and BMWs for sale and rent, with a large and well-equipped shop. Vast space is devoted to accessory display and sales. Downstairs is a bargain basement, and overlooking the road, a bike cafe.

The Schallenberg road has open sweepers through farms that have no great commercial or tourist value, so it's a motorcycle favorite. The area is a bit less polished-looking than most parts of Switzerland. The cafe at the top, Restaurant Gabelspitz, is almost exclusively aimed at serving *Töfflers*, since all the parking close by is for motorcycles. A choice second-floor balcony lets patrons watch the road and the parking lot activity.

The east side of the Schallenberg comes down to a village called Wiggen. From Wiggen, the trip heads east in the direction of Luzern for a few kilometers. Just at the edge of a town called Schupfheim, a road to the right leads south to a town called Fluhli. This is the Glaubenbuelen Pass road, sometimes called *Panorama Strasse*. (Note: In some Swiss German dialects, the pass is spelled Glaubenbeilen). On up from Fluhli is a small village called Sorenberg with a friendly hotel called Rischli. From Sorenberg, the road is twisting, paved, one-lane across the top with lovely views of lakes and mountains and forests. But it seems like only cows are looking at the panorama. There are no restaurants, no services. The Swiss will insist that Heidi came from eastern Switzerland, but the Glaubenbuelen looks like what Heidi country ought to look like. In the fall and spring the road may be full of cows heading to or from the high pastures, with floral headdresses in the fall. In either case, the lead cow will wear a big brass bell hung from an elaborate collar. Lesser cows have smaller bells and smaller collars, down to the least with tin sheet metal bells.

The pass road connects with the main highway between Interlaken and Luzern at Giswil, just in time to climb west over the Brunig Pass in the direction of Interlaken. (Looking for the Panorama Strasse from Giswil, the only hint is a sign on the main road pointing to Schupfheim. Look for the Giswil church which sits back on sort of a nob. The Panorama Strasse goes by it.)

To extend the trip, instead of going back to Interlaken over the Brunig, take the main road in the opposite direction toward Luzern. Then at Sarnen, head back north on the Glaubenberg Pass. More below.

The Brunig isn't high, but it *did* have some great sweepers that drew motorcycles from all around. A few years ago an avalanche took out most of the good sweepers and some vehicles with it. The replacement road does the job, but has less oomph. There remains one corner, a righthander going up from the east, that has a pull-out space that fills with bikes on good days. And the several restaurants and hotels at the top often host huge crowds of motorcyclists. Friday night is supposed to be *the* night on the Brunig. The Motel Restaurant Brunig always has a sport bike mounted on a post out front, changed from time to time. Across the road, the Restaurant Silvana has a big lot carved out of the mountainside, often packed with bikes. Its front tables are right on the road for good view and sound. From the top of Brunig, a dead-end road goes south a few kilometers to an area called Hasliberg with good views of the Aare valley, including Meiringen and Reichenbach Falls, described in Trip 1.

Parallel to and east of the Glaubenbuelen Pass (the *Panorama Strasse*) is another pass road called Glaubenberg. They must have named them to confuse us. Anyway, it's at least as high, even less used, and is also one lane across the top. Don't give up, the gravel part is only one kilometer. A restaurant/ski lodge named Hotel Langis on the south slope accommodates lots of motorcyclists during the summer. It's famous as a site where motorcyclists meet to make blood donations (called "blut spenden" in German). The north end of the Glaubenberg is in the middle of a village called Entlebuch, a few kilometers closer to Luzern than Schupfheim, above. Its southeast side ends at Sarnen, a town at the end of a lake by the same name.

From Sarnen it's possible to cross the main road and catch an obscure pass called Acherli over the next mountain into the Engelberg valley. There are no signs for the pass, so follow the signs from Sarnen to Kerns and then to Sand. The only intersection in Sand is at the north edge of the village, and that's the pass road. Leaving Sand on the pass road there's a reassuring sign, DALLENWIL, the next town in the Engelberg valley. A couple of kilometers above Sand are in dark forest. Across the top and down the south side is one-lane, paved, open cattle range. There are electric cattle gates. The winding road through green vistas is lovely. It comes out on the main street of Dallenwil. Coming the other way, from the Engelberg valley there are no signs for the pass either. Just follow the main road into and through Dallenwil.

From the Engelberg road it's only a few kilometers on the autobahn toward the St. Gotthard to Beckenried, where a ferry crosses the Vierwaldstatter See to the Axenstrasse and the roads of Trip 4. There's a fine hotel restaurant, Sternen Hotel am See, right at the ferry with a terrace overlooking lake and mountains. Ferries run about once an hour. A less romantic connection from Beckenried to the roads of Trip 4 is the autobahn tunnel, four lanes, about five kilometers through the cliffs above Vierwaldstatter See. A marvel, but no view.

Or head back over the Brunig Pass to Interlaken.

The west side of the Brunig has a connecting road to the Susten and Grimsel Passes, the roads of Trip 1. Weekend bikers often head that way.

Trip 7 Gurnigel

Distance *About 120 kilometers, round trip from Interlaken*
Terrain *Lakeside road, then a climb through woods to high pasture*
Highlights *Handsome lakefront, woods, maybe military artillery, Gurnigel Pass (1,608 meters)*

Riggisberg, about 15 kilometers northwest of the town of Thun, is the access key to a loop west of the Thuner See. From Riggisberg, this loop heads south on back roads to the summit at a restaurant called Berghaus Gurnigel. The easterly leg of the loop is a full two-lane road. The westerly leg is partly one-lane and is a bit rough, although paved. Both are fun. Both have good views, as does the restaurant at the top. The restaurant terrace has views over the low mountains to the south, often used for military exercises.

Friendly hotels and biker stops await you atop nearly every pass in the Alps. Invariably, there are also many other motorcyclists.

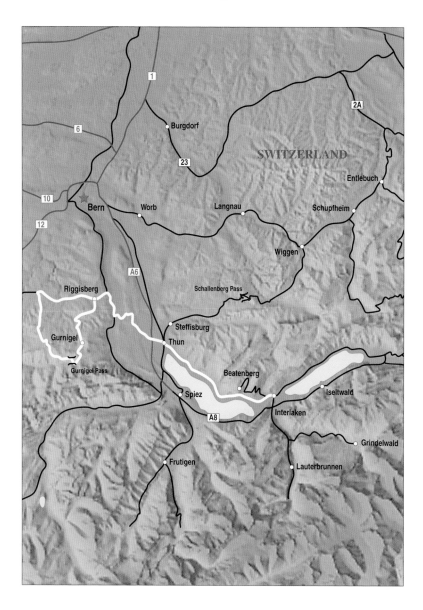

Trip 8 Trimbach bei Olten

Distance *About 140 kilometers, one way from Interlaken*
Terrain *Highway and autobahn*
Highlights *Thousands and thousands of motorcycles*

Friday night is the meeting night on Brunig Pass, but the biggest gathering of riders is usually on Thursday night at Trimbach bei Olten (Trimbach is just north of Olten), about 80 kilometers straight north of Interlaken, south of Basel, and west of Zurich. To get to Trimbach bei Olten from Interlaken, head north over the Brunig Pass and continue on the autobahn past Luzern. Olten is just off the autobahn, about halfway between Luzern and Basel. Or take the autobahn from Interlaken to Thun and Bern and then to Olten.

A huge parking lot next to a modest Gasthaus named Eisenbahn (railroad) accommodates about 3,000 motorcycles, and on good nights they spill out over neighboring fields. No events. No program. Only tire kicking. Special parking is reserved for any and all Harleys. The latest everything will show up, along with customized and restored bikes of all kinds. Every Thursday. Unfortunately, there aren't any recommended hotels nearby. There are a couple of serviceable ones in Olten.

On Thursday nights, thousands of motorcyclists gather for tire kicking at the Eisenbahn restaurant in the Swiss village of Trimbach bei Olten. Bikes fill the parking lot, and the rest spill over adjoining fields and roads.

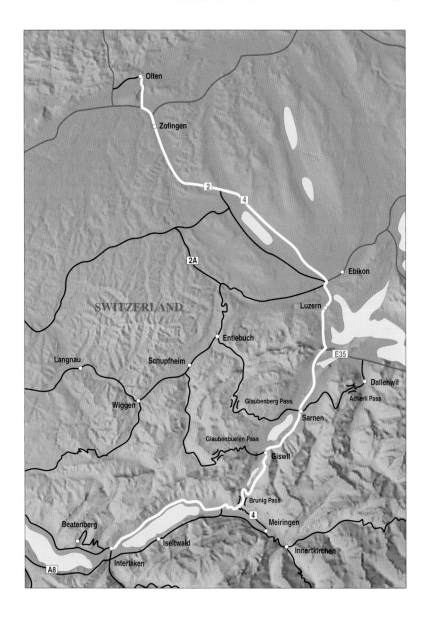

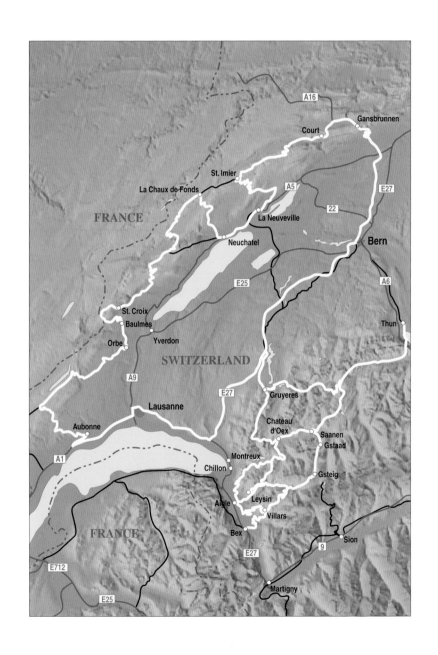

Leysin/Villars

Hung on a mountainside at about 1,200 meters, Leysin is a village with a view and a lot of hotels, and it's off the beaten track. It's in canton Vaud, and French, *s'il vous plait*. From most any point on the one road through town, from any balcony on any hotel, and from any terrace, there's a view across the Valley of the Rhone River (that started at the glacier on the Furka Pass) to the eternal snows of Mont Blanc and its neighbors.

Leysin is about six kilometers off the Col des Mosses road, the one road into Leysin, above the Rhone Valley town of Aigle. A cog train runs down the mountain from Leysin to Aigle.

A small family-run hotel near the top of the town, with views and good hearty cooking, is the Hotel Mont Riant. Another is modest La Paix.

Since there's a Swiss hotel school in Leysin, there are many other hotels, some quaint and some more grand. In case you need a wash cloth, there's even a Holiday Inn.

An alternate to Leysin is Villars, a village hanging on an adjacent mountain-side above Aigle at about 1,200 meters. It's signed from Aigle and from Bex and is the jumping off place for the Col de la Croix. A good hotel bet is the international style Eurotel.

Villars is home to a handy hotel guide for the budget traveler in Switzerland called E and G Hotels. "E" and "G" stand for Einfach and Gemutlich, which gets translated, "simple and cozy." It's published every year and lists about 175 or so modestly priced hotels all over Switzerland. Each listing has a color picture along with prices, hours, address, phone, and a clever symbol system that describes showers, pools, view, and other amenities. Naturally, a cheaper hotel in the city may prove less attractive than one of similar price in the country. The book is available at all Swiss tourist offices, or write E and G Hotels, Case Postal; CH-1844 Villars; 024 495-1111.

On the Sannenmoser road, just above Saanen and Gstaad is giant Steigenberger Hotel with views and every facility.

Trip 9 Simmen Tal and Jaun Pass

Distance *About 145 kilometers from Interlaken to Leysin via Jaun Pass; about 110 kilometers via Saanenmoser*

Terrain *Easy sweeping climbs over low passes*

Highlights *Picturesque villages and covered bridges, lush pastures, forest, medieval walled town and famous cheese factory (Gruyeres), Jaun Pass (1,509 meters), Saanenmoser (1,279 meters)*

The picturesque Simmen Tal (valley) feeds into the south shore of the Thuner See, just west of Interlaken. From the lake, the road up the valley winds past quaint wooden covered bridges and through small villages. Unfortunately, it's marked "no passing" (double white, not double yellow) for practically its whole length. And the many little villages are famous for strict enforcement of the speed limits.

Up the Simmen Tal about 15 kilometers from the Thuner See is a tiny one-building village called Weissenburg (don't confuse it with Weissenbach, farther upstream). The building is the Hostellerie Alte Post at Weissenburg, a

Almost down on the east end of the Juan Pass there are fine views of very green Simmen Tal.

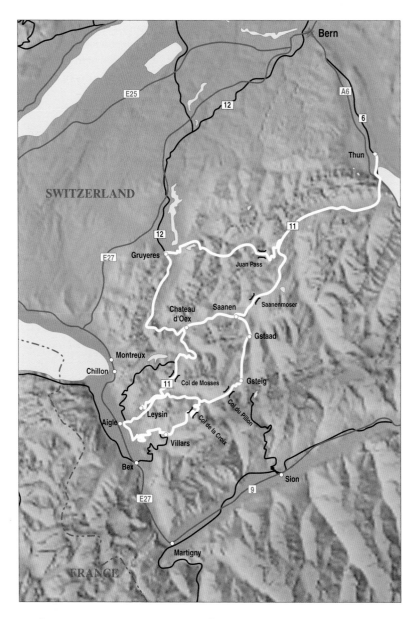

joy for any antique connoisseur as well as anyone ready for a genuine Swiss meal. It's famous for serving coffee cream in chocolate cups that melt into the coffee.

At Zweisimmen, a dead end road climbs south about 25 kilometers into the mountains to a nice waterfall.

The top of the Simmen Tal is called Saanenmoser with several gasthof hotels. On the way down westerly the road passes the Steigenberger Hotel overlooking a lush green valley and then curves into a village called Saanen with a dominant church steeple and many cute log houses. At Saanen, the road forks, with the left tine leading right into Gstaad. The rich and famous are supposed to ski or play tennis at Gstaad. There's a tunnel under the town so as not to bother the rich and famous. On through a log village Gsteig, the road sweeps up the Col du Pillon where all of a sudden everything is French. Then it twists toward Leysin.

The right fork at Saanen goes immediately into French speaking Switzerland through Rougemont over the Col des Mosses to Leysin.

For Villars, take the Col du Pillon down to Les Diablerets, then over Col de la Croix right into Villars. These roads are more completely described in Trip 10. The road up the mountain to Leysin is just about where the Col du Pillon road and the Col des Mosses road intersect.

In some parts of the Alps, churches have steeples that sort of look like witch's hats. This one is at Gsteig.

In the fall, cows come down from the high summer pastures. The lead cow is usually decorated with flowers. Of course, it has the biggest bell. Coming at the cows, it's best to pull over and let them pass. Then enjoy the road well-sprinkled with cow pies. Approaching them from behind, the cow pies will give fair warning of what's ahead. But it is difficult to pass through the herd from the rear.

But should you chose the longer route over the Juan Pass, the turnoff is before the Saanenmoser, out in the country in a meadow at the edge of the Simmen Tal village called Reidenbach. Jaun Pass (say "yawn," not "whawn") runs between the Simmen Tal on the east and Gruyeres (like in cheese) on the west. Nice views and an easy climb to the top where there are restaurants.

Gruyeres, on the west end of the Jaun Pass, is a preserved old walled city on a hill. No vehicles. It's worth the short walk in to visit. Bikes can park right by the city gate. Too many restaurants offer almost any concoction or most any kind of berry with the thickest, richest cream imaginable, cream that comes from the cheese factory for which the town is known. On through plaza and shops of the walled village is a castle, for which an entry fee is charged. The factory is at the bottom of the hill and is open to visitors in the morning. Do the town rather than the cheese. In case you hadn't guessed, Gruyeres is French speaking.

South from Gruyeres is the Col des Mosses, leading to the road to Leysin, or on to Aigle and Villars.

Trip 10 Three Cols and a Route

Distance   *About 144 kilometers from Leysin*
Terrain   *Fun sweepers over lower passes, mostly modern highways, modest height and difficulty*
Highlights   *Well-known resorts (Gstaad, Chateau d'Oex), log village (Saanen), German/French culture border, Col du Pillon (1,546 meters),* ★*Col de la Croix (1,778 meters), Col des Mosses (1,445 meters), Route Militaire*

The Col des Mosses climbs out of the Rhone Valley from Aigle, past a handsome private castle, and past the dead-end road to Leysin.

Chateau d'Oex (sounds like "shat oh decks") and Rougemont are attractive tourist towns at the north end of the Col des Mosses. The highway now bypasses both villages. The medieval church at Rougemont is worth a stop if you're passing by. Although the village is French speaking, the church is of Germanic style, because the diocese was controlled from nearby Germanic Saanen.

Rougemont has a comfortable log hotel restaurant that's called Hotel de Commune.

An interesting and fun alternate route parallels the Col des Mosses from Aigle. It's a military road and is open only on Saturdays, Sundays, and holidays. The south end, out of the valley village of Corbeyrier, climbs through handsome

Heading to Les Diablerets from Col de la Croix on a morning after an early fall snow.

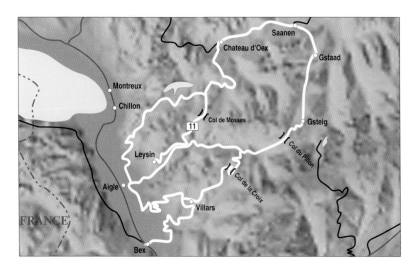

vineyards, then some narrow, steep hairpins and a twisting, one-way-at-a-time tunnel.

The north end cruises by a lake, then over many bridges. Some pass roads number the hairpins. This one numbers the bridges: forty some. Unfortunately, part of the road has a low speed limit.

At the lovely log house village of Saanen (also the westerly base of the Sannenmoser) the road heads south for Gstaad, and then starts climbing the Col du Pillon through the village of Gsteig, which has one of the nicer Germanic-Swiss church steeples, shaped much like a witch's hat.

As the name Col du Pillon implies, the top of the pass is in French-speaking Switzerland. In the few kilometers between Gsteig and the top of the pass, the buildings and menus change from Germanic to French.

The attractive restaurant at the top of the Col du Pillon, with a terrace viewing the highest peaks in the area, is called Les Diablerets. So are the peaks. So is the next town. At the next town, Les Diablerets, the Col de la Croix road heads southwest. Somehow, the Col de la Croix is uncluttered, with sweeping turns and sweeping views. It has gotten rough in spots. The Col road comes down to the village of Villars, one of the few Swiss towns that is anxious to sell condos to foreigners.

At Villars, the Col de la Croix road forks. One leg, the main road, heads for the Rhone Valley at Aigle. The other, the nicest, winds down to the valley at Bex, following much the same route as the trolley-train (mind the tracks) through chalet-filled villages and vineyards with views across the Rhone to the high Alps around Mont Blanc. From either road, it's just a few kilometers back up the Col des Mosses road to Leysin. Looking for the Col de la Croix from the Rhone Valley, follow signs to Villars from either Bex or Aigle.

Trip 11 The Swiss Jura

Distance *About 390 kilometers round trip from Leysin or Villars, about half on autoroute (freeway), about 200 kilometers from or to Col de la Faucille*

Terrain *Some autoroute, farm land, lower wooded passes with narrow, non-tourist roads, French culture*

Highlights *Good views of Lac Leman, Lac du Joux, Lac du Neuchatel, famous Castle of Chillon, Col du Mollendruz (1,180 meters), Col de Marchairuz (1,447 meters), ★Col de l'Aiguillon (1,293 meters), Col des Etroits (1,152 meters), Vue des Alpes (1,283 meters), Col du Chasseral (1,502 meters, toll), Weissenstein (1,279 meters), Col du Mont Crosin (1,227 meters)*

Cobblestones like these remain only on short historic pieces of road. These cobblestones help preserve the atmosphere in front of the Castle of Chillon on Lac Leman (Lake Geneva). The castle was made famous in English literature by Lord Byron's poem, The Prisoner of Chillon. The nearby autoroute (freeway) is fast and smooth.

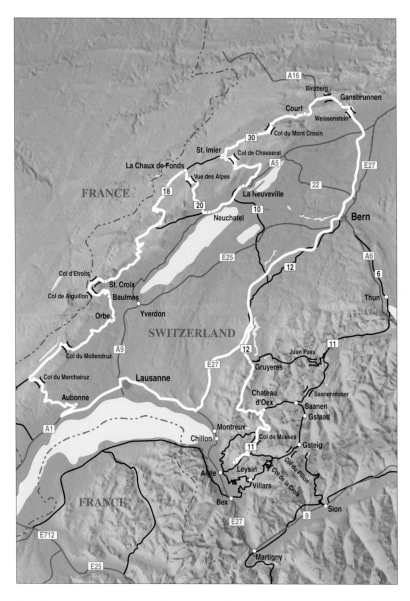

The Jura is a range of mountains just northwest of Lac Leman and the lower Rhone River. About half the Jura are in the French-speaking part of Switzerland and half are in France. They're pretty mellow compared to the rugged Alps, more like the Smokies in the U.S. This trip covers all the good riding in the Swiss Jura, all reachable from the Leysin/Villars base. The French Jura are in Trip 16.

Many roads in the Alps slink through narrow, twisty gorges.

Or maybe stay at a spectacularly sited mid-point hotel, La Mainaz, just in France at the Swiss border, high in the Jura overlooking Lac Leman and Geneve. From the hotel room, you can see all of Geneve, the Jet d'Eau, a major portion of the lake, and beyond that, Mount Blanc itself. The hotel is all by itself on the Col de la Faucille, just twenty minutes from the Geneve airport. On one side of the hotel are the Swiss Jura, the French on the other. La Mainaz is a *Relais de Silence* . . . a quiet hotel, but motorcyclists have enjoyed it.

Arcing west from Leysin and Aigle for about 100 kilometers, the north shore of Lac Leman harbors the major cities of French-speaking Switzerland: Montreux, Lausanne, and at the west end, Geneve (Geneva). Suspended above the lake, sometimes on spectacular viaducts, an autoroute (freeway) whisks right by the Castle of Chillon (made famous by Lord Byron's poem) on the east end of the lake to Geneva on the west end.

The Castle of Chillon is a real medieval castle that seems to rise right out of Lac Leman. It can be visited from the lake shore road below the autoroute, just east of the city of Montreux. One American visitor was overheard wondering, "Why did they build this nice castle so close to the railroad tracks?"

To get to these passes, it's best to avoid traffic along the lake shore road by taking the autoroute west toward Geneve, past Lausanne, exiting at Aubonne, then climbing northwest over the Col de Marchairuz. The restaurant atop Marchairuz has a hand washing machine. It's been in place for years yet seems unique. Put your hands in the opening. First warm water. Then soap. Then more warm water. Then warm air. North of the col, the road descends to the Lac du Joux.

Follow the lake shore east, then up the low Col du Mollendruz. Just across the top head east to Orbe, then northeast to Baulmes, a pleasant small village nestled in a nook of the mountains. Into and through Baulmes is the Col de l'Aiguillon road. It climbs through forests and into meadows, a little road where no tourist has gone . . . at least not many. It meets a more main highway near the French border. Go east, staying in Switzerland, over the Col des Etroits to a town called St. Croix, then on east to La Chaux de Fonds, where a jaunt south goes over the Vue des Alpes, then merge with the autoroute to Neuchatel and follow the autoroute east under (that's right, under) the city of Neuchatel exiting at La Neuveville beside Bieler See. Cross under the autoroute (to the north side} to an intersection. Turn east and follow the signs for Le Chasseral. There's a toll. At the col (1,502 meters), take a dead end road on up a couple of kilometers to a large restaurant (1,607 meters) with a view toward Mont Blanc. Down northerly through St. Imir turn northerly again through meadows up over Col du Mont Crosin, then on east through Court and Moutier to Gansbrunnen (the road straight from Court to Gansbrunnen is not paved). At Gansbrunnen, there's a sign pointing south up the twisting road over Weissenstein where there's a restaurant. Or, cross the same mountain a few kilometers farther east at Welshenrohr up by Balberg. No tourists here for sure. Back down at Solothurn, the autobahn leads by Bern and Freiburg to Villars and Leysin.

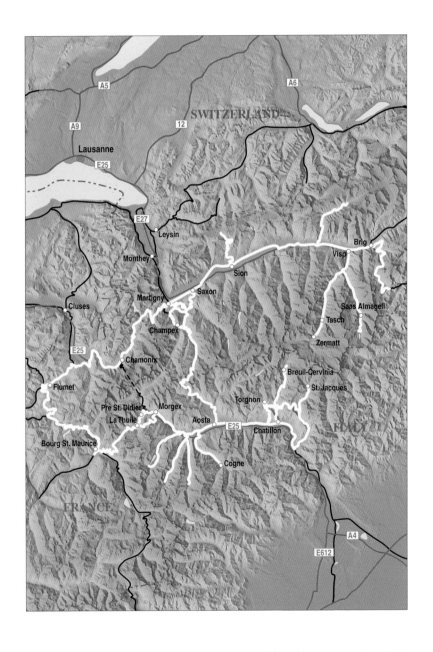

Mont Blanc Region

The Rhone Valley makes a 90-degree bend at a pretty good sized Swiss town called Martigny. Quite French. It's where two pass roads head out to encircle the eternal snows of the highest mountain in the Alps, Mont Blanc, 4,807 meters (15,779 feet!). From Martigny the Col de la Forclaz road heads toward France, and the Grand St. Bernard road heads toward Italy.

Martigny, or any of the villages hung on the mountains around it, are good bases for the Mont Blanc trip. Right where the two pass roads come together in Martigny is the hotel La Porte d'Octodure; *Malhereusement,* it's a Best Western!

A little village called Les Marecottes, atop a spectacular road just eight kilometers from the Martigny town square, has a variety of hotels that have served motorcyclists well. Go northwest from the square, over a covered wooden bridge, and keep climbing. The road climbs a traverse overlooking the Rhone Valley, then crosses to the north side of the Gorge du Trient on a high bridge. From that point on, the road barely hangs on the cliff edge overlooking the gorge. A train up the gorge goes through to France. The road doesn't. Les Marecottes is near the end of the road. One hotel is called Aux Mille Etoiles.

From the autoroute in the Rhone Valley, the pass roads are signed via a bypass road that misses downtown Martigny.

The trips in this chapter are accessible from Leysin or Villars.

That white hut in the middle of the road up there is the border crossing from Italy into Switzerland. Many stop for lunch on the Italian side.

Trip 12   Valley of the Rhone

Distance   *About 160 kilometers between Martigny and Andermatt, one way; about 110 kilometers between Martigny and Tasch (Zermatt), one way; about 100 kilometers between Martigny and Simplon Pass, one way*

Terrain   *Fairly straight valley road and sweeping mountain climbs on good modern highway*

Highlights   *Sweep up a finger valley toward the Matterhorn, over a high mountain pass (★Simplon, 2,006 meters), Col du Sanetsch (2,251 meters, dead-end), some concrete roofed highway, some narrow*

From the high passes at Andermatt, the Rhone Valley makes a pretty straight shot down to Martigny. The higher eastern part of the valley, called the Goms, is an amusing ride through log cabin villages. The lower part is more commercial and boring. It does make a functional east-west connection, about 150 kilometers long, with such high mountains on both sides that there's hardly any way out. From the Grimsel Pass back by Andermatt, there's no through road going north until the Col des Mosses by Leysin. It is possible to put a bike or car on a train and take it through a tunnel toward Interlaken. Switzerland is slowly extending an autobahn/autoroute easterly up the valley.

Two dead-end roads north make for interesting escapes into high valleys: Lotschen Tal climbs up to the glaciers behind Lauterbrunnen (turn off at the signs for the train tunnel to Goppenstein), and the Col du Sanetsch from Sion almost makes it across the top to Gsteig, but doesn't.

One road out of the Rhone Valley to the south toward Italy, the Simplon Pass, starts at Brig, 50 kilometers below the Furka. The Simplon is one of the major passes of the Alps between Italy and France, through Switzerland. The first major Alpine train tunnel went under the Simplon to carry the Orient Express. Both sides of the pass road are in Switzerland, with good quality sweepers to the summit on both sides. The north side has an amazing "S" curved poured concrete suspension bridge. On the summit is a giant stone eagle monument and a couple of serviceable restaurants. One regular menu item is goulash soup, a spicy, meaty specialty of the Germanic Alps that tastes something like chili.

An elaborate two-lane (on-coming traffic) freeway and tunnel now lead from the Goms around, through, and under Brig, with well-signed connections for the Simplon Pass.

(For good road connections from the south side of the Simplon, see Trip 33, "Simplon Pass".)

Several dead-end valleys go south from the Rhone Valley. The most famous valley is Matter Tal to Zermatt and the Matterhorn, but no vehicles are allowed into Zermatt. The Rhone Valley turnoff for Zermatt and the Matter Tal is at

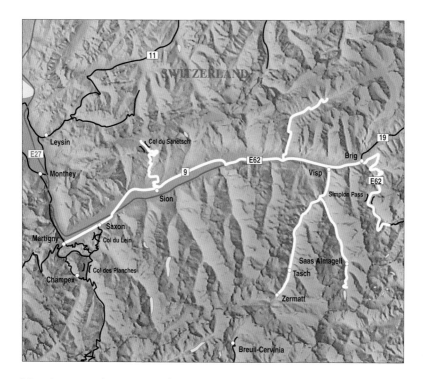

Visp, into a newly constructed tunnel that by-passes some commercial clutter. From the tunnel, it's a fine sweeping ride up the Matter Tal as far as Tasch, where one of the biggest parking lots in Europe accommodates tourists taking the cog train the rest of the way to Zermatt. There is underground and indoor parking at Tasch. Outdoor bike parking is available right next to the train station.

The village of Randa, just below Tasch, bears witness to the terror of the Alps. In recent years a whole mountain collapsed into the valley, burying everything—the stream, parts of the village, the road and railroad—under granite boulders. The road and railroad now go around the site.

About ten kilometers up the Matter Tal from Visp, there's an intersection. The west fork continues to Tasch and Zermatt, while the east fork goes all the way up to the towns of Saas Fee and Saas Almagell. The road to the former is interesting, with glaciers right at hand, but it's a walk-around-only village. Motorcycle parking is free.

Just downstream from Visp in the Rhone Valley, without a sign, everything changes from German to French: architecture, menus, bread, even cars.

Visible from the autoroute near Sion are castles and vineyards and airstrips with airplane hangars in the mountainsides. The autoroute by-passes Sion, the capital city of canton Wallis, only here it's French and the canton is called Valais.

Trip 13 All Around Mont Blanc

Distance *About 300 kilometers from Martigny*

Terrain *Circle the greatest mountain in the Alps, Mont Blanc; from low valleys with some congestion, climb to empty mountain roads; three major Alpine passes and several lesser ones; some narrow, tight, steep hairpins*

Highlights *Three countries, famous passes and ski resorts, Roman ruins, plus some quiet, remote, twisting stuff, ★Col du Grand St. Bernard (2,469 meters), ★Colle San Carlo (1,971 meters), ★Col du Petit St. Bernard (2,188 meters), ★★Cormet de Roselend (1,922 meters), ★Col du Pre (1,703 meters), Col des Saisies (1,633 meters), Chamonix, Col des Montets (1,461 meters), Col de la Forclaz (1,526 meters), Col des Planches (1,411 meters), Col du Lein (1,656 meters), Champex (1,486 meters)*

Three amusing little roads start near Martigny. Just toward downtown a few hundred meters from the Hotel La Porte d'Octodure, a tiny road, the Col des Planches, climbs up the mountainside. It isn't high, but it does lead up and over

The top of the Great St. Bernard on the Italian side is fairly gnarly, although rebuilt recently. Here, a couple of bikes are clearing that stuff for the more open area.

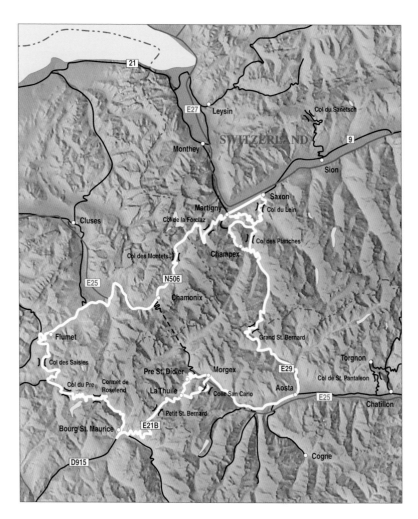

to a high resort at Verbier, 1,390 meters. Up the Grand St. Bernard a few kilometers, at Les Valettes, another small road makes a twisting climb up to a mountain lake village called Champex. The road goes through and winds back down to the Grand St. Bernard road at Orsieres, where an interesting dead-end valley road, Val Ferret, heads up toward some glaciers at 1,705 meters.

The third amusing little road is the Col du Lein, crossing the mountain behind Martigny between Saxon in the Rhone Valley and the Grand St. Bernard road near Sembrancher. Saxon is about ten kilometers east of Martigny, and the turnoff is from the center of the village, marked Col du Len, not Lein. Sembrancher is 12 kilometers up the Grand St. Bernard road from Martigny. The little col road climbs to about 1,600 meters, one lane, with about four kilometers unpaved.

Down a few curves from the top of the Petit St. Bernard, the French side, is a village called La Rosiere hanging on the side of the mountain. On the down hill side with great views of the Val d'Isere and food too is Hotel Le Plein Soleil. If the umbrellas are out it must be a good day.

There are two St. Bernard Passes, a Grand (big) and a Petit or Piccolo (little) St. Bernard. The big one goes between Martigny, Switzerland, and Aosta, Italy. It's where the dogs are. The little one goes from Aosta in Italy to France. There's a statue of St. Bernard on both of them.

The Grand St. Bernard Pass is fairly commercial and has high-speed sweepers so well engineered that it's hard to realize how quickly you're up among the glaciers. But it goes by tunnel into Italy. Motorcycles want to stay on the pass road, so turn off just after entering the tunnel, where a sign, COL, points to the right. Sometimes the col is labeled OUVERT, open, on the Swiss side, but the border crossing just over the col is closed. Sometimes it's closed with huge concrete blocks. The restaurant on the Swiss side is French. It will have sandwiches (try a croque-monsieur, grilled ham and cheese) and plates of cold cuts (assiette); the Italian, fresh pasta and salad and cappuccino. Most of the dogs around are stuffed toys. On the Italian side, the 14 kilometers between the pass and the Italian entrance to the tunnel are fairly challenging and wild. Approaching the pass from Italy, the pass road leaves the tunnel road just before a long viaduct that leads to the tunnel entrance. There's a place to change money at the complex of offices just across the viaduct. Euros are needed for cash purchases in Italy, Swiss francs in Switzerland. The rest of the route down into Aosta has commercial traffic.

Approaching Aosta, a new tunnel takes traffic from the pass to the autostrada well east, down stream, of Aosta. To avoid this and get to Aosta and the Little St. Bernard, follow signs for a sharp right turn before the tunnel. Once in the tunnel, enjoy the view, and upon reaching daylight, turn back toward Aosta.

Aosta center has some significant Roman ruins, an arch, walls, and a theater. On the east end of town, past the airport, is a very large motorcycle shop called America. It does not sell Harleys. It does fit tires quickly.

Even though it's in a fabulous Alpine valley, Aosta has a lot of traffic and smog, alleviated recently by the newly completed Monte Bianco Autostrada that bypasses the town taking most trucks and busses with it.

There is a serviceable hotel in Aosta. Hotel Valle d'Aosta is on the east end of town (see Trip 14 for riding in the vicinity of Aosta). An exceptionally attractive hotel, the Miramonti, is at Cogne, the end of a road south out of Aosta into the Gran Paradiso National Park. Cogne, and the hotel furnished with lovely and comfortable antiques, are worth a special trip. The hotel's working language is French. Another hotel, carefully more business-like, is at Chatillon, miles east (downstream) of Aosta. It's called Relais du Foyer. Located well above the valley on the north side, it is near the road that climbs to Monte Cervino, the Matterhorn (see Trip 14 for more about the roads near these hotels).

To get to the Piccolo St. Bernard Pass from Aosta, follow the signs to Courmayeur and the Italian entrance to what used to be the longest vehicle tunnel in the world under Mont Blanc. Commercial truck traffic to the tunnel is terrible. An elaborate autostrada is under construction, but . . . . Fortunately, motorcyclists need not go through the tunnel. From the smog-filled highway there are occasional glimpses of Mont Blanc, huge and white, before the turnoff at the village of Pre St. Didier, 30 kilometers from Aosta, where the Piccolo St. Bernard goes south and leaves the traffic behind.

Or better yet, before the Piccolo St. Bernard turnoff at Pre St. Didier, there's a long cut over an obscure pass called the Colle San Carlo. It's recently been improved with new retaining walls and pavement. Escape the traffic early by turning up the Colle at a village called Morgex. The pass isn't marked. The sign is to Arpy, a town on the pass. After a great climb twisting through the forests, the road descends into the village of La Thuile, on the Piccolo St. Bernard road.

The rest of the Italian side of the Piccolo St. Bernard is a delight. Often the road cuts through deep banks of snow well into mid-June. The only village, La Thuile, has a good ristorante called Grotto, and another called Les Marmottes just across from the little and only parking lot in town. Try tortellini carne in garlic and walnut sauce.

Some American motorcyclists have noted that French road repair crews use a lot of gravel. They dump a load in a hole and wait for traffic to pack it down. In the meantime, they mark the site with a sign that profiles a car spraying stars from its wheels.

Past the statue of St. Bernard, on the French side of the col, a mountain village called La Rosiere has a couple of pleasantly sited hotel/restaurants. Hotel Le Plein Soleil has nice views of the Val d'Isere. Several hairpins below La Rosiere is a shortcut in the direction of the Val d'Isere (Trip 17). It's in a hairpin signed MONTVALEZN (D84). The French base of the Petit St. Bernard is a town called Bourg St. Maurice. Southwest of its center is Hotel l'Autanic.

One of the *plus joli* (prettiest) roads in France, the Cormet de Roselend (sounds like "core may") starts at a traffic circle on the east end of Bourg St. Maurice (D902). On its way out of town, the road passes a very fine restaurant, L'Arssiban.

The Cormet de Roselend has no commercial activity. No ski activity. Parts are only one lane wide and bumpy, but it feels like no one else has ever been there. Near the top should be herds of the handsome red-brown cows, source of the famous cheese that comes from the other side of the mountain at Beaufort.

On the north side of the Cormet is a beautiful lake with a couple of satisfactory mountain restaurants. The lake results from a dam (barrage in French) with a road across it. Turn down across the barrage to another pass road with no significance except views so wonderful that even the most enthusiastic rider will pause to look. It's mostly one lane wide, paved, and is called Col du Pre. Near the top a restaurant called la Pierra Menta is justly proud of its *tartelettes aux*

On the way down to Beaufort off the Col de Pre, there are nice views of fields and houses and winding lanes.

myrtilles, mountain blueberry tarts, and its terrace with views of mountain meadows and the lake, and beyond a very white Mont Blanc.

In France, what we call a menu is called a carte. Menu in French is a multi-course meal. *Terroir* on a carte means locally grown. Omelets are lunch items in France. Try one.

On over the col, the road winds down through open pastures surrounded by snowy peaks into Beaufort, the town of cheese fame.

Three kilometers below Beaufort is the turnoff for the Col des Saisies (say coal day sigh zee) heading up and north (D218). Cross-country skiing events for the Albertville Olympics were held on the col and there's a lot of ski-oriented development. It's a north-south pass, with the north end daylighting at Flumet, a little village on the main valley road between Albertville and Chamonix.

But wait. There's a more fun and more beautiful way up the Col des Saisies. The signed road three kilometers down from Beaufort (D218) heads up a finger valley in the direction of Hauteluce. But just one kilometer further downstream is a sign for a village called Villard. Go into Villard (D123) and keep climbing, back and forth switchbacks up the face of the mountain with views for miles and kilometers. The road eventually makes it up to the col and joins the main road. Just across the col, at a mini-traffic circle, there should be a sign for Crest Voland, a little village down on the edge of the mountain. It's a fun alternative to the main road into Flumet.

From Flumet, traffic for Chamonix is directed through St. Gervais (D909) with a lot of traffic, before winding laboriously down into a valley and on to the Mount Blanc Autoroute (N205). The autoroute marches audaciously up the mountain on stilts out over the top of everything. Finally, at Chamonix, the huge glaciers of Mont Blanc come into view. And the tunnel entrance to Italy. Chamonix is a summer and winter tourist center with all the accommodations and traffic to prove it. One of the most exotic cable car rides (*telepherique* in French) in the world goes from Chamonix to the Aiguille du Midi on the Mont Blanc massif. From the main highway through the city, an underpass takes you to the parking lot of the cable car. The ride up is exciting if the weather's clear.

Most of the traffic is going through the tunnel to Italy, not to Switzerland. For Switzerland, follow the signs to Argentiere and Col des Montets, a hardly noticeable pass, and on to the Swiss border.

The Swiss side of the border crossing has all kinds of services, including money exchanges. Across the border there's a turnoff to a town called Finhaut. A road climbs through Finhaut to dead-end at a lake called Emosson at 1,930 meters. The road's good and there's a restaurant with a terrace and view of the whole Mont Blanc massif.

Back at the foot of the mountain, the road on to Martigny climbs over the Col de la Forclaz. The Martigny side of this col has a couple of restaurants with good views of the Rhone Valley and surrounding vineyards.

Trip 14 Val d'Aosta

Distance *About 78 kilometers from Martigny to Aosta, one way, plus about 50 kilometers from Aosta to Breuil (the Matterhorn, called Monte Cervino in Italy) one way, plus about 25 kilometers from Aosta to any of the valleys in the Parco Nazionale Gran Paradiso, one way*

Terrain *Once out of the Aosta valley, quiet, twisting narrow roads into high forgotten valleys surrounded by glaciers*

Highlights ★*Breuil, as close to the Matterhorn as a road goes (2,006 meters), glaciers and peaks of Gran Paradiso National Park,* ★*Col di Joux (1,640 meters), Col de St. Pantaleon (1,645 meters)*

Just west of Aosta, up stream, on the traffic-jammed autostrada to Courmayeur and the Monte Blanco tunnel, four roads dead-end south into the Parco Nazionale Gran Paradiso. The closest to Aosta is Val di Cogne, the next is Val Savaranche, the third, Val di Rhemes, and the fourth, Val Grisenche. They are signed from the autostrada and quickly leave traffic and civilization behind. Each twists and climbs into high Alpine valleys. Fun roads. Lovely views.

Val di Cogne is a good base for hikers and climbers and offers beautiful views of Monte Bianco and the Gran Paradiso. At the top of the valley, surrounded by Gran Paradiso Mountains, is the village Cogne at 1,534 meters, a painstakingly preserved mountain village and the home to lovely Hotel Mirimonti. The village is much as Zermatt would like to be.

Twenty-six kilometers downstream from Aosta toward Torino is Chatillon, a town hung on the north slopes of the valley and the base for good roads that need exploring. Chatillon has a nice hotel, Relais du Foyer. The most prominent of the good roads climbs north up Val Tournenche to 2,006 meters, the

Another view of Monte Cervino (the Matterhorn) across Lago Bleu.

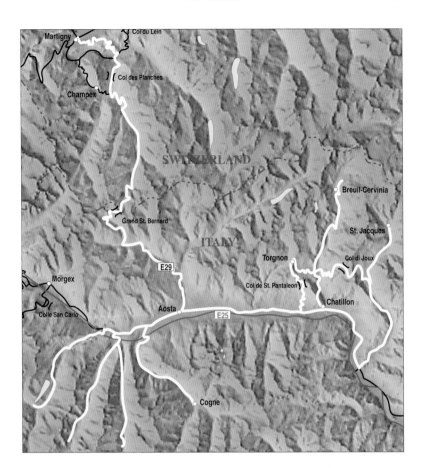

very base of the Matterhorn. Of course, in Italy, it's Monte Cervino. The village up there, Breuil, has a lot of ski hotels that are usually closed in the summer.

Just short of Breuil and opposite a small hotel called Stella Alpina (that's the Italian name for what Germans call Edelweiss) is little Lago Bleu. Hike up over a little slope for a picture to treasure, Cervino reflected in the lake.

On the way back to Chatillon, turn up the west side of the valley to Torgnon, and on over Col de St. Pantaleon. St. Pantaleon daylights in the Aosta valley, just five killometers from Chatillon.

Easterly from Chatillon through St. Vincent, the Col di Joux road makes a nice loop. From St. Vincent it climbs over to the next valley where a road, not nearly as interesting as the one to Monte Cervino, climbs to St. Jacques at 1,689 meters. Just west of the top of the Col di Joux is a restaurant with views to die for: the whole Aosta Valley west to Mont Blanc, er, Monte Bianco. The owner studied English in Buffalo! Coming the other direction, the col and St. Jacques are signed from the autostrada exit at Verres.

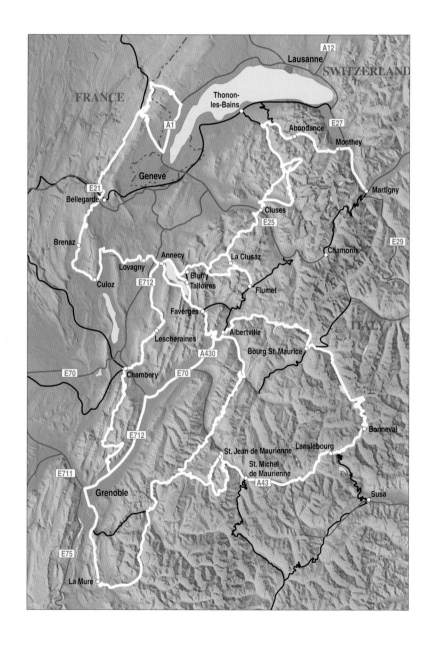

Lac d'Annecy

In France, south of Mont Blanc, are some of the highest passes and wildest country of the Alps. Exciting to explore. The '92 Olympics at Albertville highlighted some of them. France alone of the Alpine countries has good, prominently marked route numbers. (Ns are national roads; Ds are departmental roads. Department road numbers may change from one town to the next.) The only trouble is, the numbers disappear in cities where there are sure to be many confusing intersections. As you approach a city in France, there may be signs like POUR FLUMET SUIVRE ALBERTVILLE, "for Flumet follow Albertville." So there won't be route number signs, but there will be signs for Albertville. And France has a lot of roundabouts, always preceded by a sign, VOUS N'AVEZ PAS LE PRIORITE. Entering the roundabout "you don't have the priority." Any vehicle to the left does. But once in the roundabout, you have the right of way and can go around as many times as it takes to check signs and plot an escape. Remember, signs may point at the road as well as, or instead of, the direction of travel. In France, freeways are called "autoroutes." Some have tolls.

Many stop to take a picture of the sign at the top of Col de l'Iseran.

Although they're pretty well developed for winter sports, the French Alps seem to close down during the summer season. Facilities, almost endless in number and variety elsewhere in the Alps, are a bit harder to locate in France, and some pass roads aren't open until late in June.

But facilities are always open at Lac d'Annecy, one of the loveliest lakes in the Alps, just a few kilometers northwest of Albertville. Passes south of Lac Leman lead to Annecy, as do the autoroutes south from Geneve and west from Chamonix. The French province that includes Annecy and most of these good passes is Haute Savoie. Its flag looks almost like the Swiss flag, a white cross on red. On Savoie's flag, the white arms of the cross reach the edge of the flag.

Here, some bikes are closer to the top on the north side of the Col de l'Iseran.

With the coming of the European Union, most national border crossings are no longer manned. About the only manned crossings left in the Alps are at Switzerland, which is not in the EU. Swiss guards will be pleased to sell you a "vignette," the sticker which is good for one calendar year and must be affixed to any vehicle using a Swiss freeway, autobahn,

The town of Annecy, at the north end of the lake, has all services, including a variety of large and helpful motorcycle shops, even Harley. Annecy has a colorful walking old town with little canals, and a smart modern lake front promenade and beach. The whole city presents a very clean, neat, pleasing aspect.

Hotels for all tastes are located around the lake. On the eastern shore is a village called Talloires (say Tal whar). Tufts University has a campus in Talloires. There are some pricey places like George Bise, and La Cottage, fairly pretentious. The owner of nearby Hotel le Lac is a biker and he also owns a ski hotel high in the Val d'Isere. Next door is the Hotel la Charpenterie, attractive and more modest, and Hotel Beau Site. Some American motorcyclists like la Villa des Fleurs.

A couple of good and reasonable hotels can be found east of Annecy at La Clusaz where the Col des Aravis meets the Col de la Croix Fry; Alp Hotel and Hotel Sapins. Don't get confused. This town is La Clusaz and north of it on the autoroute is Cluses.

The south shore of Lac Leman is French with familiar names like Thonon les Bains and Evian les Bains. Worth a visit is Yvoire, a small medieval walled town at the tip of a promontory into the lake just 40 kilometers from Geneve, Switzerland. There is a very nice, very French hotel, Le Pre de la Cure.

Trip 15 Lac d'Annecy

Distance *About 230 kilometers from Martigny to Annecy, one way*
Terrain *Sweeping and twisting over seven non-commercial passes*
Highlights *Farms, forests, high meadows, some narrow roads, ski resorts, Pas de Morgins (1,369 meters), Col du Corbier (1,237 meters), Col des Gets (1,163 meters), ★Col de Joux Plane (1,712 meters), Col de la Colombiere (1,613 meters), Col des Aravis (1,486 meters), Col de la Croix Fry (1,467 meters), Col de Joux Verte (1,760 meters)*

Annecy's old city is one of quaint canals and shops.

Several passes south of Lac Leman make fun connections between Switzerland and the high roads of the French Alps. On most of them there is no traffic. Start out of the Rhone Valley in Switzerland on the Pas de Morgins. From the town of Monthey, just a few kilometers downstream from Martigny, it climbs through pleasant Swiss countryside and crosses into France at the top. The operator of the motorcycle shop in Monthey is an enthusiast who has biked all over the world, including North America and Baja.

Coming down into France below the town of Abondance, the little pass road of Col du Corbier (D32) heads up and south into a wonderful set of switch-backs on the northeast side. It leads to the next valley and the road up the Col des Gets. To the east of Gets is another little pass road called Col de Joux Plane (D354). It's a one-lane road that twists up from the town of Morzine on the north to Samoens on the south. It's not conspicuously marked at either end, but it's popular with French and Swiss motorcyclists and is worth the effort to find it. A restaurant at the top is called Relais des Vallees.

A high loop out of Morzine to Super Morzine (that's its name) climbs easterly to the Col de Joux Verte (D338) at 1,760 meters and comes down at Montriond about five kilometers downstream from Morzine where it started. The northerly leg is through rustic country.

The whole loop adds about 30 kilometers.

All this leads down to a fairly large city, Cluses, on the autoroute to Chamonix. Signing through Cluses is circuitous.

Across the autoroute from Cluses, the Col de la Colombiere (D4) leads up and over the mountains toward Annecy through St. Jean de Sixt and Thones. Colombiere is a noncommercial play road. Oil spills have been noted, though. There is a restaurant at the top.

From Flumet, on the loop around Mont Blanc (north end of the Col des Saisies (Trip 13), the Col des Aravis (say are uh VEE) goes up and over toward Annecy. The Col des Aravis has a nice restaurant with a terrace view of Mont Blanc. Just down a little on the north side of the Col des Aravis, near the ski resort of La Clusaz, the Col de la Croix Fry heads up and west (D16). It's a good road with little traffic leading over to the town of Thones and the main road to Annecy. From it, a shortcut to Talloires turns south at Bluffy (D169).

Up in the high Alps the Cols meet. Col de Glandon goes left, Croix de Fer goes right.

Spring days are warm and long, yet last winter's snows are still deep in the high country. Here, a snowblowing plow has opened the road.

There are many roads in the Alps where you might think you're the only one riding them. Even so, there will usually be a restaurant or hotel awaiting you.

Trip 16   **The French Jura**

Distance   *About 210 kilometers from Annecy to Col de la Faucille, one way*

Terrain   *Mostly small rural roads, some rough, pleasant mountain vistas*

Highlights   *Walk in gorge, Grand Colombier (1,531 meters), Col de la Faucille (1,320 meters), Col de la Givrine (1,229 meters), Col de Richemond (1,060 meters)*

Just west of Annecy (and the autoroute) through Lovagny are the Gorges du Fier and a fine looking castle named Montrottier. You can park and walk through the gorge, not the castle.

Continue on across the Rhone Valley to Culoz, and climb the steep ascent of the Montagne du Grand Colombier. There's a rustic restaurant near the top at about 1,500 meters, l'Auberge Le Grand Colombier, with a view southerly over the Lac du Bourget.

Wander along the Grand Colombier, northerly through Brenaz, and over the Col de Richemond which has a marker explaining that the col is named for World War II resistance martyrs.

Continue north across the autoroute near Bellegarde, where there are signs for Col de la Faucille. Climb a pleasant long valley then jog through some woods over the Col de la Faucille (1,320 meters) (see Trip 11 for Hotel La Mainaz, dramatically sited on the col). Geneve, Lac Leman, Swiss autoroutes are just over the col.

An alternate route, just before the Col de la Faucille, is to turn north, crossing into Switzerland after a couple of kilometers over the Col de la Givrine (1,229 meters). The col road and the border crossing meet in a triangle, but you have to go around two sides of it to get across the border.

To continue in the Swiss Jura, see Trip 11.

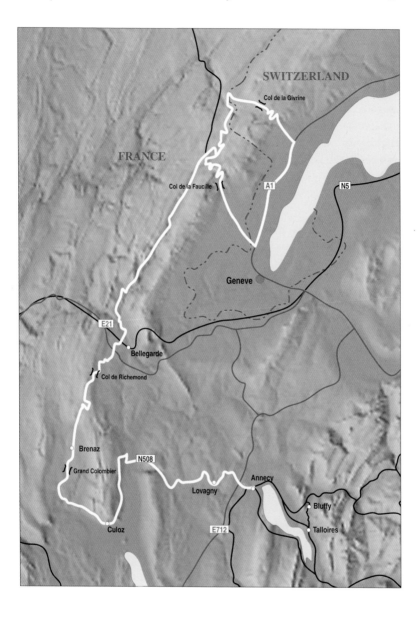

Trip 17   South of Lac D'Annecy

Distance   *About 250 kilometers round trip from Annecy*

Terrain   *From commercial valleys to mountain highs on every kind of paved road, limited facilities*

Highlights   *Ski resorts, one of the highest and loneliest roads of the Alps* ★★*Col de l'Iseran (2,769 meters), Col de la Forclaz (1,150 meters),* ★*Col de la Madeleine (1,984 meters), Col du Glandon (1,951 meters), Col de la Croix de Fer (2,068 meters), Col de Tamie (902 meters), Col du Mollard (1,638 meters)*

Some of the highest and most awesome passes of the Alps are south of Albertville, but their lower slopes are less forested and the heights seem grayer. In fact, they are often called the Gray Alps. Civilization seems further removed.

In addition to the main highways linking Lac d'Annecy with Albertville to its south, it's possible to take one of several low but interesting passes. Col de la Forclaz (same name as the pass out of Martigny, Switzerland) climbs right up the mountainside out of Talloires. In just a few kilometers, the restaurants at the summit provide views of the lake and of Talloires far below, as well as lunch, hang gliding, and parasailing. From the south end of the col, head for Faverges.

Descending southerly from the Col de l'Iseran to the little village of Bonneval.

From La Clusaz, the Col de la Croix Fry leads to Faverges.

A new highway takes through traffic around Faverges on the north side. From it, head south and cross through Faverges to the pleasant little Col de Tamie (D12). It connects to N90, an autoroute. Head east, upstream on N90 in the Isere Valley (no toll in this direction), passing Albertville and numerous dead-end routes south into ski resorts like Courchevel, all the way to Bourg St. Maurice. There, past the turn for the Petit St. Bernard, the climb up the Col de l'Iseran starts in earnest. (You could get to Bourg St. Maurice from Albertville by crossing over the Cormet de Roselend, a bit longer, and much twistier, all described in Trip 13).

A couple of bikes head up the north side of the Col de l'Iseran. Note the sturdy guard rails. The Val d'Isere ski areas are all way down right.

The Col de l'Iseran, named after the Isere River and its valley, the Val d'Isere (the river is L'Isere in French, so it sounds like "lee zayer," and the pass sounds like "coal duh lee zay RAHN"), is one of the highest in the Alps. The valley is where all the skiing events took place in the Albertville Olympics. The col connects the upper reaches of the Val d'Isere with the next valley south, the Val d'Arc, which sort of parallels it. Both flow to the Rhone.

The ski center at Val d'Isere, about 86 kilometers from Albertville, looks naked and uninviting in the summer, with its concrete highrises set in big gravel parking lots, and most everything closed. Above the ski center though, the road climbs and climbs through beautiful and ever-wilder looking country. As the deep snows melt in the early summer, the meadows are carpeted with flowers.

Cross the col—the mountains look even starker and wilder—into the Val d'Arc. The first village, Bonneval, has a couple of small hotels. One is the Bergerie where a big poster of Marilyn Monroe presides over the dining room. Further down, at Lanslebourg, a few more services are available and the Col du Mont Cenis heads up south to the roads of Trip 22. A good hotel at Lanslebourg is the Alpazur.

Farther down the Arc at St. Jean de Maurienne, past St. Martin and the turn up Col du Galibier, turn south and climb up the twisty Col de la Croix de Fer (D926), which bends west and meets the Col du Glandon near its summit. There's a tinier road up the Croix de Fer starting from the east side of St. Jean, and crossing the Col du Mollard on the way up. (D80). Atop the Croix de Fer is a small restaurant. And there is a cross of iron.

Up over the top of the Col de Glandon ride down its curves in open country to Le Chambre in the valley of the Arc. Straight across the main valley road is the road up the Col de la Madeleine. The south side of the Col de la Madeleine is fairly modern alignment with ski resorts. A restaurant at the top has a deck with views to Monte Blanc. The north side is narrow and more rugged. A possible lunch stop on the north side is the Hotel du Grand Pic at a village called Celliers at about 1,300 meters. Near the north end of the Col de la Madeleine, almost back in the Val d'Isere, there's a village quaintly called Pussy. It's not far back to Albertville and Lac d'Annecy. The Col de Tamie makes a good connection, bypassing Albertville.

Trip 18 Straight South over Three Cols

Distance *About 175 kilometers from Albertville to south of Grenoble*
Terrain *High mountains, twisting high pass roads, some narrow, few services*
Highlights *Almost a straight shot across three mountain ranges from Val d'Isere to Val d'Arc, to Val da la Romanche, to Val du Drac; from Albertville to south of Grenoble, Col de la Madeleine (1,984 meters), Col du Glandon (1,951 meters), Col d'Ornon (1,371 meters)*

Three passes line up, north to south, each with narrow, fairly rugged north slopes. Start about 20 kilometers up the Val d'Isere autoroute from Albertville (N90) at an exit (sortie) marked Col de la Madeleine. Wind up the narrow col past the turn to Pussy. The top of Madeleine has a good restaurant with views to Mont Blanc. Down the south side past ski facilities, cross the Arc River and the main valley road at La Chambre and start up the Col du Glandon. At the top it meets the Col de la Croix de Fer (Trip 17) then works its way down south past large reservoirs, into a gorge and back up around it, to the main road in the Val de la Romanche (N91). Four kilometers upstream along the Romanche, at Le Bourg d'Oisans, the Col d'Ornon (D526) starts its climb up south and over to Valbonnais and La Mure and the routes of Trip 21.

Motorcyclists in Switzerland wait for a green light so they can proceed through a one-way-at-a-time construction area. "LU" is canton Luzern, Switzerland. "VA" is Italian.

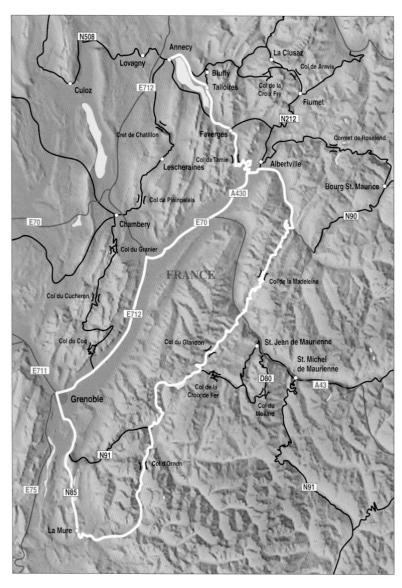

This trip could be combined with Trip 19 for a round trip of about 300 kilometers.

Trip 19 The Crest Route South

Distance *About 150 kilometers, one way*
Terrain *Rural roads, little traffic*
Highlights *Cret de Chatillon (1,699 meters), Col de Plainpalais (1,174 meters), Col du Granier (1,134 meters), Col du Cucheron (1,139 meters), Col du Coq (1,434 meters), Massif de la Chartreuse*

The Cret de Chatillon road starts right in Annecy. From the lakeside in Annecy, head uphill, west. The second roundabout should have a sign for Semnoz to the south. That's the one (D41). Immediately, you're out of traffic in a forest. After winding through the forest, the road comes out on a mountain crest where there's a restaurant with a terrrace view across lake and mountains to Mont Blanc. Then it's down through some hairpins and through several villages to one called Lescheraines where a road starts to climb up the Col de Plainpalais (D912). South, across the col, the road comes down to Chambery, a pretty good sized city. Follow the main road (not the autoroute) toward Grenoble a few kilometers and pick one of several roads (like D12A) climbing the Col du Granier, only about 20 kilometers up. The col has a pleasant restaurant and a wood carver. Down through a gorge and on up over Col du Cucheron, (D512)

This Austrian sign says, "Give your guardian angel a chance."

skirt the Chartreuse Massif. Just past the village of St. Pierre-de-Chartreuse, the Col du Coq climbs east up over the massif and wends down to Grenoble . . . a big city.

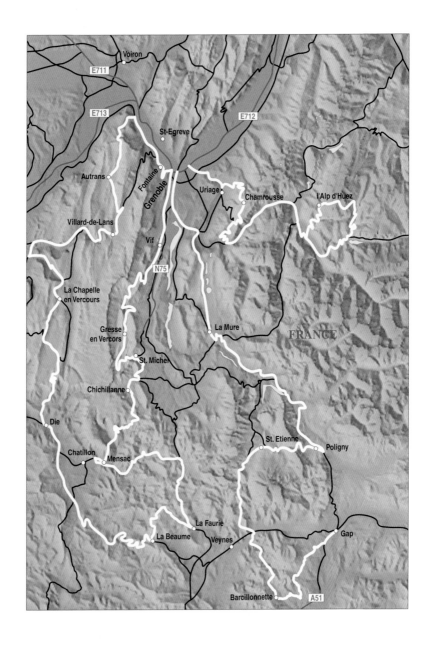

Grenoble Highs

Grenoble is a city surrounded by mountain massiffs, each worth exploring. To the north is the Massiff de la Chartreuse (Trip 19). To the east is the Chamrousse, and beyond that, l'Alpe d'Huez, famous in the Tour de France. To the south is the Vercors Massif.

An autoroute comes into Grenoble from the northeast and exits to the northwest, looping south of the old city. The first exit (sortie) on the northeast side of the loop has a cluster of chain hotels. One, the Ibis, is a little nicer than a Motel 6, others are even more modular than Motel 6. In fact Motel 6 is owned by the same French company, the Accor Group, that owns Ibis. Quite serviceable. (There are over 500 Ibis hotels around France).

At the other end of the loop around the old city, the northwest side, is an exit (sortie) named Fontaine. Fontaine is a suburb and it's main street, on the south side of the autoroute, has a line of motorcycle shops.

Many sources tell of the history and wonders of Grenoble, an Olympic city. Here, we'll concentrate on roads, some of which have already been described in Trips 18 and 19.

North of Grenoble is a mountain area known as Chartreuse. Immediately east of Grenoble is a mountain known as Chamrousse. South of Grenoble is a mountain mass known as the Vercors Massif. On the east side of the Vercors is Chichilianne with Hotel Chateau de Passiers, and Gresse-en-Vercors, with Hotel Chalet. On the south side on the Col de Menee is Le Mont Barral Hotel-Restaurant. On the west side of the Vercors in Villard-de-Lans is Best Western Grand Hotel de Paris. Then at Autrans is Hotel La Buffe.

An autoroute heads south out of Grenoble and immediately starts branching. One branch, N91, follows the Romanche River east toward Alpe d'Huez and on to trips of Chapter 7. One branch, M85, is the Route Napoleon to Gap. One branch, N75, skirts the Vercors Massif.

When Napoleon escaped from the island of Elba, he marched on Paris through the Alps, Gap, and Grenoble. A hundred days later he was defeated at Waterloo and got shipped off farther than Elba. The route he took through the Alps is known now as the Route Napoleon.

Trip 20 Alpe d'Huez

Distance *About 170 kilometers round trip from the Grenoble area*
Terrain *Nice sweepers through forested mountains; some arduous switchbacks*
Highlights *Forest roads, famous climb of Tour de France, Chamrousse (1,650 meters), Col Luitel (1,262 meters), l'Alpe d'Huez (1,860 meters), Col de Sarenne (1,989 meters)*

The Chamrousse is a high mountain immediately east of Grenoble with a scenic loop road to a ski resort. To find the road, take the autoroute sortie for Uriage on the east side of Grenoble (D524). From Uriage, a handsome residential area and spa, the Chamrousse loop starts (D111).

Looping clockwise, the descent meets the tiny Col Luitel road which works it's way down south to the valley of the Romanche River (N91). Turn east, upstream, through the Gorges de la Romanche. A couple of kilometers past le Bourg d'Oisans is the turn for the famous switchback climb to l'Alpe d'Huez (D211). It's immediately apparent why the road is such a famous challenge on the Tour de France. It climbs north up the face of the mountain, relentless through a series of traverses, connected by switch backs; about 700 meters up in thirteen kilometers. No problem for a motorcycle. Alpe d'Huez at the top sports

On the west side of Grenoble, the suburb Fontaine has a motorcycle shop row.

a bunch of impressive looking ski hotels, firmly closed in the summer. The road through Alpe d'Huez climbs farther over the Col de Sareene, leaving the ski resorts behind. It narrows, and a bunch of deep, rock-paved cross-gutters welcome you to remote pastures of sheep. It then works it's way down to the valley of the Romanche at a nondescript intersection with N90.

The Col du Lautaret and the roads of Trip 22 are 25 kilometers further upstream. Grenoble is downstream.

Trip 21 Route Napoleon

Distance *140 kilometers round trip from Gap, 70 more south of Grenoble*
Terrain *Fairly rugged, very lonely passes all above and west of Route Napoleon*
Highlights *A sense of exploring tiny roads with some wonderful views and little villages, Col du Noyer (1,644 meters), Col du Festre (1,441 meters), Col d'Espreaux (1,142 meters), Col de Foureyssasse (1,040 meters), Col du Villar (1,039 meters), Col Bayard (1,248 meters)*

Head south about 70 kilometers from Grenoble toward Gap past La Mure (Trip 18) on the Route Napoleon, or north from Gap about 14 kilometers over Col Bayard, to an insignificant village called Poligny where there are signs for the Col du Noyer (D17) to the west. Almost aimlessly, the road from Poligny wanders through farms and farm yards for several kilometers before starting its persistent climb back and forth up the col. Views across the farms to the high Alps beyond are wonderful. Across the col, the road comes down a little way into the village of St. Entienne and then down through the Defile des Etroits, before climbing southerly over the Col du Festre to meet a main east/west road (D944).

Nobody rides Col du Noyer, even though it affords sweeping views of the high Alps.

Jog west just half a kilometer and turn south under the railroad tracks on D20. A couple of kilometers through farm lands leads to the more intricate climb up over the Col d'Espreaux, and down to a tiny village, Barcillonnette (not to be confused with Barcelonnette, 75 kilometers east). Turn east on D420 for 8 kilometers, then north on D19 toward Gap over Col de Foureyssasse and Col du Villar.

Gap has most services including motorcycle shops. There are signs for Grenoble.

Trip 22 **All Around the Vercors Massif**

Distance *300 kilometers round trip from Grenoble*

Terrain *Up and down again on fairly narrow twisting mountain roads, with a couple of sweepers*

Highlights *Spectacular gorge ★★Grand Goulets and Gorges de la Bourne, favorite motorcycle roads, some possible hotel stops, Col de l'Arzelier (1,154 meters), Col de l'Allimas (1,342 meters), ★Col de Menee (1,457 meters), ★Col de Grimone (1,208 meters), Col de la Haute Beaume (1,268 meters), Col de Cabre (1,180 meters), ★Col de Rousset (1,367 meters), Col de St. Alexis (1,222 meters), Col de Proncel (1,100 meters), Col de la Croix-Perrin Jaume (1,220 meters)*

In the Grand Goulets, the two way road is cut into the vertical granite cliffs of the gorge.

Vercors Massif is about 100 kilometers long north to south and about 2,500 meters high. Even though it's only a few kilometers wide east to west, no road climbs across its vertical mass. It appears to be fairly flat on top, but no road goes there. The roads on this trip circle its flanks in a clockwise direction, having a lot of fun trying for the top but not making it. The top is the "Reserve Naturelle des Hauts Plateau du Vercors." Some of the roads are regularly on the Tour de France. The l'Isere River makes a sharp bend to the north at Grenoble to get around the Massif.

South out of Grenoble on N75, just a couple of kilometers at Vif, D8 starts up the Vercors Massif over the Col de l'Arzeilier and on to Gresse-en-Vercors and Hotel Chalet. Through Gresse over Col de l'Allimas and on to N75 nine kilometers to the turn back up the Vercors to Col de Menee (D7) past Chichilianne and the Hotel Chateau de Passieres. The col road is marked difficult on some maps. Famous for vintage car races, it's fairly intricate through forests to a tunnel at the top. Then it's more open on its way down past Le Mont Barral Hotel to Mensac where there's a one kilometer short cut easterly to the Col de Grimone road.

The Col de Grimone is exciting as it climbs through the the narrow Gorges de Gats, sometimes in tunnels. Across the top it makes a more open descent to N75. South on N75 eighteen kilometers to La Faurie there's a turn back up the Vercors (D28) over Col de Haute Beaume, a nobody-there road. Near the top there may be herds of sheep. Just a couple of kilometers down, there's an intersection with the Col de Cabre road (D93) which climbs quickly through tight sweepers to the top and then winds down through a lot of tight sweepers into the valley of the Drome River which it follows northwesterly through open country to the town of Die.

The west side of the Col de Grimone snakes through the Gorges de Gats.

The traverses of the Col de Rousset are famous in local motorcycling circles.

Just west of Die, the famous Col de Rousset road turns north up the west flank of the Vercors Massif. In a series of open traverses connected by hairpins it climbs the col. Very photograph-able. Just over the top, left at a fork climbs back over the Col de St. Alexis (D76), and then over the Col de Proncel through La Chapelle en Vercors to the Grand Goulets.

Turn into the Grand Goulets, and immediately the road is in tiny tunnels and terraces chiseled into vertical granite cliffs. Another photographic must. Two way traffic. Down through the Grand Goulets and then through the Petit Goulets there's an intersection with the Gorges de la Bourne road (D531) back up east, almost as spectacular as the Grand Goulets, but a little more open, leads right into Villard-de-Lans. Villard-de-Lans has been an overnight stop on the Tour de France and is the site of the Best Western Grand Hotel de Paris. The hotel might have been grand once. It is pleasantly sited. From Villard-de-Lans, there's a more direct road down through the Gorges d'Engins into Grenoble, or one at Lans, over the Col de la Croix Pernin Jaume to a village, Autrans, with the Hotel La Buffe, and on down to the Isere River and Grenoble.

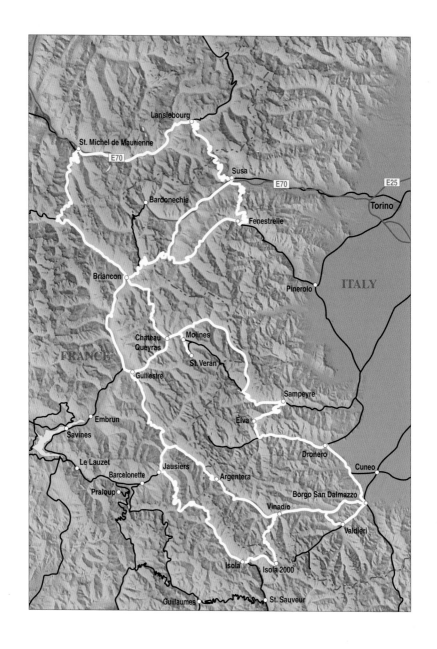

The Gray Alps

A succession of kings and emperors pushed the French border east across the southern Alps at the expense of Italy, so that much of the high country is in France today. A few minor passes cross down into Italy. The countryside is bleak and the few towns are walled fortresses, left over from the defense budgets of past centuries. Here are some of the highest passes in the Alps, several of which are known today as the Route des Grandes Alpes.

While the northern Alps abound in tourist accommodations, restaurants and hotels are few and far between in the southern Alps, and often closed. The small village of Guillestre, at 1,000 meters, offers the best amenities. It's one of those fortress towns with stone works that boggle the mind, left over from Louis XIV. Guillestre is south of Briancon and east of Gap, and the base of two passes on the Route des Grandes Alpes, the Col de Vars and the Col d'Izoard. Les Barnieres is a nice modern hotel with a good restaurant, even tennis and a pool in season. No English!

A little closer to the center of Guillestre and a bit less formidable is Hotel le Catinat Fleuri. To an American eye, it looks more like a U.S. style motel, with a parking lot in front.

A huge stone fortress, Mont Dauphin, of Louis XIV's time, dominates the valley at Guillestre. Cross the moat, ride through the gates, and check it out.

Why not stay at the highest hotel in the highest village in the Alps? Upstream, east of Guillestre, in the Parc Regional du Queyras, is a rustically preserved village called St. Veran at 2,257 meters. At the village limits is a NO VEHICLES sign, except those on business. You have business. Past the little village church there should be a sign pointing up to the Chateau Renard above the village. English spoken. The owner's wife is from Tasmania. To get to St. Veran, head up the Col d'Izoard and turn east at the fortress, Chateau Queyras. A couple of kilometers past the fortress, turn south to Molines and then St. Veran (see road description for Trip 19).

Southwest of Guillestre at Embrun is Hotel les Bartavelles, known to accommodate international motorcyclists. Where the Col di Sampeyre and the Col Agnel roads meet in Italy is large comfortable Hotel Monte Nebin.

Trip 23 Around Guillestre

Distance *About 250 kilometers*

Terrain *High, rugged mountains and roads, limited facilities*

Highlights *Exotic wild scenery, ★★Col d'Izoard (2,361 meters), Col de Montgenevre (1,850 meters), into Italy, Sestriere (2,033 meters), Col de Finestre (2,174 meters), Col du Mt. Cenis (2,083 meters), Col du Telegraphe (1,578 meters), ★★Col du Galibier (2,645 meters), Col du Lautaret (2,058 meters), Col de l'Eschelle (1,760 meters)*

East from Guillestre the Col d'Izoard road (D902) enters the Parc Regional du Queyras following the gorge of the Guil River. The road twists and tunnels through the gorge (this part of the road often seems to have gravel on it, not always conveniently placed) and climbs to a fork at a fortress on a mountain, the Chateau Queyras. The north fork is the Col d'Izoard. The right leads to St. Veran and Trip 19. The Col d'Izoard snakes up through very strange formations and barren gravel, an area called the Casse Deserte, to a summit with an obelisk monument, and winds down past a refuge with minimal facilities dating from Napoleon III, coming down right into Briancon, a pretty good sized city with another fortress.

This rider is starting down the south side of the Col du Galibier below the short tunnel. The glaciers are those of the Massif des Ecrins.

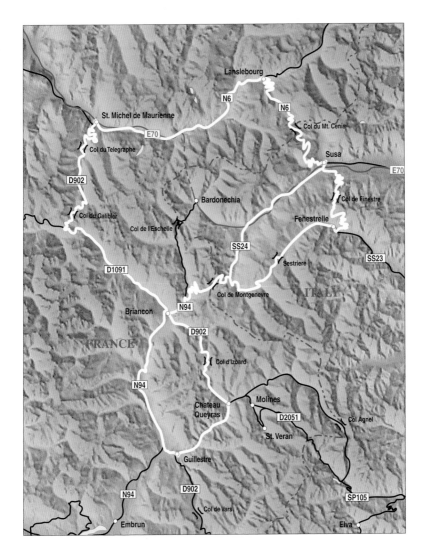

Loop through the city to get on the main road and take the road east to Italy (N94) and the Col de Montgenevre, only 15 kilometers up.

Then, six kilometers down into Italy, the road splits. A south leg climbs to a ski resort, really a pass, called Sestriere, then goes down toward Torino, passing Fenestrelle where there's a tempting climb north on a partly paved pass road, the Col de Finestre, which comes down near Susa.

Or, starting up the Col de Montgenevre road out of Briancon, just 4 kilometers, there's a turn north to Nevache, and then over obsure Col de l'Eschelle into Bardonecchia and then down to Susa. Below Bardonecchia, there's a connection to the Tunnel du Frejus (toll) back to France and the Val d'Arc.

Coming into Italy over the Col de Montgenevre, at the split where the south leg goes to Sestriere, the north leg goes past the connection to Bardonecchia and on to Susa. At Susa, the Col du Mt. Cenis climbs back north into France, then along a lake and down into the Val d'Arc, just below the Col de l'Iseran at Lanslebourg, Site of Hotel Alpazur (Trip 17).

There are two parallel east-west roads through Susa, a few blocks apart. The Col de Finestre and the Col de Montgenevre are signed from the southerly one. The Col du Mt. Cenis is signed from the northerly one. The Col de Finestre rates a brown sign a bit east of the centro, city center.

Head downstream, west, in the Val d'Arc (N6) as far as St. Michel de Maurienne, where one of the wildest passes of the Alps (D902) climbs right up south, the Col du Galibier. Before tackling the wonderful high stuff, the road climbs the Col du Telegraphe to a village, Valloire, where there's a hotel called Relais du Galibier. From Valloire begins the real climb over the Col du Galibier. Near the top, there's a short cut tunnel. Real motorcyclists (and bicyclists) take the road on over the top. Coming down the south side of the Col du Galibier there are views of the glaciers across in the Parc National de Ecrins, and down below of the junction with the top of the Col du Lautaret, which is an east-west road.

From the junction (N91), it's a sweeping ride on down to Briancon and Guillestre.

Looking down on the north side of the Col d'Izoard at the Refuge Napoleon.

From the top of the Col du Galibier there's a good view down to the tunnel entrance that cuts off the last part of the fun.

The Col d'Izoard, between Briancon and Guillestre, has strange rock formations.

Trip 24 Agnel, Sampeyre, and Lombarde

Distance *230 kilometers*
Terrain *Little roads over high passes*
Highlights *Four high passes, two unknown, seldom traveled ★★Col Agnel (dell'Agnello, in Italian) (2,744 meters), ★★Col di Sampeyre (2,284 meters), Col de Larche (Maddelena in Italian) (1,996 meters), Col de Vars (2,111 meters), ★★Col de Lombarde (2,351 meters), Madonna di Colletto (1,304 meters)*

Head out of Guillestre on the road to Col d'Izoard, and turn at Chateau Queyras toward St. Veran (D5). (There's a rough dead-end road that climbs up behind the Chateau fortress to 2,257 meters.) Before St. Veran, turn through the village Molines, which doesn't believe in street repair. Not to worry. Above the village is smooth narrow asphalt, climbing very high in a broad valley above the tree line to the Col Agnel and the Italian border. This little road is one of the highest in the Alps. Sometimes, back at Molines there's a FERME, closed, sign. But the road is opened for the Giro d'Italia bicycle race very early in June. So go for it. Down below the pass, in Italy, there may be a bar across the road, but just join the locals driving around it.

The highest hotel in the highest town in the Alps is Chateau Renard above the village of St. Veran, France.

Down about 35 kilometers into Italy at a village called Sampeyre is Hotel Monte Nebin, a large and comfortable inn. (Interesting how Sampeyre in Italian sounds like Saint Peter in French.) The mountain, Monte Nebin, is high above the village on the Col di Sampeyre which snakes up the mountain south of the village. Col di Sampeyre is not much traveled. There's an interesting metal sculpture of the Madonna at the top, and views of distant snow capped peaks.

The pavement on the road down south is sort of broken up, but passable. On the south side in the village, Elva, there's a little church with a very fine Renaaissance fresco. What's it doing here? The ristorante in Elva will lend you a key to the church while it prepares your very Italian lunch. The descent south from Elva is spectacular. The artist must have come up through this gorge 400 years ago.

Back on the valley road, below Elva and the gorge, head downstream to Donero, a town about out of the mountains with tree shaded streets. Then south to Borgo San Dalmazzo, avoiding Cuneo, a fair sized city to the east. At Borgo, head west to France on the Col de Maddalena road. There are a couple of ways to cross into France from Borgo. Most traffic signs point southerly to France and Monaco through the Col de Tende tunnel. If that's not your intention, be sure to head west toward Argentera, a village near the border on the Col de Maddalena. If you should find yourself on the road to Valdieri, which is a dead end valley parallel to, but south of the Argentera road, not to worry. At the village, Valdieri, there's a good little pass road going north called Madonna di Colletto. It crosses north and comes down on the road for Argentera. Once you cross into France from Argentera, Col de Maddalena is called Col de Larche. There are a couple of good bends on the way down to the valley road which it joins just south of the Col de Vars and north of Jausiers. Head back over the Col de Vars for Guillestre and St. Veran.

If you're riding up hill into Sampeyre toward the Col Agnel and France, the turn for the Col de Sampeyre is clearly marked. But coming down from France, it can't be seen.

A group of bikers pauses near the little monument atop the Col di Sampeyre, Italy, looking at those French peaks in the distance.

Or, instead of crossing back into France on the main Col de Maddalena road, connecting to the Col de Vars, it's possible to cross the border on a seldom traveled high pass, the Col de Lombarde, which ties in with the south end of the passes in Trip 24. West from Cuneo toward the French border on the Col de Maddalena road, after the village of Vinadio, the narrow Col de Lombarde heads south. It is a lot of fun on the Italian climb to the summit. (At about 2,000 meters elevation, the road straight ahead dead ends. The pass road cuts back to the left.) A few kilometers down into France, the road enters a ski resort called Isola 2000, apparently the elevation. On into Isola, in the valley below, the road is aligned to get busloads of skiers up to Isola 2000. The lower Isola is on the south end of the Col du Restefond, which leads north to the Col de Vars.

More roads to the south are in the next section, Some High Stuff.

8

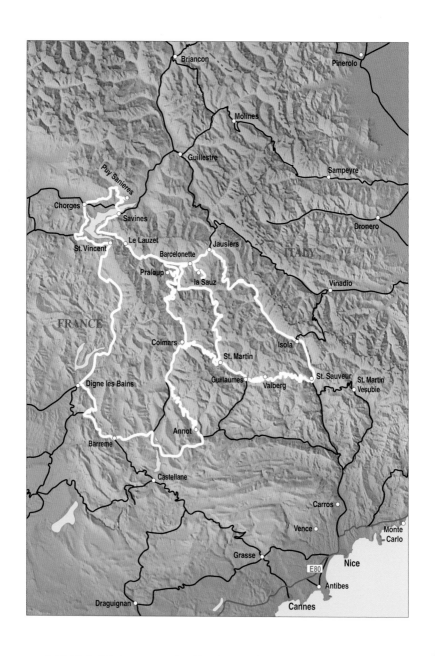

Some High Stuff

South over the Col de Vars from Guillestre is the high valley of the Ubaye River where there's a town, Barcelonnette, surrounded by high Alps. North of town, only a few trails climb a kilometer or two up the steep slopes. But south of Barcelonnette, several twisting pass roads scale the peaks of the Parc National du Mercantour. And east eight kilometers is Jausiers, gateway to the Col du Restefond and La Bonette. Downstream, west along the Ubaye are pass roads seldom explored offering marvelous vistas of lakes and mountains.

It's possible to stay in Barcelonnette. Would you believe the main hotel is called the Azteca, famous for its Mexican decor. But no Mexican food. In fact, no restaurant. In the center of Barcelonnette there is a very modest looking restaurant right next to a small fountain with delightful food, La Gaudissart. It may also feature some Mexican decor. Apparently when the French withdrew support for Maximillian as emperor of Mexico in the 1860s, some supporters who didn't relish his fate found their way to Barcelonnette.

There are hotels in nearby mountain villages. For instance, eight kilometers southwest and up on the mountainside is Pra Loup with a hotel called Prieure de Molanes. Just four kilometers up and south is the village La Sauze. (Note that in French, "at la Sauze" becomes *au Sauze*.) Au Sauze are the Alp Hotel and the Hotel Soleil et Neiges (Sun and Snow).

After a long day's ride, some bikers took a little back road into La Sauze. Armed with nice web page pictures of the Alp Hotel, they asked for it, only to be told, "I don't think you want to go there." Seems the poor owner had just fallen to his death from a high window. "Not to worry," said a lady, "my hotel, the Soleil et Neiges, will be open tonight at 6:30 and I will have rooms." Well, she did open at 6:30, and she did have rooms. After a fabulous dinner, the bikers were still the only guests. Strange. And why 6:30? Aha. By 9 p.m., the place was packed with an office party from Nice.

Trip 25 Three Highs

Distance *140 kilometers*
Terrain *High rugged mountains and roads*
Highlights *Seldom traveled narrow mountain roads through wild mountains.* ★*Col de la Cayolle (2,327 meters),* ★*Col des Champs (2,087 meters),* ★*Col d'Allos (2,240 meters)*

The road south from Barcelonnette forks a couple of kilometers above town. The tine to the west climbs the Col d'Allos. The easterly tine climbs the Col de la Cayolle. Each is a narrow, exciting road climbing opposite sides of a gorge into the Mercantour Park. Each road barely clings to the cliffs above the gorge. Over the top of the Col de la Cayolle about six kilometers down, at Estenc, there's a fine restaurant in a stone building called Relais de la Cayolle. Farther down the south side of the col at St. Martin, there's a connecting pass road, the Col des Champs. It climbs west from the town of St. Martin, connecting it with Colmar, over on the south side of the Col d'Allos. The intersections in both towns are well marked. From St. Martin, the Col des Champs road is fairly well defined, climbing past jagged peaks. But once across the top, above the treeline, the road on down to Colmar has many deep paved drainage ditches and lots of gravel trailing off the slopes.

Hardly anyone finds their way to the top of the Col des Champs.

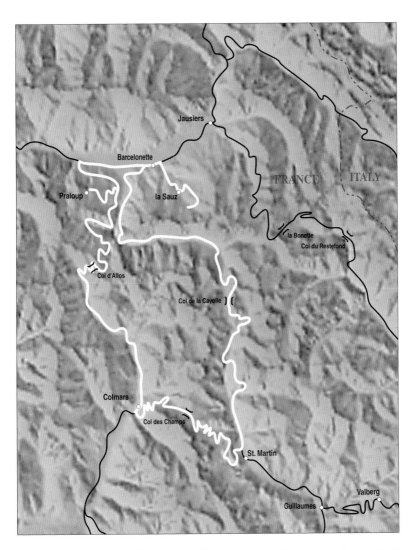

Still in the woods of the Col des Champs, a view site has a marker entitled "Un peu d'histoire," a little history, with a map of Colmar and its fortifications. Seems in the early days of Louis XIV, Colmar was on the border, so Louis ordered it fortified. Then, after a couple of battles, Louis annexed the surrounding area, so Colmar was no longer a border town. However Louis' armies did it, it's probably more fun today on a bike. It's interesting to walk inside the walls of old Colmar. Colmar and the Col d'Allos mark the headwaters of the Verdon River (see Trip 29). There's a serviceable restaurant just outside the walls of old Colmar called Cafe de France.

Take the Col d'Allos, an intricate climb, back to Barcelonnette.

Trip 26 La Bonnette

Distance *about 200 kilometers*

Terrain *Very rugged, barren mountains and a road oft called the highest in the Alps.*

Highlights *Exotic wild scenery. Col du Restefond (2,678 meters) ★★la Bonnette (2,862 meters), Col de la Couillole (1,678 meters), Col Valberg (1,668 meters), ★Col de la Cayolle (2,327 meters)*

About eight kilometers east of Barcelonnette at a village called Jausiers, the Col du Restefond road begins its struggle up the pass, which may not be open until mid-summer. It isn't a commercial route. Near the top, there's a loop road called La Bonette which might be the highest pass road in the Alps. It climbs up around a peak to a high point where many seem to have been unable to restrain themselves from leaving a mark of their visit. Near the loop junction are two arrow signs. One pointing north reads PARIS. One pointing south reads NICE.

From the col it's about 50 kilometers south, past some abandoned military buildings, a village or two, the Col de Lombarde road at Isola (Trip 24), on down to St. Sauveur. There, instead of continuing on to Nice, turn sharply

This rock marks the highest point on the highest road in the Alps, La Bonette (2,862 meters). It's a loop off of the Col du Restefond.

down across a river, for the Col de la Couillole. It really twists up a red rock gorge, past a medieval village hung on the cliff, Roubion. The road comes down in a valley and then climbs up again over the Col Valberg. At Valberg there's the Hotel Le Chalet Suisse that advertises itself as having winter sports only 80 kilometers from Nice.

West of Valberg, at Guillaumes, is the Col de la Cayolle road, heading north to Colmar, Barcelonnette, and Guillestre.

Trip 27 Around Lac De Serre-Poncon

Distance   *About 285 kilometers*
Terrain   *Some tiny, tight roads, some open sweepers*
Highlights   *Little, low passes with amazing views of lakes and mountains and fields; rural France, one major pass, Col d'Allos (2,240 meters), Col Lebraut (1,110 meters), Col de Pontis (1,301 meters), Col St. Jean (1,333 meters), Col de Maure (1,346 meters), Col de Toutes Aures (1,120 meters), Col de la St. Michel (1,431 meters), Col de Corobin (1,230 meters)*

Westerly from Barcelonnette the main road follows the Ubaye River in a pleasant sweeping fashion (D900). Just west of the village, Le Lauzet, about 24 kilometers from Barcelonnette, turn down northerly along and across the river (D954). In about six kilometers, a tiny road starts steeply north, signed for Pontis. Near the top there are sweeping views of lakes and mountains. The Pontis road comes back down, north, on D954. At Savines it joins N94. Take N94 north across a long bridge, then, for fun, take a little road up the mountain north to Puy Sanieres.

From Puy Sanieres, D9 wends through remote meadows back down to N94 at Chorges. Cross under N94 on D3, climbing over Col Lebraut to a nice view cafe, then down to D900. Take it easterly to a junction at St. Vincent where it

Short and small Col de Pontis has a nice viewpoint down over Lac de Serre Poncon.

continues a climb south over the Col St. Jean, then on south over the Col de Maure to Digne-les-Bains (say DEEN yay) where there's the Tonic Hotel.

In Digne, look for signs to "Thermal" and "Eaux Chaud" (hot water). The road goes east up a valley past the Tonic Hotel and past public baths, and then becomes a dancing climb up over the Col de Corobin and down to join the Route Napoleon (now N85). Just seven kilometers southeast at Barreme turn east on N202 around a lake and over the Verdon River (see Trip 29) and on over the Col de Toutes Aures. East of Toutes Aures, near Annot, a wonderful little road, D908, heads back north, making a dramatic climb over the Col de la St. Michel and down to the valley of the Verdon. Upstream, north, is Colmar and the Col d'Allos and Barcelonnette.

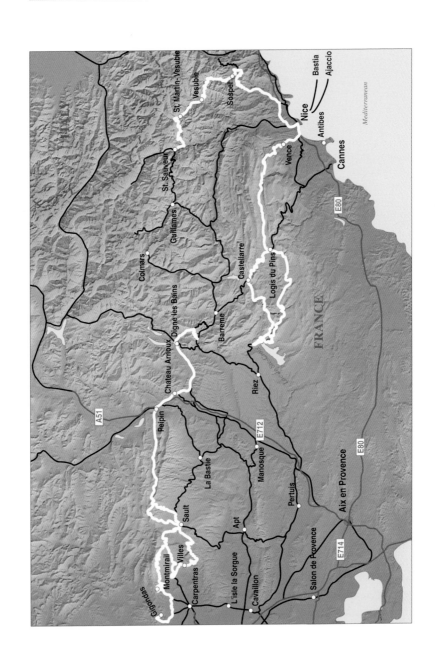

Provence

Provence in France conjurs up romantic notions and stories enough to fill a thousand books. It's where the southern end of the Alps meets the sea . . . the Mediterranean. And it *is* different. Instead of gray stone houses with gray slate (or metal) roofs, provincial houses are beige stucco with rosy tile roofs. There are indeed fields of lavender. Markets are full of blue and yellow linens. It's usually drier, sunnier, than the Alps to the north. This is the Provence of the mind's eye. It includes several political divisions.

Should you be checking out this Provence, the one in the travel books, the one in the mind's eye, there are some roads to enjoy, too.

A likely base in the east near Nice and Monaco is Vence, a city almost atop the first range of mountains, about 15 kilometers from the Mediterranean and about 25 from Nice. It has a lively provincial marketplace, a chapel designed by Matisse, a coastal climate, and it's not too far from the Grand Canyon du Verdon, a major motorcycle destination. A good modern hotel with parking and a pool is the Mas de Vence.

Nice is a big city with motorcycle dealers of all brands. (Moto Deschamps, BMW, Kawasaki, and Bimota, have all proved very helpful to travelers.)

To the west, not far from Avignon and Aix and the Rhone River and vinyards, not to mention the major motorcyle destination, Mont Ventoux (always on the Tour de France), the village Gigondas is just into the foothills from Orange (say oh RAWNGH). And there, hidden in the trees, is Hotel Les Florets. In Digne-les-Bains is Hotel Tonic.

There are a lot of roads in Provence. Here are some of the best.

Trip 28 Twisting to Vence

Distance *About 120 very kinky kilometers*
Terrain *Low mountains, but very convoluted pass roads*
Highlights *Col St. Martin (1,500 meters), Col de Turini (1,604 meters), Col de Braus (1,002)*

The south end of the Col du Restefond described in Trip 26 is at St. Sauveur where that trip route headed west over the Col de la Couillole. From St. Sauveur, there are some fairly direct roads to Nice and Vence. But here is the twisty way.

Just four kilometers south of St. Sauveur is a junction. Turn up east over the Col St. Martin (D66) to St. Martin-Vesublie. Vesublie is a river. Then south, downstream 13 kilometers to another junction. Turn up east (D70) across the Col de Turini and then south to Sospel, a pretty good sized town. North from Sospel, one road climbs to Italy via a tunnel, the Col de Tende. The one to Nice and Vence wiggles southwesterly up the Col de Braus, and then winds down to Nice, about 40 kilometers away. There are few services between Sospel and

Looking south toward the Mediterranean over traverses of the Col de Braus. Somewhere down there are Nice and Monte Carlo and lots of people.

Nice. From Nice, take the autoroute or coast road west about 15 kilometers to Cagnes, where there are signs for Vence.

Trip 29 Grand Canyon du Verdon

Distance *About 240 kilometers, round trip from Vence*
Terrain *Low mountains, rural roads, some very twisty*
Highlights *Grand Canyon, Corniche Sublime, Col de Vence (963 meters), Col de Luens (1,054 meters), Col d'Ayen (1,032 meters), Cirque de Vaumale (1,201 meters), Col de Clavel (1,060 meters)*

Don't expect the Grand Canyon of Arizona or the Copper Canyon of Mexico. But the Grand Canyon du Verdon has good paved roads that go around and through it.

The Col de Vence road climbs north out of Vence (D2) over the col and then heads west all the way to Le Logis du Pins, where a main road (N85) climbs northwesterly over the Col de Luens to Castellarre. Cross over the Verdon River, and head for its famous canyon (D952).

The Verdon flows mostly from northeast to southwest. This route is on the north side of the canyon. Parts of the road wind down a bit into the canyon. It's kind of like looking from the south rim in Arizona, the high walls are across the river. A loop road (D23) goes down deeper. There are tunnels and viewpoints. At the west end of the canyon, a large lake comes into view. It's possible to turn

Twisting to Vence. Will it ever end? Sometimes it seems the road climbs a mountain, only to start back down it.

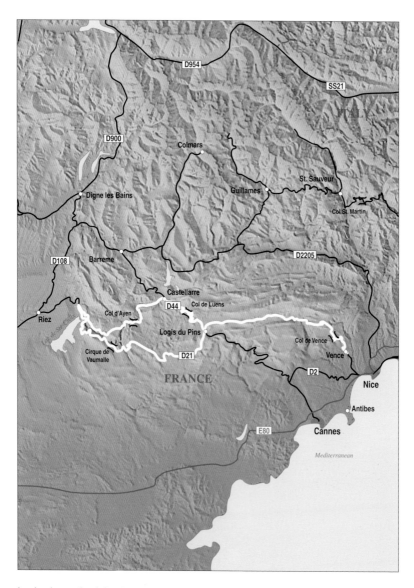

back along the lake (D957) and a few kilometers later, turn up the famous Corniche Sublime (D71) which twists quite laboriously back east along the south rim to Comps, where a road (D21) heads back to Le Logis du Pins and the road to Vence.

Should one way be enough, it's possible to go north 50 kilometers from the west end, by the lake where the north side road meets the Corniche road, to Digne-les-Bains where a very satisfactory hotel is the Tonic.

Trip 30 Mont Ventoux

Distance *About 200 kilometers from Gigondas*
Terrain *Good mountain roads, rural fields, and villages*
Highlights ★*Mont Ventoux (1,909 meters), Gorges de la Nesque,
Povincial village Sault, Col de l'Homme Mort (1,212 meters), Col de
Macuegne (1,068 meters)*

From Gigondas, a road (D90) works through a jagged mountain called the
Dentelles (laces) de Montmirail to Malaucene, the beginning of the climb up
the west side of Mont Ventoux (D974).

Mont Ventoux isn't a pass. It's a mountain almost 2,000 meters high not too
far from the Mediterranean and close to the tourist centers of Aix and Avignon
(north of Aix and northeast of Avignon). The three roads to the summit are
often used to test cars and brakes. One of the three, the one from the west (from
Gigondas and Malaucene) is usually featured in the Tour de France. It's a steady

Yes indeed, the French have a Dead Man's Pass.

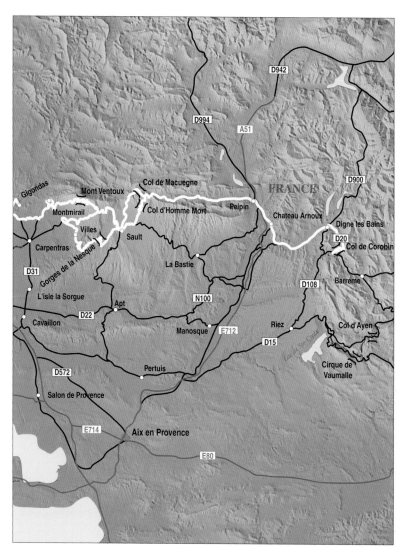

climb with mostly open sweepers, a few tighter than others, through several climate zones. A sort of missile-looking pylon marks the windswept top. There's a cafe just below the summit. Then, a few kilometers down to the east, there's a junction and a restaurant, the Chalet Reynard. South from the Chalet, the road down (D974) is tight but banked like a race track for 15 kilometers. At the bottom of the mountain, a few jogs south across little fields lead to a village called Villes, gateway to a twisting, climbing, and scenic ride through the Gorges de la Nesque (D942). At the east end of the gorge road is an interesting provincial village, Sault.

Meanwhile, the road east from the Chalet Reynard wends more roughly down to Sault. Sault sits atop an embankment, with views back to Ventoux. Some may need to stop and shop.

From Sault, two pass roads loop further east through very rural landscapes. Dead Man's Pass (Col de l'Homme Mort) is northeast from Sault (D63). It meets the Col de Macuegne (D542) which heads back to Sault.

Sixty rural kilometers east of Col de Macuegne is Digne-les-Bains and the Hotel Tonic.

South of Andermatt

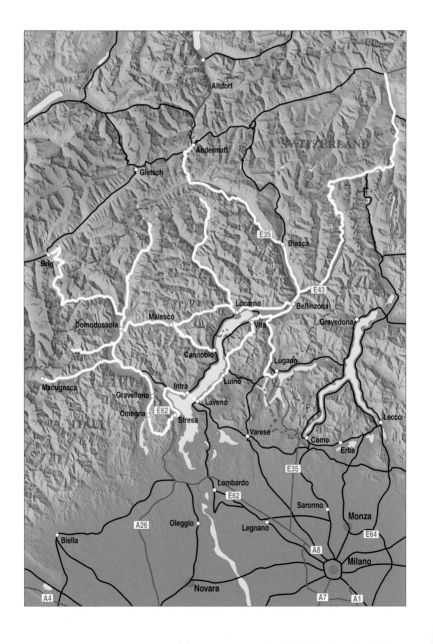

Lago Maggiore

If it gets a bit chilly or misty up in the high county, just do what the Swiss do: head for Lugano or Locarno, down in that Italian-speaking, pasta-eating part of Switzerland called Ticino. It's only an hour or two away. Hawaii, it's not. But around the lake shores there are real, if dwarf, palm trees, and oleander and hibiscus blooms—probably in pots—even while the snowy mountain peaks are still in sight. And there are some pretty good roads to get there on.

Locarno is on the north shore of a long, large lake called Maggiore. Part of the lake is in Italy, the rest in Switzerland. Lugano is on a smaller lake called Lugano, a bit southeast of Locarno. Why must the names sound so much alike? To confuse us.

Locarno, on Lago Maggiore, is small, sunny, and closer to the mountains than Lugano. It has hotels on the lake, on the hills, and in neighboring villages.

Right on the lake in Locarno is the Ramada Hotel Arcadia. Rooms with a view of the lake are a bit more than "garden views." Just a few blocks uphill and down in price is a plain, practical hotel, Hotel Carmine. Across Lago Maggiore from Locarno, about 20 kilometers around the north tip of the lake, is San Nazzaro, where a modest hotel, Albergo Consolina, is squeezed on the water's edge and has great views across to Locarno and the Alps beyond from the dining room and some of the guest rooms (the back rooms are close to a train track).

From Lugano, the southernmost Swiss city, almost surrounded by Italy, the border crossing in the direction of Lago Maggiore is signed PONTE TRESA. At Ponte Tresa there's a pleasant waterfront hotel restaurant called del Pesce.

From the high Alps there are three pass roads leading down to Lago Maggiore: from Andermatt, the St. Gotthard Pass; from the Rhone Valley, the Simplon Pass, and from Graubunden and the Rhine Valley, the Passo del San Bernardino.

Trip 31   Passo San Gottardo

Distance   *About 100 kilometers from Andermatt to Locarno, one way*
Terrain   *Modern pass road and valley autostrada*
Highlights   *Quick way to get down out of the mountains, Passo San Gottardo (2,108 meters)*

From central Switzerland, that is, cantons Zurich, Bern, Luzern, and Uri, north-south Passo San Gottardo is the link to warmer, sunnier Ticino on Lago Maggiore. Of course in these cantons it's called St. Gotthard Pass, and from Andermatt the top is just a few sweeping kilometers up and above the tree line.

Through the years, the pass road provided major commercial connections and so was regularly improved for higher speeds and weather protection. Now, the pass road itself is superseded by the long tunnel under the pass. Hurrah.

At the top of the pass, just 12 kilometers from downtown Andermatt, there's a mini diamond interchange providing access to the cluster of buildings that have always provided shelter and sustenance to travelers on the pass. One of the buildings houses a museum. In front of the buildings is a small monument to aviators who first flew over the pass.

Parts of earlier, more torturous alignments remain and some are traversable, like the link on the south slope, often called the Tremola, that starts down near the cluster of buildings. Its sweepers and hairpins hug the mountainside, supported by rock walls. And it has fine cobblestone pavement.

Meanwhile, the higher speed road heads down from the mini interchange through concrete snow sheds and tunnels with a couple of sweeping turns cantilevered in space, occasionally crossing and intersecting the old Tremola road.

About halfway down there's a view point with a little shop. The whole Ticino River valley, ringed by snowy mountains, is below. And the little village called Airolo where the pass road joins the autostrada as it emerges from the tunnel, all in an amazing collection of bridges and ramps.

Head down the valley on the autostrada, past the Nufenen Pass connection at Airolo, and the Lukmanier Pass connection at Biasca, joining the autostrada from the San Bernardino Pass at Bellinzona.

A few kilometers south of Bellinzona, the autostrada begins to climb on stilts over the next range of mountains toward Lugano, Lake Como, and Milano.

There's a signed exit for Locarno and Lago Maggiore, leading to a pretty busy standard highway, lined with commercial development, and decorated every little ways with roundabouts that keep traffic crawling.

Approaching Lago Maggiore, the road splits, one branch to Locarno, on the north shore of the lake, and the other branch to the south shore with San Nazzaro, Indemini, and Passo Alpe de Neggia.

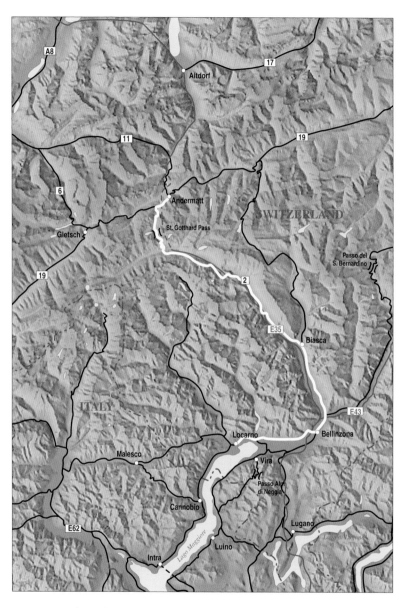

Getting through Locarno to Valle Maggia, the Simplon Pass, and Val Cannobina used to be a nightmare of congestion. Now there's an autostrada tunnel under the whole town.

Trip 32 Passo del San Bernardino

Distance *About 105 kilometers from Chur, in the Rhine Valley, to Locarno, one way*

Terrain *Tight, twisting, narrow mountain pass road, followed by high speed swooping across huge bridges to autostrada*

Highlights *Rustic cafe on top of pass, exhilarating swoops, Passo del San Bernardino (2,065 meters)*

From the Rhein (we spell it Rhine) valley in Graubunden, the San Bernardino Pass (in Ticino, Passo del San Bernardino) makes a direct and good ride connection to Locarno. The pass road is a sweeping, high-speed, two-lane autobahn most of the way from Chur in Graubunden in the Rhine Valley to Locarno. Most of the way it's possible to dodge back and forth, keeping to pieces of non-autobahn roads. There's an all-weather tunnel under the highest peaks, but there's a twisty, attention-demanding road up over the pass, above the tunnel, that's a motorcycle delight. A restaurant on a lake at the top makes a great stop, and a regular *Toffitreffpunkt*. Dine rustically upstairs if it's not comfortable sitting out.

It's a good day atop all the switchbacked, gnarly corners of Passo San Bernadino, way up over the tunnel underneath.

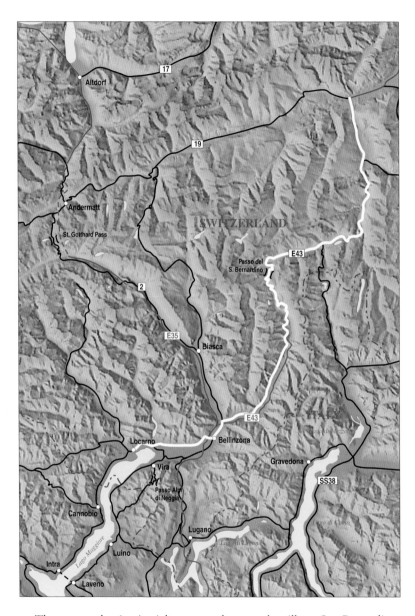

The pass road twists in tight corners down to the village, San Bernardino, where traffic can join the modern road coming out of the tunnel, or continue on the older road. In the village there is a hotel/restaurant.

The south side of the San Bernardino is on a magnificent series of sweepers with high arched bridges carrying the road back and forth over the valley below.

Near Bellinzona the San Bernardino road joins the San Gottardo autostrada.

Trip 33 Simplon Pass

Distance *About 100 kilometers from Brig in the Rhone Valley to Locarno, one way*

Terrain *High pass with high speed sweepers in Switzerland; Val Cannobina in Italy is narrow and tight*

Highlights *Narrow and tight and fun, used by locals only, leads to a lakefront road; Simplon Pass (2,006 meters), a major pass between Italy and Switzerland; charming Centovalli and Val Cannobina, Swiss Army may be on maneuvers*

From the Rhone Valley, the Simplon Pass (Sempione in Italian) is in Switzerland all the way across, then enters Italy at its southern base. From here, there are a couple of fun connections back to Switzerland and Locarno: the Centovalli and Val Cannobina. Just after entering Italy at the base of the Sempione, before the Italian industrial town of Domodossola, the Centovalli road heads up and east toward Malesco. From Malesco, the road heads into Switzerland and down to Locarno. A pleasant route.

For a more challenging ride, head up and around Malesco's village church (not the big domed basilica on the edge of town which, incidentally, has a gruesome collection of pictures of vehicle accidents) and up over a narrow pass, the Valle Cannobina road. Near a tunnel at the top, right on the edge of a lush, green, peaceful gorge, are some small memorial markers commemorating Italian partisans killed by the retreating Germans at the end of World War II. The road works down in a one-lane-wide collection of twisties through green forest to Lago Maggiore at an Italian town called Cannobio. From Cannobio it's a short ride north along the lakeshore to Switzerland and Locarno. (Lakeshore traffic can be tedious, and this little jaunt, however nice the views, may be all that's needed to illustrate the point.) Both the Centovalli and the Val Cannobina roads have rustic places to stop for refreshment.

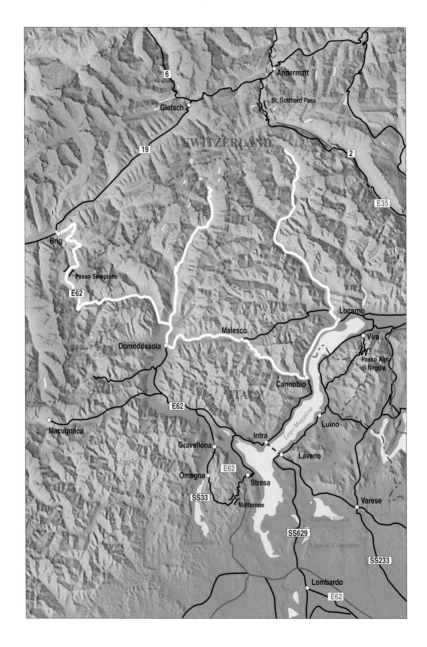

Trip 34 Valle Maggia

Distance *Valle Maggia, about 120 kilometers round trip from Locarno*
Terrain *Small, twisty roads into remote, high villages surrounded by giant mountains*
Highlights *To explore where no one goes, try these dead-end valleys*

A couple of kilometers out the Centovalli road from Locarno, it splits. The Valle Maggia road goes north and climbs through quiet villages with stone houses and roofs of huge stone slabs. The road narrows to work up switchbacks to high Alpine lakes where it dead-ends, 50 kilometers from town. Nobody there.

The upper parts of Valle Maggia above Locarno get narrow and intricate.

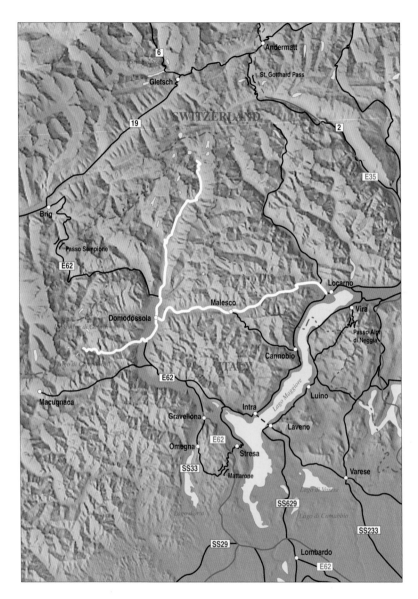

Over toward the base of Passo Sempione, on the Italian side of the border above Domodossola, the Val d'Ossola climbs north almost to the Nufenen Pass in Switzerland. There's a *rifugio* near the lake at its top. (*Rifugios* are Italian institutions, usually staffed by a resident family to serve Alpine travelers and workers.)

South of Domodossola, at Villadossola, a wild little road climbs the Val di Antrona. There's a rifugio there, too.

Trip 35 Highs Over Lago Maggiore

Distance   *220 kilometers*
Terrain   *Little mountain roads right behind the lake congestion*
Highlights   *A pass no tourist sees, Passo Alpi de Neggia (1,395 meters), ferry across the lake (toll), Mattarone (1,491 meters)*

On the east shore of the lake, south of Locarno, still in Switzerland, at Vira, take the steep little road uphill signed INDEMINI. That's a town at the Swiss-Italian border. Getting there, it quickly leaves houses behind and winds up and over the Passo Alpi de Neggia. There's a restaurant atop the pass with views to the north of Lago Maggiore, Locarno, and the snow-capped Alps. Border guards will be surprised to see you. You may be their only customers for the day. In Italy, ride down to the lake at Maccagno and south along the lake shore to Laveno, where there's a ferry across the lake to Intra on the west shore. There are a couple of ferries an hour, and the ride takes about twenty minutes.

Follow the west lake shore south to Stresa, a fairly congested tourist town. Once there, head inland on cobbled streets, west for Mattarone. It's signed.

The main street of Pontresina, Graubunden, on a busy morning. The buildings illustrate typical Romansch architecture designs with deep set windows and etched patterns on the corners.

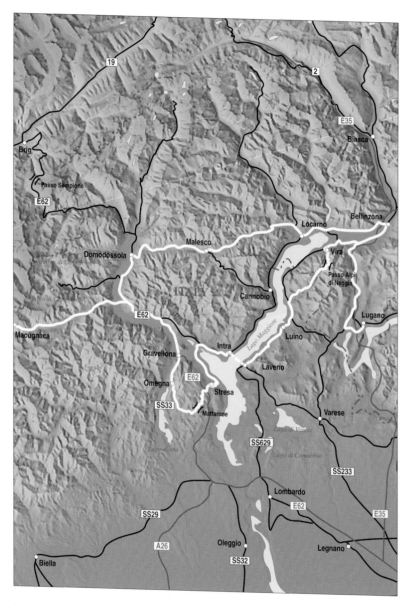

You're quickly in the woods. At the top there's a cable car and a restaurant. There's also a toll. Head down west to the next lake, Lago d'Orta, and then north to Omegna. Might as well take the autostrada from Gravellona to Piedimulera where there's a dead-end road up the Val Anzasca to a ski resort, Macugnaca, separated by Monte Rosa from Zermatt, Switzerland.

Back in the valley, take the Malesco road from Domodossola to Switzerland.

It's a long tedious ride around Lago Maggiore, so a ferry trip across the middle connecting Laveno on the east side with Intra on the west side makes sense.

East of Andermatt

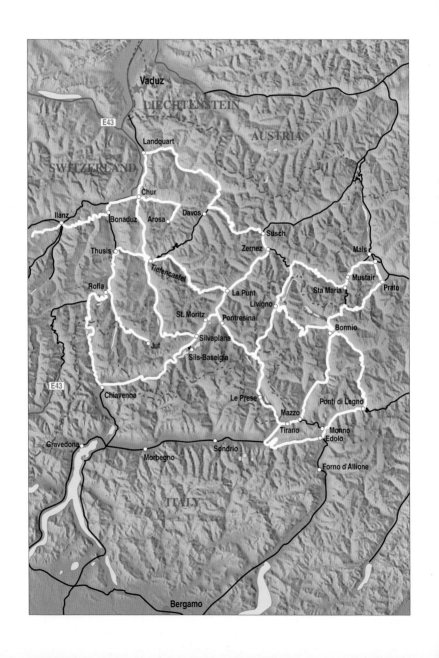

St. Moritz

East of Andermatt, over the Oberalp Pass, is the biggest and wildest of Swiss cantons, Graubunden, home of world-famous winter sports, St. Moritz, Davos, and more. Part of Graubunden is in the Rhein Tal (Rhein Valley) draining toward the North Sea, and part of it is in the Inn Tal, usually called Engadin, running toward Innsbruck, the Danube, and the Black Sea. A few parts in the south run into Italy and the Adriatic. Getting back and forth between these valleys across great mountain ranges makes for some good roads and good riding.

Climbing Passo Spluga, Italians decided to build it up this cliff face supporting the road with stones and arches. There are hairpins in those tunnels. Back down in the valley is Chiavenna and the Maloja Pass into St. Moritz. Just over the top of the passo is Switzerland.

Down stream at the Austrian border is a unique fiscal finger valley called Samnaun Tal. At a village called Vinadi, a tiny road snakes sixteen kilometers north up into the Samnaun Valley. At the end are huge complexes of hotels and shops, all supported by a tax free status. A wider road connects the valley to Austria.

St. Moritz, in the high Engadin (valley of the Inn), is higher than a lot of passes, at 1,822 meters. Even though it's high and cool and famous, St. Moritz and its neighboring resort villages are a logical base for exploring the great roads of Graubunden. Most facilities are available. Its reputation as the old-time playground of royalty means that there are old-time posh establishments, but there are plenty of places for ordinary bike riders. St. Moritz-Dorf (the German word for "village" is *Dorf*) is on the north slopes of the Engadin, up the mountainside from St. Moritz on the main valley road.

Right in the center of the Dorf, facing one of the few outdoor eating plazas (one of the few level places in St. Moritz), is the Hauser Hotel. Right behind the Hauser is Hotel Crystal. Both are modern and touristy.

Traffic through and near St. Moritz is encouraged to use the main valley road below the Dorf, but there is a good high road running east and west from the plaza at the Hauser Hotel.

Cross into Switzerland and Passo Spluga becomes Splugen Pass. Instead of the steep climb up a cliff face like in Italy, the Swiss have engineered an amazing series of traverses, stacked one atop another, connected by hairpin turns. Fortunately, they are all out on an open slope, so all is easily in view.

All this at the dead end of a narrow valley, the Samnaun Tal on the Swiss-Austria border, is because it's tax free.

For a real experience in how a Swiss hotel can coddle, and at about the cost of a modest hotel in the city, treat yourself to Hotel Le Prese in the village of Le Prese, south of St. Moritz, on the other side of the Bernina Pass, and almost completely surrounded by Italy. An old building that's been modernized, Hotel Le Prese is guaranteed to make everyone feel luxuriously cared for. There's a large outdoor pool. Almost all guests are annual regulars, with hardly a foreigner (non-Swiss) among them. Since there's a dress code, the management may discreetly arrange a table with heavy linen and silver in the handsome bar room.

Escape St. Moritz down the Engadin (northeast) about 12 kilometers to Zuoz, with cobblestone streets and beautiful quaint houses, some hundreds of years old, with shops, banks, and cows. The main valley road bypasses the town on the south bank of the Inn River leaving Zuoz high—1,716 meters—on the north. In Zuoz is the Post Hotel Engiadina, complete with an outdoor pool for the brave.

Pontresina is a lovely village just six kilometers east of St. Moritz with a fine new hotel. The Bernina Pass road skirts the village. The old main street through Pontresina, now bypassed, is one way, uphill, and on it is Hotel Allegra. Very contemporary.

Most hotels in the Engadin offer complementary transportation passes that include cable cars to the high peaks.

Trip 36 Vorderrhein (the 'Front Rhine')

Distance *About 150 kilometers from Andermatt to St. Moritz, one way*
Terrain *Narrow cliff-hanging road to major mountain highway*
Highlights *Brief glimpse at a Switzerland no tourist sees, Operalp Pass (2,044 meters), Julier Pass (2,284 meters), lonely high meadows and a cliff hanging gorge road*

The summit of the Oberalp Pass is just a few sweeping kilometers up from Andermatt. Then there's a pretty quick and tight descent as far as Disentis, followed by a long ride down the Vorderrhein valley (the "front Rhine") toward Chur, the capital of Graubunden, and the next good roads. Along the way, the Rhein goes through one of those *schluchts*. The highway has to go up and around to the north of the Schlucht through the ski resorts of Laax and Flims.

Only locals use the tight narrow road chiseled out of the cliffs and spanning gorges on awesome bridges, all on the south side of the Rhein, between Ilanz and Bonaduz.

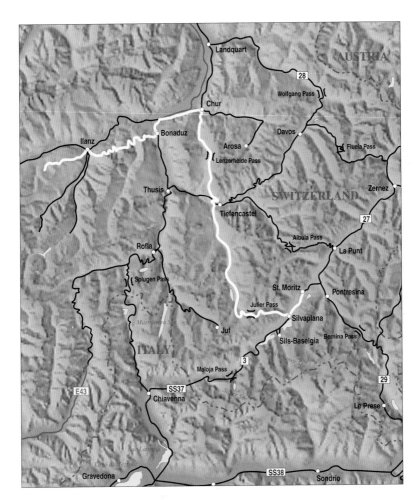

But there's a neat alternative. Chiseled out of the cliffs on the south side is a tight, narrow, cliff-hanging road known only to locals and exploring motorcyclists. It's easy to catch at Ilanz by crossing into the village from the highway and heading east, downstream, at the village square. The east end of the road is at Bonaduz, on the main route to St. Moritz. From Bonaduz, the main road goes to Tiefencastel and then over the Julier Pass. (For more information about these roads, see Trip 36.)

To extend the exploring, there's more high road paralleling the main one. Turn south off the main valley road about 20 kilometers upstream (west) of Ilanz. (At the time of the turnoff, the main road is briefly on the south bank of the Rhein.) It's marked "Obersaxon," which is a region, not a town. The road climbs through high meadows with views over the whole valley, then comes down to the main square in Ilanz.

Trip 37   Hinterrhein (the 'Back Rhine')

Distance *About 170 kilometers from St. Moritz, plus 50 to Juf*
Terrain *Narrow, tight, steep climb, hairpins, and tunnels on Splugen;
challenging, modern mountain highway on Maloja and Julier*
Highlights *Audacious mountain road, awesome gorges, rustic rifugio,
highest village in Switzerland, Maloja Pass (1,815 meters), ★★Splugen Pass
(2,113 meters), Juf and the Via Mala, ★Julier Pass (2,284 meters)*

Winding upstream (southwest) through the Engadin valley from St. Moritz, past some nice lakes, you don't feel like you're climbing. Then, suddenly, you come upon a stack of switchbacks down hill: the Moloja Pass. You're already at the top. Below the switchbacks the pass road meanders down through some pleasant Swiss villages. Then a brief piece of new alignment takes you around below a border village where there's a large gas station, and then back up to the border crossing into Italy. On down into Italy, the deep valley seems more popu-lated. There's a huge waterfall pouring off the cliff, and then you're in the larger town of Chiavenna on tree shaded streets. There's a little traffic circle with most traffic bearing left toward Lake Como. Right there, there's a brown sign, PASSO SPLUGA to the right, the beginning of a wild climb up the Splugen Pass back

Maloja Pass only has one side, down, westerly from St. Mortiz into Italy at Chiavenna. Or up only, if you're heading to St. Moritz from Chiavenna. It does sport a center line. But look, it's not double. Go ahead! Pass that bus.

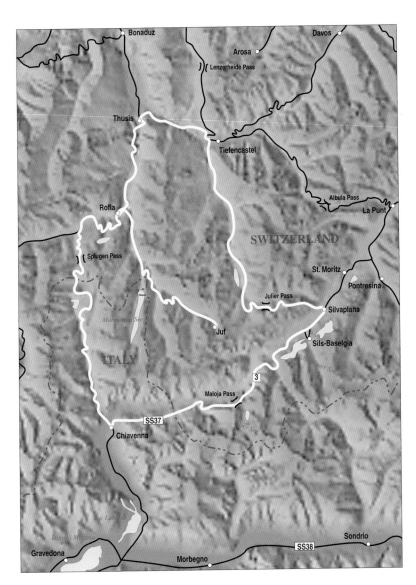

toward Switzerland. (For roads south of Chiavenna, see Trip 47).

Right in Chiavenna Passo Spluga begins the climb up. There are tight, steep hairpins in villages. The pass road often just barely hangs on a cliff, often hairpins in a tunnel, often works through stone snow shed tunnels that seem hardly helmet high and must have been built a century ago. Yet after snaking through stacks of cliff-hanging hairpins and one-way tunnels, in typical Italian fashion, the road ends in villages with people and trucks and buses, all using the road as their only connection to the world.

Climbing up from Chiavenna, the Splugen Pass road hangs precariously to mountain slopes alternating between hairpins and tunnels, or sometimes both at once.

Short of the top of the pass, just below the face of a Mussolini-massive stone dam, is a typical Italian mountain rifugio, called Rifugio Stuetta, a fun place for a lunch, cappuccino, or good Italian hot chocolate. In a rustic wood-paneled room with a tiny bar, the host family will see that some kind of food, usually pasta and salad just waiting to be made, is available to refresh a weary traveler. It's a good place to remember that *bolognese* is meat sauce and *pomodoro* is tomato sauce, that oil and vinegar is the salad dressing of Italy, and that *formaggio*, cheese, will probably be Parmesan. Almost all remote Italian passes have these inns, staffed by a family in residence, which provide shelter and food to road workers and travelers. Invariably, there's one clean, though small, toilet.

Many cafes in Italy serve no meals, but they may have panini, a grilled sandwich, or toast and gelato.

Higher and just a few switchbacks below the summit is the village Monte Spluga, at 1,908 meters, with a small, rustic hotel only 150 years old, Hotel Vittoria.

Back in Switzerland, the road pulls one of the most amazing and oft-photographed series of ladder switchbacks in the Alps. The road goes back and forth so often on the alluvial mountain slope that you can pass by the same vehicles going in the same direction time after time.

Ten kilometers over the border into Switzerland, the pass road meets the high-speed San Bernardino Autobahn, a two-lane freeway. This is the valley of the Hinterrhein, the "back Rhine," to go with the Vorderrhein, the "front Rhine" leading down from the Oberalp.

Just ten kilometers down the autobahn from the Splugen, an autobahn ausfahrt (exit) called Avers-Rofla leads to an adjoining Schlucht, and a Tofftreffpunkt at Gasthof Roflaschlucht. Opposite, a winding and deserted road leads south up to Juf, the highest permanent town in Switzerland, at 2,126 meters. You'll find no tourists on this road.

Farther down the autobahn, just before the Vorderrhein and Hinterrhein meet, is the Via Mala, the "bad way." The autobahn sweeps through the gorge of the Via Mala in tunnels and bridges that make it easy to miss the narrow, deep gorge that for centuries was the "bad way." Take the Via Mala Ausfahrt and look down on what a frightening journey it must have been.

Below Via Mala and Bonaduz (Trip 36) at Thusis, take the road toward Tiefencastel and the Julier Pass. The first part is another engineering tour de force, sweeping through an impossible gorge, playing back and forth at times with the Glacier Express train. Tiefencastel, wedged into a tiny valley, has gas, hotels, and a church typical of Romansch style: square stucco bell tower with an octagonal belfry topped by a dome.

The Julier road starts in Tiefencastel and climbs long, snaking up a gorge, then by a lake. Facilities at the top are good only for a postcard. Because the Engadin around St. Moritz is so high it's not far down to them from the top of the Julier into Silvaplana, a town with cute hotels and restaurants, and on into St. Moritz.

Trip 38   Albula Pass Connections

Distance   *About 190 kilometers from St. Moritz*

Terrain   *Four high passes and one medium high pass*

Highlights   *Cute Romansch villages, views of Glacier Express trestles, ski resorts, ★★Moonscape on Albula Pass (2,312 meters), Lenzerheide (1,547 meters), Wolfgang Pass (1,631 meters), ★Fluela Pass (2,383 meters), Arosa (1,775 meters)*

The picturesque Romansch village of Bergun is more than half way down the north side of th Albula Pass. The Glacier Express train makes a climbing loop inside the mountain above the village. Just ahead of these riders, the pass road makes a sharp right turn.

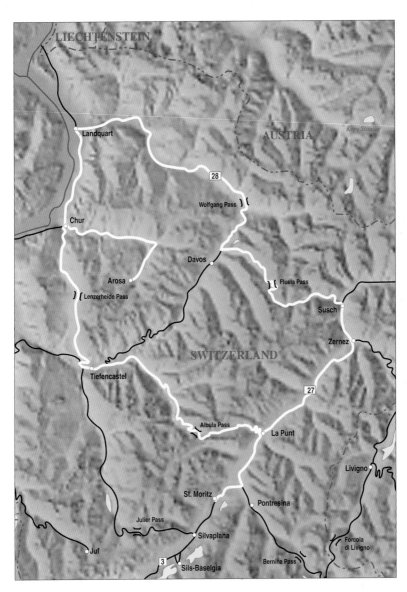

Right in the middle of a little village called La Punt, 12 kilometers down the Engadin (north) from St. Moritz, is the Albula Pass turnoff. It looks like a street of no significance between two buildings. The Albula is a back road. It climbs quickly above the tree line and then dips and jogs and weaves across a wild, rocky no-man's land to the summit, where there's a pleasant restaurant, before starting down through lovely remote Romansch villages. Sometimes, it barely squeezes through a gorge, or barely hangs on a cliff.

Across the top, Albula is almost a moonscape, and just a few kilometers from St. Moritz.

While the Julier Pass is considered the main auto road into St. Moritz, the train takes the Albula. Several of the bridges used by the Glacier Express along the route are famous on postcards and travelogues. Around the town of Bergun, the train makes several climbing loops inside the mountain, and below Filisur, the train crosses a gorge on a high stone arch viaduct, only to disappear at a right angle into the sheer granite cliff face.

The Albula leads down to Tiefencastel, quite a crossroads in its narrow gorge. The Albula Pass meets the Julier Pass to continue the main connection toward Thusis and the rest of Switzerland, working through another gorge also used by the railroad. Another road out of Tiefencastel climbs north over Lenzerheide. And there's a shortcut road across to Davos, base of the Fluela and Wolfgang Passes.

Up above Tiefencastel, a really fun but short piece of road connects the road from Davos with the Lenzerheide road.

For some reason Lenzerheide is never called a pass, even though it's always listed as one. It's where the book *Heidi* is supposed to have taken place. It is very pretty country, but not exotic. The area centers around Chur, the canton capital, a large city with motorcycle shops and services, but the Lenzerheide road stays on the hillside above Chur and connects directly to the San Bernardino Autobahn.

East above Chur is Arosa, a well-known ski resort, accessible only by a very twisty road that follows the arc of a mountain stream called Plessur for 30 kilometers. Arosa, at 1,775 meters, is the end of the road. It's necessary to go into Chur to catch the Arosa road.

A 15-kilometer jaunt north on the autobahn brings the rider to Landquart and the Wolfgang Pass road to Davos. Just short of the summit of the Wolfgang Pass is Klosters, where some members of the British royal family have been known to ski. A most spectacular bridge is under construction along this stretch, part of a plan to bypass Klosters. It looks like something designed by Disney.

A couple of kilometers over the Wolfgang is Davos, with a one-way loop street that makes for an easy return to the Fluela Pass road. The Fluela, which has a pleasant, rustic restaurant at the top, crosses back to the Engadin below St. Moritz.

Once, 500 motorcyclists, on a rally sponsored by Michael Krauser, paraded through Davos past a reviewing stand with some notables, while the Davos town band played and replayed Queen Liliuokalani's "Aloha Oe," "Farewell to Hawaii."

Fluela Pass Hospiz is always a favorite bike stop. Note the prominent "WC" sign. There's a charge for using it. There's a free one for customers in the hospiz.

Trip 39   Italian Connections, Stelvio

Distance   *About 230 kilometers*

Terrain   *Endless tight hairpins on Stelvio, one of the highest passes in the Alps; a short unpaved section on Umbrail Pass, and a challenging modern pass road on Bernina Pass*

Highlights   *Good sweepers over ★Bernina Pass (2,328 meters) into Switzerland's farthest corner; a major motorcycle goal, the ★★Passo dello Stelvio (Stilfser Joch) (2,758 meters), with restaurant terraces, and hotels, vendors on top; Swiss national park, Umbrail Pass (2,501 meters), Ofen Pass (2,149 meters)*

The Bernina Pass, south from St. Moritz, swoops down and around, bypassing Pontresina, a popular resort. Then after climbing the first switchbacks, and just over some railroad tracks, there's a view point with the best views of Piz Bernina (the highest peak of the area) and its glaciers. The restaurants at the top are serviceable. Just across the top is an intersection with a border crossing into the isolated Italian valley of Livigno (see Trip 40).

The sweeping southerly descent of the Bernina stays on good Swiss pavement. Below the town of Poschiavo is the little village of Le Prese, notable to bikers because of the train tracks that go down the middle of the street—well,

Motorcyclists pass themselves coming and going many times when working up the Stelvio.

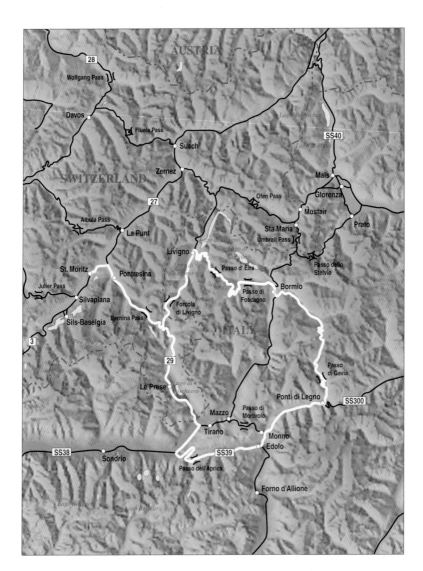

almost the middle. It would be easier if they stayed in the middle. At the downhill end of the village, just as the tracks pull off to the side, is the Le Prese Hotel. Stop for lunch or refreshment on the lakefront terrace.

Recently an avalanche took out the road around the lake, below the hotel. Travelers had to take a boat across the lake until a precarious wooden ramp could be built. The ramp served until the permanent road could be rebuilt.

The Italian border is just a few kilometers on, with a steady parade of Italian cars crossing into Switzerland, tanking up on less expensive Swiss gas, and making a U-turn back to Italy. Not a bad idea.

Conservationists loudly lament the clutter of shops and restaurants and motorcyclists atop the Stelvio. But it seems that everyone is either having a good time, or is making money. Bikes from all over the world stop here to kick tires. There's a sense of camaraderie. "We've all made it to the top." Only one way to go now. Down.

Just into Italy is the Italian town of Tirano, where a turn north by the big yellow church starts the climb to the most famous motorcycle destination in the Alps, the Passo dello Stelvio, known in German as the Stilfser Joch (say yoke.) At 2,758 meters, it's one of the highest pass roads in the Alps. Every motorcyclist has to climb it. The collection of stalls, shops, restaurants, hotels, and even a bank at the top of the Stelvio probably does violate environmental sense, but the convenience is unmatched.

Italy is building a two-lane freeway up the lower part of the valley from Tirano as far as Bormio, but the road over the pass above Bormio can only be described as *laissez faire* Italian determination. It seems like half the hairpins in the Alps are on the Stelvio, 40 or so on each side. And they are hairpins, with practically zero inside radius. Where there's room, the road may be almost two lanes wide, but much of the time, one narrow lane seems to strain the limits of the slope. In some places, the hand-laid rock retaining walls have obviously been pushed beyond their limits, and the road has slipped a bit down the mountainside. The Italian solution is to bridge the gap by pouring asphalt in the crack.

The Stelvio clearly illustrates the problem of mountain road building and maintenance. Surrounded by high cliffs, the alluvial slope is the only possible place to hang a road. And the alluvial slope is inherently unstable. The alternative, often used elsewhere in Italy, is a tunnel deep inside the mountain. But that surely spoils the view.

There's a road sign repeatedly seen in Italy: LAVORO IN CORSO, "work in progress." It perhaps should read "work needs to be in progress."

Whether it's sunny or foggy or snowy or rainy, there are always bikes on Stelvio. It's a must-stop for lunch or cappuccino or just tire-kicking. The postcard vendors know their market: there are plenty of cards showing the road, some with bikes in the hairpins. Skiers are permitted and there's summer skiing on the glaciers. There are even a couple of hotels on the top: Hotel Stilfser Joch (also known as Passo dello Stelvio Hotel) and Stelvio Hotel Perego, recently remodeled.

The northeast side of the Stelvio is equally exciting. It is often marked *chiuso,* "closed," but traffic is usually going around the barricade.

Just short of the top of the Stelvio, on the southwest (Bormio) side, is a border crossing back into Switzerland. This is the Umbrail Pass. From the border crossing it's all downhill. A reasonable portion of it is not paved, but is maintained in good condition. It goes down to the main Swiss road in the handsome Romansch village of Santa Maria, where the Ofen Pass climbs back toward the Engadin.

A fascinating alternate route to Santa Maria is to continue on across the Stelvio and, at the Italian base town of Prato, head north on a beautiful side road past the Castle of Lichtenburg to Glorenza (and the German is Glurns), a very attractive walled village with cafes and shops. From Glorenza, it's 20 kilometers to the Swiss border and the Ofen Pass road.

There are always vendors atop the Stelvio selling heiss wurst in a bun. Tastes good with senf, mustard.

Just north of Glorenza (in Italy) there's a wonderful hotel in the village of Mals. (It's actually on the Reschen Pass road.) With spacious rooms, views of the valley and mountains from every one, including the indoor pool, Hotel Garberhof is a good base for exploring the Passo dello Stelvio.

Just inside the Swiss border, above Glorenza, is the Swiss village of Mustair. Right on the road is a small church dating from the time of Charlemagne, famous for some of the earliest frescoes in Europe. Most of the frescoes tell the story of John the Baptist. The main ones focus on the gruesome aspects: tied up before Solome, then his head on the platter, etc., in the almost comic-book art style of the Middle Ages. The parking lot is across from the church, but bikes can usually park on the sidewalk by the gate.

Santa Maria has Hotel Stelvio, a good hotel just above where the Umbrail Pass comes down into town. It has good parking, WCs, an outdoor terrace, and goulash soup.

The Ofen Pass, heading back toward the Engadin and St. Moritz, passes through the Swiss National Park. The park area seems very arid by Alpine standards, looking much like western parks in the U.S. From the Ofen Pass road, there's a one-way-at-a-time toll tunnel back into Italy and the Livigno valley (Trip 40). The small, narrow tunnel is several kilometers long. Traffic signals control the direction of traffic flow.

Look ahead, up (or down) the road ahead when approaching any of the hairpins on the Stelvio. Most, like these on the east (Sud Tirol) side, have almost zero radius and vehicles will require all of the road.

Traverses are stacked midway down the Bormio (west) side of the Stelvio, each connected with a hairpin.

Below the traverses, the Stelvio Pass road must cling to these unstable alluvial slopes.

Trip 40 Duty-Free Livigno & Passo di Gavia

Distance *About 230 kilometers*

Terrain *Rugged, high, challenging mountain roads*

Highlights *Forcola di Livigno (2,315 meters), Passo d'Eira (2,210 meters), Passo di Foscagno (2,291 meters), Passo dell'Aprica (1,176 meters), a high valley of Italy where everything is tax-free, including gasoline; also one of the Alps' more famous challenges, the ★★Passo di Gavia (2,621 meters), ★Passo di Mortirolo (1,896 meters), unknown to most map makers*

Just over the Bernina Pass from St. Moritz is a border station, open during the day, into Italy. It opens to a nicely paved Italian Alpine pass road, Forcola di Livigno, that descends to an Alpine curiosity, the duty-free high Alpine valley of Livigno. The valley is pretty well surrounded by Switzerland. The only Italian road out is up over two passes. Everything in Livigno is tax-free, including gas.

Free enterprise has not treated Livigno with gentleness. It's a hodgepodge. Most of what merchants think visitors should buy won't fit too well on a bike. Hotels and restaurants are adequate, but nothing special.

Besides the road from the Bernina Pass, there are two other ways out of Livigno. Straight down the valley, through the town and out the other side, a road winds around a lake to the toll tunnel back into the Swiss National Park. It's a one-way-at-a-time tunnel, controlled by lights (Trip 30).

Spray-painted signs for bicycle racers on the Giro d'Italia cover the pavement on Passo Mortirolo.

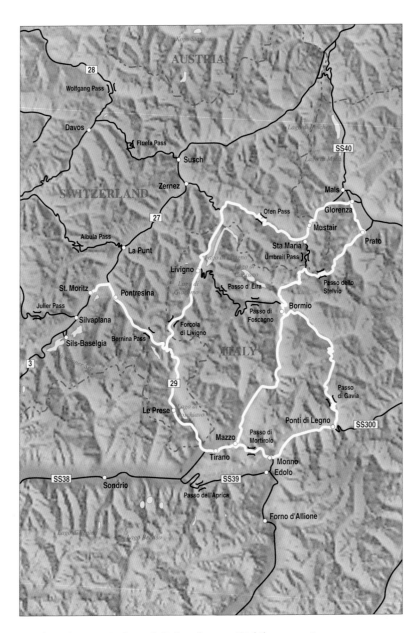

The other way is through Italy, a bumpy 50-kilometer trip over two passes, the Passo d'Eira and the Passo di Foscagno, that few tourists or visiting motorcyclists see. These pass roads lead to Bormio, the base of the Passo dello Stelvio and also the take-off point for Passo di Gavia, one of the higher roads in the Alps. Follow the brown signs for the Gavia in downtown Bormio.

This south side of the Passo di Gavia has just been paved to almost one full lane width. It was graded dirt and rocks.

The Gavia is a north-south pass. From Bormio, south bound, the first 15 kilometers are standard highway. Then at Santa Catarina the road narrows, with hairpins leading to a high wind-swept valley where there's a restaurant. There's another restaurant at the top that accommodates many motorcyclists on a good day. Then the fun begins. The south side is very narrow and has just seen its first asphalt, maybe three meters wide. It hangs on little ledges with tight hairpins supported by flimsy old rock walls with hardly a piece of string or a tree branch for a guard rail. Passing four-wheel vehicles is a squeezing experience. Four wheel vehicles passing each other is an engineering experience.

This is another of those roads where "chiuso" (closed) probably means "travel at your own risk." Even when the road is closed, the rifugios near the top may be open, but there are no other services on the 35-kilometer crossing to Ponte di Legno.

Ponte di Legno is on a main east-west highway. Head west in the direction of Edolo. (Edolo is a few kilometers north of Trip 46.)

About five kilometers before (east of) Edolo is the turn for a fantastic little road used on the Giro d'Italia bicycle race, but otherwise forgotten, Passo di Mortirolo. No maps show this road correctly. It is paved but narrow, and goes across the mountain between the villages of Monno and Mazzo. In Mazzo, its north end, it's signed PASSO DI MORTIROLO. At the other end, near Edolo, the only sign is MANNO. At the top, a small road leads west, while the pass road zigzags down, one lane of narrow pavement covered with painted slogans for the bicycle racers. Mazzo at the north end is in the Adda Valley. Downstream, west, is Tirano and the entrance to the Bernina Pass. Upstream, east, is the Passo dello Stelvio.

Should you choose to continue on through Edolo, instead of Passo di Mortirolo, the Passo dell'Aprica is straight ahead. The Aprica isn't high but has some ski hotels and restaurants right on the road through town. The west side of the Aprica has sweeping views of the Adda Valley which leads toward Lake Como. But before that, about seven kilometers below Aprica, just after a tight curve that reverses the traverse, a little sign saying STAZZONA points at a little road into the woods that works down the mountain to the main road toward Tirano.

At Tirano, the big yellow church marks the gateway back to Switzerland, Le Prese, the Bernina Pass, and St. Moritz.

Be wary of train tracks. They may create a hump in the highway that can surprise the unwary rider if there's no train on them.

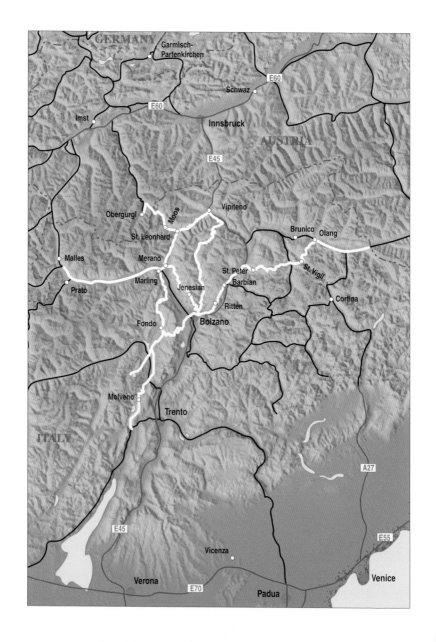

Sud Tirol

Hairpins and traverses on the south side (Italian) of Timmels Joch demand attention. In the distance are the peaks called Giogaia de Tessa.

Handsome is the word to describe Merano, Alto Adige, also known as Meran, Sud Tirol. Giant trees shade its streets. A mountain torrent, the Passiria in Italian, Passeier in German, regularly used for whitewater racing pours through its heart. Flowered promenades with coffee houses and *gelaterias* (ice cream parlors) follow the edge of the torrent. Its little medieval section has narrow arch-shaded streets lined with shops selling everything: bananas, nuts, pastries, leather goods, toys, the latest fashions. Behind the shops are beer gardens with the best Austrian and Italian food. Mountain peaks surround the town, lower slopes laden with apples and pears and vines. It's been the favorite spa of kaisers and kings. Yet Americans never stop in Merano. Say "Merano" to an American travel agent and you will be corrected, "You mean Milano." No, Merano.

Merano is one of those places that has become Italian instead of Austrian only in the twentieth century. Much of the culture is both Austrian and Italian, and most everything has a name in both languages. You'll find pasta right beside Wienerschnitzel on many menus.

The mountainsides are lined with hotels. Hotel Augusta is a handsome yellow structure in a sort of Austrian Victorian style, secluded in a shaded garden just off the promenade.

The giant old time hotel "spa" of Merano is the Kurhotel Palace. It looks like a palace, sitting well back from the street. It has huge halls and lots of gilt, only slightly faded. In low season prices are reasonable, especially for rooms facing the town. There's an outdoor-indoor pool with an electric eye to open the glass

Climbing above St. Leonhard, the Jaufen Pass road is pretty narrow. Motorcycles can pass, but when a couple of cars meet, things can back up.

Above the tree line, like here on the north side above Sterzing, it's easier to see what the traffic is doing. Motorcycles can usually maintain an entertaining pace.

door between them as you swim up to it. Across the street is a shady park with a statue of the Empress Elizabeth, wife of Franz-Joseph. (Remember, she was assassinated in Geneve by a guy wielding scissors.) Coat and tie required at dinner!

Up the Passeier 20 kilometers is St. Leonhard (San Leonardo, in Italian), a village with several good Tiroler style hotels, like Hotel Stroblhof. It's right on the main street where all the bikes pass.

Thirteen kilometers west of Merano in the direction of Reschen Pass and Stelvio, just past the village of Naturns, a great road called Schnals Tal (Val Senales) climbs north toward the glaciers. The road's another alpine wonder. At the top of the road, a cable car takes skiers up to summer skiing on the Similaun Glacier where the multi-thousand-year-old ice man was recently found.

Hotel Garberhof is on the Reschen Pass road at Malles (just Mals in German), about 50 kilometers west of Merano.

Up the mountain east of Merano is Hafling, famous for the small horses called Haflingers. From Hafling, a small road hangs on the mountain south to Bolzano (coming from Bolzano, follow signs to Genesio to reach Hafling). (See Trip 44).

Merano is a delight to be in, but it can be a pain to ride through. Brown signs do mark routes through town to the nearby passes.

Trip 41 Timmels Joch

Distance *About 100 kilometers round trip to top of the pass*

Terrain *Some congestion near Merano, narrow twisting climb, dark tunnel, on Italian side; more moderate on Austrian side*

Highlights *Exhilarating views of glaciated peaks, connection to Austrian Tirol and Germany (toll),* ★★*Timmels Joch (2,509 meters)*

The raging river through Merano is the Passiria (Passeier in German). Follow it upstream, north from Merano, 20 kilometers to St. Leonhard, at the base of the Timmels Joch. On the way, the road passes the home of Andreas Hofer, a sort-of George Washington of the Sud Tirol (only he didn't win). The house is now a Gasthaus.

The Timmels Joch is the lower leg of the fork in the road at St. Leonhard. It's a secondary road, narrow, tight, and twisty, hanging over deep canyons with a horizon studded with snowy peaks, and with some dark, rough-bottomed tunnels at the top.

Sometimes fog plays around the road, like here on Timmels Joch.

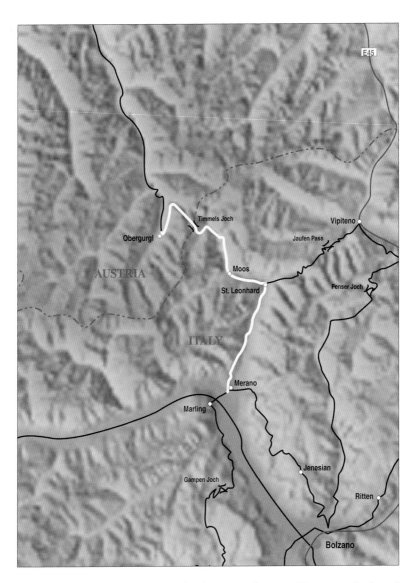

In St. Leonhard there's a little bridge across the river. You may take it and follow a mini-one-laner through the forests as far up as Moos where it rejoins the main Timmels Joch road.

Across the border at the top, on the Austrian side, there's a good restaurant. The road quality improves—as well it should, because Austria collects a toll. It leads in a few kilometers to ski areas at Hochgurgl, Obergurgl, and Untergurgl, then into a long, pleasant Austrian valley (see Trip 61 for a hotel in Vent Tal, below the "gurgl's").

Trip 42   Reschen Pass

Distance *About 160 kilometers round trip to top of pass*
Terrain *Gentle climb on Italian side, a little more precipitous on Austrian side*
Highlights *Orchards and farms, toll-free connection to Germany, leads to Stelvio, Reschen Pass (Passo Resia) (1,504 meters)*

The main highway skirts around Merano on the west, then crawls up past the huge Forst Brewery, followed by about 50 kilometers of gentle climbing through lovely Sud Tirol country: farms and apple orchards by the road, substantial houses on the hillsides, snowy mountains in all directions, cute villages with hotels and restaurants and far too much traffic. Because the pass is low and toll-free, it's a favorite of Germans pulling house trailers (wohnwagens) with low-powered sedans. Significant effort is being made to bore tunnels through adjoining mountains in order to bypass the congestion in villages. For all this distance, the only intersecting roads wind into mountain valleys, and then end. One valley road to the north, just 13 kilometers from Merano, near Naturno (Naturns in German) makes a wonderous climb up among glaciers. Called Val Senales (Schnals Tal in German), it has a cable car at the top that takes summer skiers to the Similaun Glacier, where the multi-thousand-year-old ice man was found.

The first through road intersection, about 50 kilometers upstream from Merano, is the well-marked turn for Passo Stelvio, the hairpin champ of the Alps, and a motorcycle favorite. A new intersection has just been opened west of the village, Prato (see Trip 39, Italian Connections).

Then nine kilometers further upstream is Malles with a turn down into the valley through the quaint walled village of Glorenza to the Swiss border and the Ofen Pass into the valley of the Engadin. Hotel Garberhof is on the main road through Malles.

Above Malles the road zig-zags between concrete igloos, forts built by Austria to defend the pass from Italy in World War One. The road skirts a lake famous for the church steeple that rises out of it, all that shows of a submerged village. Just four kilometers into Austria a short-cut road hairpins down into the Engadin and Switzerland. On into Austria, the once tedious road has been improved with multiple lanes and a long tunnel that connects directly with the Austrian Autobahn in the valley of the Inn River. Before entering the tunnel, make sure you have an Austrian vignette. Avoiding the tunnel, the old road goes into the large town of Landeck. From either route, downstream leads to Innsbruck and the Tirol. Upstream on the old road leads to Switzerland, the Engadin, and St. Moritz. Up on the autostrada leads to the Arlberg and the roads of Trip 62.

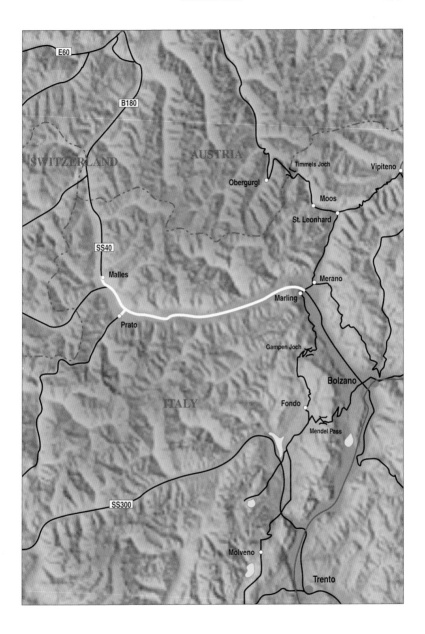

Trip 43 Merano

Distance *About 170 kilometers*
Terrain *Steep climbs and descents with hairpins, some narrow roads, over four high passes*
Highlights *Neat farms, forests, prosperous villages, Tirolian culture,* ★*Jaufen Pass (Passo di Monte Giovo) (2,094 meters),* ★*Penser Joch (Passo di Pennes) (2,214 meters), Mendel Pass (Passo di Mendola) (1,363 meters), Gampen Joch (Passo di Palade) (1,518 meters)*

At San Leonardo, 20 kilometers upstream from Merano, the road forks. The left tine, along the river, leads to Timmels Joch. The upper tine climbs Jaufen Pass, a tight and narrow road through forests that finally bursts out above the tree line. There are only sandwich shops on the top, and then a quick, steep descent into Sterzing (called Vipiteno in Italian). Sterzing is on the Brennero-Modena Autostrada, the major route between the cities of Italy and Germany.

Sterzing has an interesting but gotta-walk-in-to-see-it arcaded old street from the Middle Ages, similar to that in Merano, with many good restaurants. Try the four-cheese linguini.

The junction of the Jaufen Pass road with the Penser Joch road is before Sterzing, so it's not necessary to go into the town unless you want to check it out. The Penser Joch road is marked with one of those brown pass signs. It's a great twisting climb to the top, back up above the tree line, where there's a good rifugio restaurant. Then there's a long descent southerly, almost like a trip back in time, past flowering meadows and little villages and sturdy farmhouses. The valley, called Saren Tal (Val Sarentino in Italian), is completely Austrian in culture. Then some arched tunnels through a gorge and by a castle on a peak into Bolzano, a prosperous industrial city.

Bolzano (Bozen in German) is at the bottom of the deep canyon used by the Brennero-Modena Autostrada. It's just a couple of hours north to Munchen, and less than that south to Venezia. Bolzano has good motorcycle shops.

Keeping to the west through Bolzano, follow the brown signs to Passo di Mendola (Mendel Pass), and the regular signs to Eppan and Kaltern, towns on the way.

Mendel Pass climbs along cliffs with views of the deep canyon, the autostrada and railroad in it, and the river that made it, the Adige. Then it climbs into park-like green forests. A good picnic area. The culture is very Austrian.

Just over the pass where it's Italian again, turn toward Fondo, and from there onto the Gampen Joch road. The Gampen Joch (Passo di Palade in Italian) climbs up, over, and down, with arched stone barriers on the edge of the pavement, typical of the Austrian Empire days. The pass road approaches Merano through a pleasant Tirolean village, Marling (Marlengo in Italian).

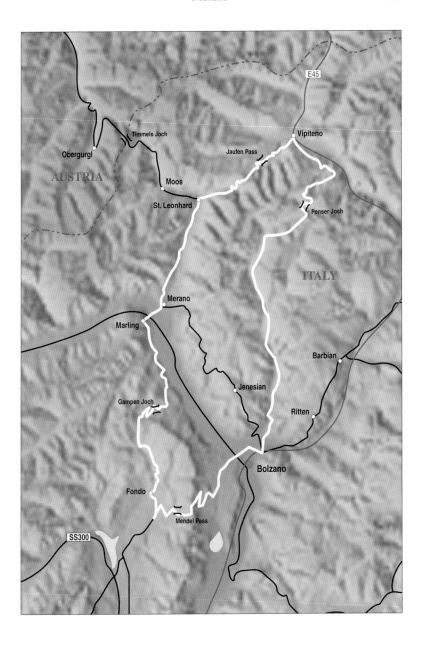

Trip 44 One Lane Roads Across Sud Tirol

Distance *About 240 kilometers*

Terrain *A couple of high passes, more modest heights, attention demanding narrow paved roads and the wonderful and handsome farming culture of the Sud Tirol. Weaving one lane mountain roads, some of them found in Trips 41, 43, 54, and 57, starting from the Austrian Ost (east) Tirol near Lienz, across Italian Sud Tirol to the Austrian Tirol near Imst. (Because the culture is Austrian, the German names for places are used here, even though the country is Italy. Where Italian names might be helpful, they're mentioned.)*

Highlights *Green forests, very neat farms with sturdy barns, and quaint villages all in park-like settings. Nothing flat. No busses. Plenty of facilities.* Take this route and discover the magic of the Sud Tiroler culture. For centuries the area was Austrian. At Versailles after World War I, it became Italian. Now, everything has an Italian name and the best map is the Italian Touring Club

It's one lane through St. Peter, and a tight squeeze around the church, but there's plenty of space at Hotel Kabis for lunch and to enjoy the Dolomitenblick, the view of the Dolomites.

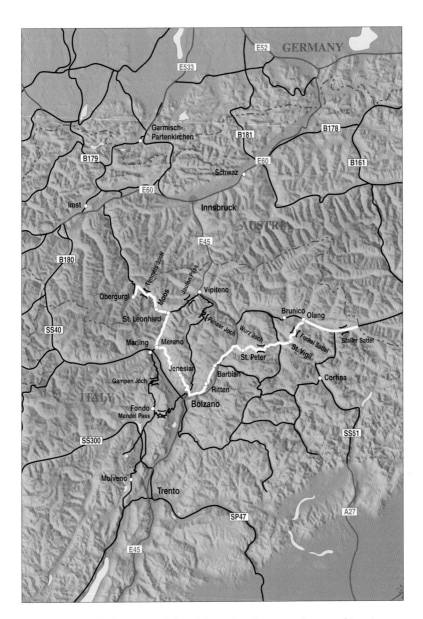

(T.C.I.) one called Trentino/Alto Adige. On the ground, everything is very Austrian. Village churches have Austrian steeples, not Italian campaniles, restaurants have Wienerschnitzel rather than pasta. The flag of semi-autonomous Sud Tirol is red and white, remarkably similar to the Austrian flag. It is flown proudly from house, barn, and church tower on special days. The route description here is from east to west.

Start at the east end of the route, where the Sud Tirol meets the Ost Tirol, which happens to be the Austrian/Italian border, atop the Staller Sattel (NW of Lienz). It's one-way down into Italy for 15 minutes starting on the hour (on the half hour coming up from Italy) (see Trip 66).

Sweep down off the mountain. In about 23 kilometers, cross the main valley east-west road by jogging a few hundred meters west and then turning down through the village, Olang (Valdaora, in Italian). Then you're climbing the one-lane Furkel Sattel, which after field and forest and a ski tow, comes down to St. Vigil. Turn downstream northwest (upstream dead-ends) to Zwischenwasser (Longega in Italian) where in a tight little valley our road meets the main north-south road. Turn south, upstream, toward Corvara for only one kilometer, then take the little bridge that crosses the adjacent stream, west, signed WELSCHELLEN. After about ten kilometers of one-lane, the road meets the one-lane "main" Wurz Joch road (Trip 54) coming up from St. Martin. Climb the sweepers and hairpins of the Wurz Joch, past the attractive rifugio at the top.

About eight kilometers west of the rifugio, the one-lane forks. The north tine goes down to Brixen. Take the south, the left tine, down to St. Peter.

At St. Peter is the Tiroler hotel restaurant Hotel Kabis with a plaza terrace just as the road hairpins around a building. (The area is called Vilnoss, Funes in Italian.) Here, as all across the Sud Tirol, the hotel and plaza will be full of locals in special Tirolian costume on Sunday morning.

From St. Peter it's but nine kilometers down west to the main valley canyon. Cross under the Brennero Autostrada, over the river, and go south, toward Bozen for a whole eight kilometers of two-lane road. (Coming eastbound from the autostrada, be sure to turn north at St. Peter. The turn is signed WURZ JOCH. Straight ahead dead-ends.)

At Ponte Gardena, after eight kilometers of two lane, take the one lane west to and through Barbian. From Barbian, it's one lane southerly (two-way) traversing the edge of the mountain to Lengmoos. Along the way are some strange formations below the road: pointed peaks with rock caps.

Lengmoos has a popular restaurant terrace, the Sporthotel Spogler. From Lengmoos it's two lanes to Klobenstein where there's a good hotel, the Dolomitenblick. As its name suggests ("blick" is German for view), the hotel has views of the Dolomites, across the great canyon that contains the Brennero Autostrada way down below.

From Klobenstein, there's a two-laner down to Bozen in the valley. Don't take it. Take the one lane across the mountain to Wangen, a high point in the area with more views of fields and forests and Dolomites. A hotel at Ritten is the Berg Gasthof Plorr. Then there's sort of a pass called Oberinn at 1,300 meters.

Twist down to Saren Tal—the Penser Joch road (Trip 43). Turn south downstream to Bozen. (Coming the other way, from Bozen, the turn up the mountain is marked "Ritten".)

This is how to explore a new road. Persuade friends to check it out with you. In this instance they all followed and they all discovered that the road around the west side of Lago Molveno that shows as paved on the map is not paved on the ground.

In just about eight kilometers, after some tunnels, there's a castle on a pinnacle called Runkelstein. Just past Runkelstein, before Bozen, there's a turn up and west marked "Jenesian" (Genesio in Italian). Take it up the mountain, swooping through tunnels and loops, past Jenesian to Molten (Moltina in Italian). Stay up on the mountain heading north to Hafling (Avelengo in Italian). Between Molten and Halfling there's another pass of 1,357 meters at Flaas. From Halfing it's two lanes down to Meran. There's no way but to wend through Meran to the Passer Tal, the road to St. Leonhard, and the Timmels Joch.

St. Leonhard is a Tiroler style village lined with several hotels and restaurants and it's where the Timmels Joch road and the Jaufen Pass roads meet.

At the fork in the road, the easterly fork is the Jaufen. Take the westerly one, which seems to go down along the rushing river. It's the Timmels Joch road. Once down along the river, there's a bridge across it. Take it. This is the beginning of a remarkable one lane steep climb through forests to a community called Moos. From Moos, it's possible to cross the raging stream and continue the one lane climb up the Timmels Joch to Austria and the Tirol.

Trip 45   Adamello Brenta National Park

Distance *135 kilometers, with an additional 40 into Lago di Tovel*
Terrain *Comfortable two lane road, moderate curves*
Highlights *Rural Italy with orchards and forests and views of the national park. Passo di Palade (Gampen Joch in German) (1,518 meters), Lago di Tovel (1,177 meters), a mountain gem with red water, peaks of the national park, Adamello Brenta*

The valley roads and autostrada connect Merano with Riva, to its south. This way is more fun.

Leave Merano through the town just southwest of it, Lana, and the Gampen Joch (Trip 43). Across the Joch, there's no more Sud Tiroler culture. It's pure Italian. From Fondo, head on south to Sanzeno where there's a pleasant Italian style hotel-restaurant, the Albergo la Mela d'Oro (the golden apple).

Next to the hotel is a rural church and beside it, a small war memorial monument in a contemporary style. Most every village in Europe has a war memorial honoring the local dead. This one recalls "the martyrs of the whole world." Nice thought. Southwest of Sanzeno, deep in the mountains of the Adamello Brenta National Park, is a lovely secluded Alpine lake with unique red water reflecting the surrounding peaks.

To find it, go south of Senzano about four kilometers, then westerly about

Those buildings across the piazza are Best Western Hotel Europa Riva at the north end of Lago di Garda. Behind the hotel, between it and the mountains, is the main road down the west side of the lake.

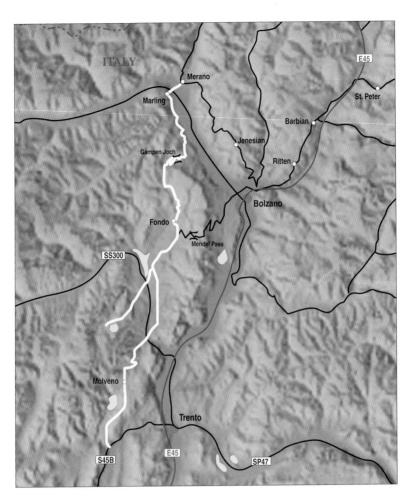

six kilometers to Tuenno where the road into the park and lake is marked. The road ends at the lake, about 12 kilometers upstream from Tuenno. There is a visitor's center, but no services. The park is reported to have bears.

Back at Tuenno, head south for Molveno. Since the main roads tend toward the Brennero Autostrada, it's necessary to avoid it by making several turns in a westerly direction back into the mountains toward Molveno. Molveno is a nicely sited Italian mountain-lake resort with hotels and restaurants well off the foreign visitor routes. There's the Hotel Belvedere. The road around the west side of Molveno's lake is not paved.

South from Molveno the main road hangs high on a cliff edge and then descends into Ponte Arche where there are signs for Riva.

To come the other direction, north from Riva, follow signs for Ponte Arche, the high road, and then on to Molveno.

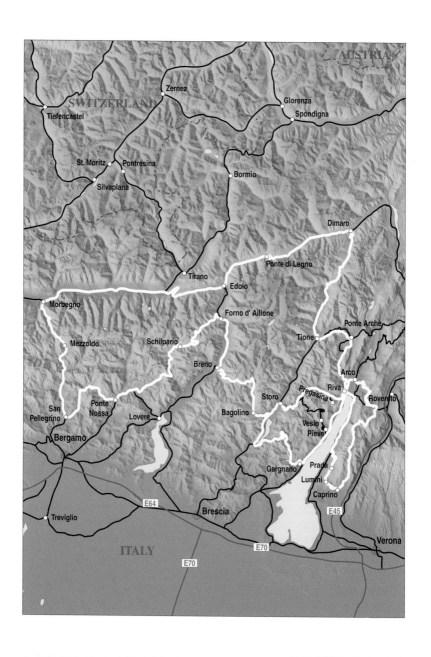

Riva and Lago di Garda

The south end of long Lake Garda, Lago di Garda, is down in the flats of the Po Valley of Italy, near historic cities like Verona and Montova. But the north end of the lake is in the Alps, surrounded by giant vertical cliffs, sometimes seeming to rise straight out of the lake. At the north point of the lake, surrounded by the cliffs and mountain roads, is the Middle Ages town of Riva del Garda, a lovely destination. It claims to be the wind surfing capital of the world.

Riva is a small lakeside resort with all the amenities needed to serve the traveler—lots of hotels, shops, and restaurants all stuffed inside some walls from centuries ago. It's only 20 kilometers west of the Brennero-Modena Autostrada and about 80 kilometers south of Bolzano, but a world away in spirit. It's signed from Rovereto on the autostrada, but it's a lot more fun to come from the north through Tione or Ponte Arche over little Passo Ballino. From a forest, the Ballino road winds down with nice views of Riva and the lake.

Riva sits at the north end of Lago di Garda, surrounded by high Alps and twisting roads. The road hugging the west shore of the lake is often in a tunnel chiseled through high cliffs that rise straight from the lake.

Coming from the Dolomites and Passo Manghen, the main road to Trento descends dramatically and loops north of Trento over the autostrada and the Adige River and the railroads to a traffic circle. Believe it or not, it is necessary to go around the circle twice to get in the right lane to exit toward Riva. It's signed. After starting up the mountain westerly from the traffic circle there's a turnoff for Monte Bondone, a step climb through countless hairpins. Up on Bondone at about 1,500 meters is Hotel Montana. Beyond it, the main road hairpins down westerly toward Riva. Straight past the turn off for Monte Bondone, the road west from the traffic circle leads to Ponte Arche and Tione.

In Riva, traffic gets pushed away from the lake. Keeping to the west, the road eventually gets to the shoreline road on the west side of the lake. Keeping to the east gets to the shoreline road on the east side of the lake. There are some opportunities to turn into the old city, but its center is closed to motor traffic. Note the blue signs with white arrows that designate the directions it's okay to go at intersections. Both shoreline roads are congested, but the westerly one winds for miles through tunnels in the cliffs that rise a thousand feet or so out of the water. Every driveway and intersecting road must be chiseled from the granite. Every spot where a wheel can fit has a restaurant or hotel. One town, Campione, has a complete interchange tunneled into the adjoining mountain.

The main road climbing the cliffs from Lago di Garda to Pieve is either hanging on a ledge or tunneling through a mountain. Honking is okay on blind, narrow corners.

The balcony of the Hotel Paradiso hangs way out a thousand feet or so over Lago di Garda. It's worth a visit.

Lake steamers, ferries, and hydrofoils come into Riva at a pedestrian square. The square is surrounded by gelaterias where elaborate ice cream concoctions are to be consumed leisurely, taking time to indulge in that great European sport, people watching. The sport is European, but Italians are the champions.

Right on the pedestrian square is Hotel Europa in several adjoining ancient buildings, all remodeled on the inside. The front door is on the square, but the back door is on the westerly road around the town, so the hotel has enclosed parking at the back. Also on the square is Hotel Sole, but it has no vehicular access. Behind the Sole, on the lakefront is Hotel Bellavista and it's possible to ride to it from the other side. Facing the square with no vehicular access is Hotel Centrale. Beyond the Bellavista away from the lake, but with vehicular access is the Grand Hotel Riva. Just uphill from the Centrale and the Europa, away from the lake, is Hotel Villa Miravalle with lovely furnishings, an outside pool, and parking.

A couple of dramatically located hotels in the mountains above Lago di Garda are mentioned on trips that connect to them.

Trip 46   Pieve and Passo di Tremalzo

Distance   *About 85 kilometers*

Terrain   *Gentle lakeshore with tunnels, steep, very narrow gorge, and dark tunnels; steep, rocky, unpaved section between Vesio and pass, smooth sweeping asphalt around Lago di Ledro*

Highlights   *Scenic lakeshore, exotic gorge and views from heights, rugged unpaved mountain climb, pass-top rifugio, ★★Pieve and Passo di Tremalzo (1,894 meters) and Lago di Ledro*

As the lake shore road on the west side of Lago di Garda approaches the turn into the tunnel for Pieve, it opens up.

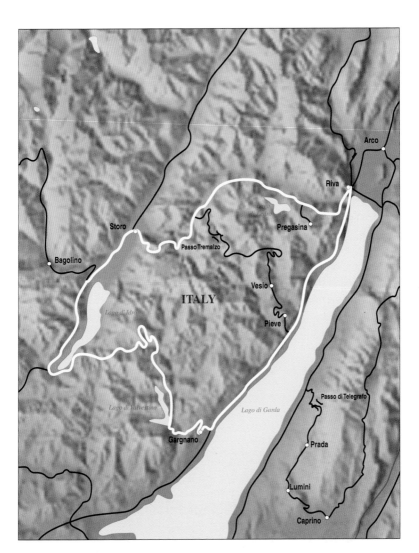

Sited on the tip top of the 1,000-foot cliff, straight up over the lake with a balcony cantilevered into space, is Hotel Paradiso at Pieve. And the road to it is an absolute must. Follow the west shore road south about five kilometers past Limone, where the road suddenly opens up with no houses or businesses in sight. Take the 90-degree turn into a tunnel. The road climbs out of the tunnel, makes several hairpins, and goes in another long tunnel—parts of it in full width, parts in tight, narrow curves—to reach a narrow gorge with overhanging cliffs, dripping water, a grotto to the Madonna, and a little monument to Winston Churchill, who must have painted there. Honk the horn on one-lane blind corners. Traffic is two-way, but there's space for only one lane.

The road circles around at a little opening in the cliffs and crosses over itself. At that spot is a good restaurant specializing in trout—pick yours out of the tank.

In another couple of kilometers, at the top of the cliffs, is the village of Pieve. The uphill road from the traffic circle at the gas station climbs past the town piazza, church, and school, and there's the Hotel Paradiso, down a long drive to the cliff's edge. Swimming pool, tennis, and food.

Once, a group of Americans at the Hotel Paradiso was supplied a menu in English. "What's this item, creamy noodle?" they asked. The hostess got out her Italian-English dictionary, which clearly translated "lasagna" into English as "creamy noodle." If you're lucky, they'll have "creamy noodle" as the first course.

If you stop just to look—and you should not miss it—buy something to eat or drink.

Passo di Tremalzo from Pieve became a dual-purpose legend when it was featured in *Motorrad,* the German motorcycle magazine. BMW was seen testing the GS models there. But it is now officially closed to motorcycle traffic. Some still risk official wrath and ride it. It's narrow, rocky, and unpaved, with hairpins hanging in space. A riding miscalculation could have very unsatisfactory results. It never was for uncertain riders, but all sorts of persistent street bikes have

These south slopes of Passo Tremalzo became too popular with motorcyclists, so it's sometimes closed to them. The road is not paved.

These American riders discovered that this Tremalzo hairpin had not been cleared of winter snow.

conquered it, most preferring to ride up rather than down it. From the rifugio at the top, down north, it's paved and open to all traffic. To find the pass from Pieve (not every intersection is marked), follow the signs from the gas station toward Vesio. The first several kilometers into a narrowing valley from Vesio are paved.

About halfway up, in a grove of trees, the pass road makes a hairpin into a fork going straight ahead, with some signs reading VIETATO, "forbidden." Whether or not it's forbidden, the straight-ahead fork isn't the right road.

The asphalt descent from the rifugio ends on the Lago di Ledro road. It swoops around the lake of that name, and starts to descend the cliffs into Riva. That's where the old road's been replaced with a 90-degree sharp turn into the mountain and a tunnel several kilometers long into the back side of Riva.

An alternate, much easier, and legal route crosses the mountains from the west shore of Lago di Garda at Gargnano. From the lake shore road, 12 kilometers south of the tunnel turn for Pieve, it crosses to Lago d'Idro from which roads lead north to Storo and the Lago di Ledro road back to Riva. The paved north slope of Passo di Tremalzo, open to all traffic, is signed from the Lago di Ledro road.

Trip 47 Monte Velo and Monte Baldo

Distance *About 160 kilometers*

Terrain *East of Riva, steep narrow twisting roads, through forests and tunnels, over several passes above Lago di Garda, mostly smooth asphalt, two way traffic*

Highlights *Exotic views of Lago di Garda and Alps. Some forest, some high meadows. Super lunch stop with views to die for. Passo Santa Barbara (1,169 meters), Passo San Valentino (1,425 meters), ★★Bocca di Navene (mouth of Navene) restaurant/hotel about 5,000 feet straight up over Lago di Garda, Cavallo di Novezza (1,433 meters), Passo di Telegrafo (1,134 meters)*

These riders are making the way through a lot of hairpins coming down off Passo di Telegrafo toward Lago di Garda.

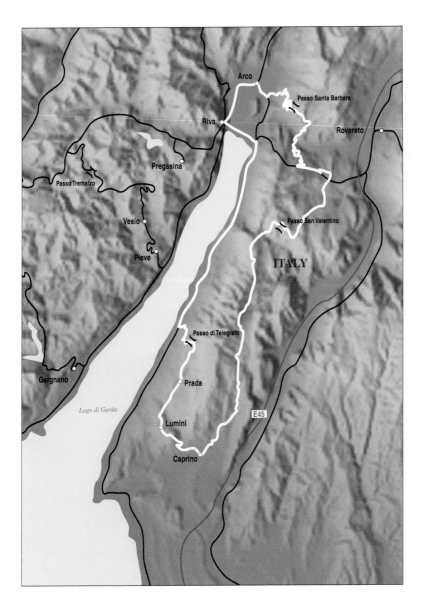

(Note: This trip can be accessed from the south by exiting the Brennero Autostrada at Affi; from the north at Rovereto).

This trip is a day's loop ride from Riva. Monte Velo is northeast of Riva. Monte Baldo is the huge mass towering to 2,200 meters in the few kilometers between Lago di Garda, only 60 meters above sea level, and the deep canyon of the Adige River. The autostrada and railroads to the Brenner Pass are in the Adige Canyon.

Head out of Riva following signs to Arco, just 6 kilometers north. The main road circles Arco to the east, connecting with a bunch of traffic circles. From one of the circles, take an exit south toward Torbole for a half a kilometer or so. Then a brown sign, MONTE VELO points left, northerly. That's the only reference to Monte Velo. The road curves and sweeps through a very pleasant residential neighborhood, then narrows and the hairpins start. Back and forth, the road climbs through a forest with occasional glimpses down on Arco and Riva and the lake. Fun. The road bursts into a high meadow with a few houses as it tops Passo Santa Barbara. From there, it becomes a wider road sweeping down to the south through the Val de Gresta. There's a junction at a village, Chienis. Left heads north through a region called Bordala. Turn right, on downhill to the junction with the main east-west road connecting the Brennero and Riva.

Turn left on it toward the Brennero. In about four kilometers, the road enters a tunnel bypassing the village, Mori. Just before the tunnel, exit into Mori. From the main street of Mori, turn right, uphill. The only sign reads BRENTONICO, but this is the Monte Baldo road, at this point, a smooth two lane road with broad hairpins. At occasional intersections keep right. After some elevation, there's a minor ski area and the lovely Hotel Giacomo. Past Hotel Giacomo, keep right as the road gets more narrow, finally twisting through

Above Hotel Giacomo, the Monte Baldo road crosses a high valley and begins to narrow. Not far ahead are narrow tunnels leading to Bocca Navene.

From the deck at Bocca Navene, the view across Lago di Garda to the Alps can take some time to absorb.

some very narrow tunnels over Passo San Valentino into a popular hiking area. Then all of a sudden, around a bunch of blind corners, there's the rifugio Bocca Navene in a new building. Park for lunch or refreshment, and walk out on the deck for the stupendous views 5,000 feet down to the lake, across to its western shore, and beyond, to the Alps. Usually most of the customers are motorcyclists.

Leave Bocca Navene heading on south on the little road following signs to Caprino about 25 kilometers down the mountain. At Caprino the little road merges with a real two-lane one. Down, through Caprino, there's a right turn for a town called Lumini. Straight ahead would lead to congestion at the lake shore. Lumini is northerly, back up along Baldo's flank. Through Lumini follow signs for Prada. North through Prada the pavement deteriorates a bit, over Passo di Telegrafo, where the excitement starts. Startling views of the lake between tight hairpins as the road snakes down off the mountain. Finally a bit of civilization at Castello, where the road splits. Either way goes quickly down to the lake shore road. It's about 25 kilometers north along the lake to Riva, passing through the sailing mecca, Malcesine, and wind surfing beaches including Navene, just 5,000 feet under the rifugio above. North Sails of San Diego, California, are prominent.

Trip 48 The High Road West

Distance *About 230 kilometers to Morbegno*
Terrain *Three narrow, steep, paved, high passes; and three less high*
Highlights *Rushing streams and high meadows with no traffic, rustic rifugios, ★★Passo di Croce Domini (1,943 meters), ★Passo di Vivione (1,828 meters), Passo di Presolana (1,294 meters), Col di Zambla (1,257 meters), ★Passo di San Marco (1,992 meters)*

A high route west from Riva uses remote passes known and used mostly by locals. Even those persistent explorers, German motorcyclists, seldom venture this way. This route crosses three high ridges between several roughly parallel valleys running south out of the Alps.

Cross the first ridge via the Lago di Ledro road out of Riva, going through the long tunnel, past the Passo di Tremalzo turnoff, and across to Storo in the next valley.

Storo appears a drab country village, but it has a first class coffee house that would do any city proud. It has marble and stained glass and comfortable booths and tables. It's at the main village intersection where a small road heads south.

Especially in Italy, Alpine roads can be pretty narrow, maybe just one lane wide, but with two way traffic. But usually they have smooth asphalt and white stripes like these on Passo Vivione that mark the edge of the pavement.

Eight kilometers south of Storo on the main valley road, alongside Lago d'Idro, is the turn up Croce Domini. It's a 170 degree right hander, a hairpin. After some scenic climbing, the road crosses a valley and there's a fork. Left goes down around and below the mountain town of Bagolino. Right goes through the old town's narrow streets. Both forks come together further up the mountain. The lower fork does provide a turn toward Passo Maniva and thence to the Po Valley.

The little rifugio on Passo Vivione was caught flying an American flag.

From Bagolino, the Croce Domini road becomes one lane of dancing and climbing asphalt that runs beside torrents of water and rises out of the forests to cross the top above the tree line. The rifugio at the top serves refreshments in front of, or practically inside, a giant fireplace.

The dirt road south from the Croce Domini rifugio is not recommended. In fact, it usually has a dirt berm across it to discourage trespassing. West from the rifugio, the Croce Domini road has recently been rebuilt with elaborate concrete and rock retaining walls. It's still very narrow in spots. If the rifugio's family is absent, there are two albergos just a couple of kilometers down west.

Breno is a pretty big town at the western base of the Croce Domini. Coming the other way, looking for the Croce Domini road, turn into Breno. There are two turns up the pass; one with a fading sign is between two high walls enclosing fading villas. It goes staight up before twisting into the mountain. Apparently authorities prefer you to take a more circuitous route, more clearly signed, through a village called Bienno. The two routes merge further up the mountain. The valley north from Breno is surprisingly industrial (for a narrow Alpine valley), but it's only 20 kilometers to the Passo di Vivione, one of the most ignored delights of the Alps. Passo di Vivione starts westerly at Forno d'Allione (which is just nine kilometers south of Edolo, see Trip 49). The pass road turns down across the valley stream, past a smelter furnace. Since *forno* means "kiln" and "furnace" as well as "oven," the turn is well named. In fact, the pass road is inconspicuous around and beyond the parking lot of the smelter. The pass is one-lane, paved, and devoid of traffic.

It's possible to cross over to the south end of Passo Vivione, then cross it south to north. To do this, from the main road below Breno, turn west toward Borno. (How come all those "B" towns? Breno is the main valley town. The next town southerly is Bienno. The turn west toward Passo Vivione is Borno. Look out, the next town further south is Boario, and the county seat, further south, is Brescia.) The road west to Borno climbs nicely with two lanes. At Borno it narrows to one lane (two-ways) and dances down the mountain across a valley to intercept the Passo Vivione road toward Schilpario.

Because the Vivione road has so little traffic, it's easy to assume the whole road is available. But there can be other vehicles.

There's a little rifugio at the top of Vivione with fresh pasta, maybe lasagna, and mountain berries. It has been known to fly an American flag. Around it are views of empty meadows and jagged mountain peaks.

Vivione comes down southwest to Schilpario, a ski resort. Below Schilpario, resist the temptation to turn down into the deep valley. Rather, stay on the higher road which leads right up Passo di Presolana, in the direction of Bergamo. The road passes through a resort area popular with Italians, but unknown to most foreigners. There are several good hotels and ristorantes in towns like Rovetta and Clusone, but no English is spoken.

Five kilometers below Clusone, just below the village of Ponte Nossa, the Col di Zambla road climbs west, while the valley road continues to the large city of Bergamo. (Bergamo was home to Montessori and is home to Acerbis.) The Col di Zambla road comes down in the next valley by Terme San Pellegrino. Terme means spa or "bad." This is the San Pellegrino of bottled water, often rated the best of bottled waters (better than Perrier?). The bottles and their plastic carriers and the trucks hauling it all will be in evidence. The spa itself looks well past its prime. The International Six-Day Trials were once held in the area.

Passo di San Marco is a rarity: no other bikes. It's not marked. Follow the valley north from San Pellegrino, taking the forks toward the town of Mezzoldo (some maps erroneously show the pass from the area of a town called Cusio, but that's the wrong valley). The high road from Mezzoldo is the pass. It crosses over and comes down into the town of Morbegno in the Adda Valley (the valley that could be seen from Passo dell'Aprica, upstream from Lago di Como). From Morbegno, there are good connections into Switzerland via the Splugen Pass and the Bernina Pass (see Trip 38, Maloja Pass, Splugen Pass, etc., and Trip 39, Italian Connections).

Trip 49   The Low Road West

Distance   *About 210 kilometers to Morbegno*

Terrain   *Three modest passes; occasional hairpins and grades, mostly main roads*

Highlights   *Faster route west than Trip 48, more interesting than autostrada in Po Valley; Passo Durone (940 meters), Passo Campo Carlo Magno (Madonna di Campiglio) (1,682 meters), Passo del Tonale (1,883 meters), Passo dell'Aprica (1,176 meters)*

Taking the higher road north from Riva toward Ponte Arche and over Passo Durone to Tione leads to the north-south Passo Campo Carlo Magno (that's Italian for Charlemagne) through the ski area Madonna di Campiglio, both in the woods below the tree line. Just over the pass is a new hotel restaurant, Casa del Campo, on the west side of the road, with views of the mountains to the east.

At Dimaro, the pass road intersects the westbound road over Passo del Tonale. For some reason, there's a Holiday Inn at the corner. (East from the corner is Fondo and the roads of Trip 43.) Tonale doesn't hairpin so much as zig-zag in a fun climb. There's a World War I sacrario (cemetery) at the top, and several closed hotels waiting for snow and skiers. Down west it's a little more curvy to the intersection with Passo di Gavia and Ponte di Legno, and further down, the intersection with Passo Mortirolo. There's a short tunnel into the pretty good sized town, Edolo. Passo Vivione (Trip 48) is just nine kilometers south. Remember, a sandwich is a sandwich, but a grilled sandwich is panini.

On the map, Passo Tonale and Passo dell'Aprica seem to line up almost straight east and west, with Edolo in the middle.

So, from Edolo, it's another zig-zag climb up west on the Aprica. Some believe that ristorantes on Aprica have the best hot chocolate in the world. Down west of the Aprica is the Adda Valley, Morbegno, Tirano, and the roads outlined in Trip 40.

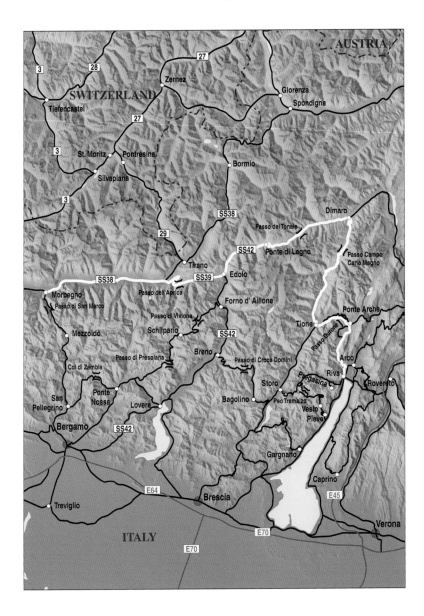

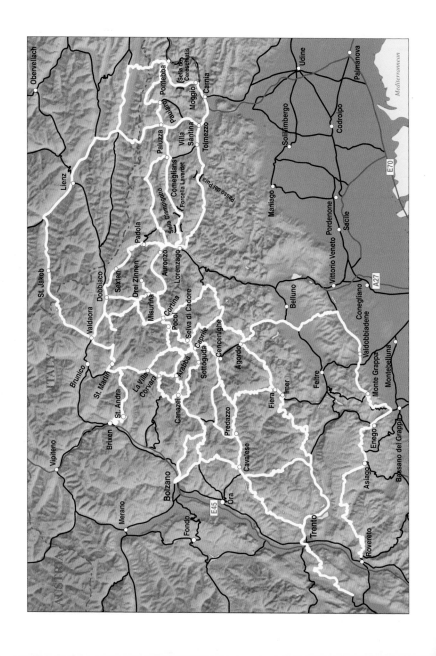

The Dolomites

The Italians call them Dolomiti, and the Germans, Dolomiten. Whatever they're called, the first view of the Dolomites will take your breath away. No matter how many mountains you've seen, no matter how many times you may have seen the Dolomites, that first glimpse—maybe as you emerge from a tunnel, or maybe as you accelerate out of a hairpin—will be an almost religious experience. The vertical massifs set in feathery green forests are duplicated nowhere. And there are more good roads than a good rider can cover in a week of hard riding.

Draw a straight line on the map between Venezia (Venice) and Munchen (Munich). There in Italy, just below the middle of that line, are the Dolomites. They're east of that giant canyon known as the Brenner Pass, the great divide made by the Adige River which is used as the major and lowest north-south route across the Alps.

No matter how wonderful the riding, the Dolomites can cause a rider to pause and look. Here they sport a dusting of snow.

There are good low-level routes around the Dolomites, so no one has to go through them to get anywhere. The only people there are there because of them. The Dolomites are a skier's and motorcyclist's dream.

The Dolomites are in Italy, with Italian laws, stamps, and money, but it was not always thus. Until World War I, they were in Austria, part of the Tirol. The Austrians were on the Germans' side in World War I, and the Italians were on the Allied side. The Austrian and Italian generals ordered up battles much like the horrible ones in France, only these were in the mountains. Little known in our history books are the costly battles fought between Austria and Italy in the Dolomites. Once one side or the other had charged up or down a mountain at great loss of life, they had to build a road to supply the dearly bought area. They built roads and tunnels that didn't seem to go anywhere except to serve some strategic need of the moment.

Now those roads make up a fantastic network for motorcycle exploring. Besides the roads, the war left only *sacrarios* (cemeteries) and some huge stone forts.

History doesn't indicate that the costly battles in the Dolomites decided anything, but at Versailles the victorious allies awarded the Sud Tirol (South Tyrol) to Italy. In the 1920s, some of the Tirol voted to return to Austria. The rest, including the great Dolomite range, is now known in Italy as the Alto Adige. Some of the World War I monuments and cemeteries (sacrarios) are mentioned on the trips here.

Vast areas of the region still remain Germanic. Many towns have Austrian-style buildings and food and are known by their German names. Typically, one side of a pass, usually the south and east side, will be completely Italian, while the next village, just a pass away, will be Austrian-Germanic. A quick clue: besides the pictures painted on the sides of the buildings, Austrian villages will have a church with a steeple, while an Italian town will have a church with a campanile.

Once some American riders on German registered bikes approached the Dolomites while the Giro d'Italia bicycle race was passing. A police officer stopped them and addressed the group in German. The Americans responded in English. The police officer asked, "Where'd yuh wanta go?"

Every Dolomite Pass road has a rifugio at the top.

Whether the village is Italian or Austrian, it'll have fresh pasta and great cappuccino. The Austrian ones will have Wienerschnitzel as well. A hotel or restaurant in either will have a dining room set with fresh linen and glasses, and another with bare tables. A meal may be available only in the room with the tablecloths, but there will always be a cover charge for sitting there. Noon time is siesta time and full meal time in Italy, and pasta is just the first or second course. (If pasta and salad is enough for lunch, make that clear, or the courses will keep coming.)

Cortina d'Ampezzo, usually known simply as "Cortina," is the most famous village in the Dolomites. It's spectacularly set on the eastern edge of the Dolomites and has been the site of winter Olympics. Regularly reviewed in travel magazines, it's the summer resort of choice for the wealthy of Milano. (It's a lot cooler than Milano.) Cortina's central pedestrian zone has pricey shops, and a department store with everything, called the Cooperativa. *The New York Times* once said something to the effect that the place to be seen is the bar of Hotel della Poste in Cortina. Motorcyclists have been seen there, and also watching the scene from the narrow terrace in front of the hotel. It's a treat to have a drink, especially if the owner, S. Manijgo, is around to talk about the history of the valley. His family has owned the hotel for more than a century, and he has the photos to prove it. Cortina is nice, but expensive.

There's a figure eight loop, lying on its side, in the heart of the Dolomites just west of Cortina. The loop includes six major passes. Just as at Andermatt in Switzerland, it's possible to ride the figure eight and expand into the almost endless variations beyond it without ever coming down into lowlands or big cities.

Each of the villages on the trip has hotels and restaurants, many nicer, and all cheaper, than those in Cortina d'Ampezzo. The middle of the figure eight is Passo di Campolongo, only ten kilometers across. The towns at each end of the pass have good accommodations.

The south anchor of Passo di Campolongo is Arabba, a completely Italian town with good food and a variety of comfortable hotels.

Spacious rooms and a parking garage can be found at Hotel Evaldo in Arabba. It features a comfortable bar, a lovely dining room, a jacuzzi, an indoor pool with water spouts, and a sauna in several flavors. Usually meals feature serve-yourself ante-pasta and deserts. The pasta course and main course are served by waiters in black ties. The Evaldo makes a point of accommodating motorcyclists. There's a high pressure wash beside the garage. Several in the family have motorcycled in the United States.

All of the hotels listed in the Appendix actively solicit motorcycle business. You will find the vast majority of their customers are on bikes. Note that "Gasthof" in German is often translated into Italian as "albergo," and calling a hotel a "Pension" has nothing to do with "demi-pension." It usually means that the hotel restaurant is for residents only.

In some spots, the jagged peaks of the Dolomites look like dribbled sand castles.

Above Arabba on the Campolongo road is the Hotel Olympia. It's a nice place with a pleasant view and it solicits motorcycle business.

Ten kilometers north across Passo di Campolongo, at Corvara in Badia (usually called just "Corvara"), things are a bit more Germanic. Actually, signs may be in three languages, Italian, German, and Laden, the local dialect that is related to Romansch in Switzerland. A variety of hotels includes Hotel Posta-Zirm, an old-time place that's been modernized and has grown in all directions to include a lovely dining room, an indoor pool, and a ski lift at the side door. Dinners include an elaborate salad bar at the Zirm, a good place to mix the American custom of eating salad before the main course with the European one of having it afterwards. Breakfasts are bountiful by Euro standards.

Very popular with motorcyclists is Pension La Fontana in Corvara. Food in the attractive dining room may be about the best in the Alps. Bountifully and beautifully served. Prices are very reasonable. The road up the Passo di Campolongo goes right by it.

Right in the center of Corvara is the Hotel Col Alto, popular with some motorcycle travel groups.

In the fall you may see some *cacciatores* . . . hunters.

Trip 50   Dolomite Figure 8

Distance   *About 90 kilometers*

Terrain   *Climbs and descents with lots of hairpins and switchbacks; some cobblestones*

Highlights   *Six major passes encircle fantastic vertical massifs; many cafes and hotels. Includes: ★Passo di Valparola (2,192 meters), ★Passo di Falzarego (2,105 meters), Passo di Campolongo (1,875 meters), ★Passo di Gardena (Grodner Joch) (2,121 meters), ★Passo di Sella (2,244 meters), ★Passo Pordoi (2,239 meters)*

(Note: There is a gas station 5 kilometers east of Arabba, two in Corvara, and one in San Cassiano. Passo Sella has been especially congested at times, and rumors suggest that a toll may be charged. Sella is Italian for saddle.)

    Passo di Valparola starts just five kilometers north (down stream) of Corvara, in a village called La Villa in Italian (Stern in German). In Italy, directional signs for passes are brown in color. Signs to towns are in blue. The brown pass sign for Valparola points easterly. After twisting down to cross a stream, the pass road climbs southeasterly by-passing a village called San Cassiano in Italian (St.

From Passo Valparola there is a great view of the Passo Falzarego road snaking down to the west between Dolomite peaks.

Kassian in German). Some sweeping hairpins climb to the top, where there's the ruin of a massive World War I fort built by the Austrians. The Italians call the fort Tre Sassi. It's now a museum full of artifacts (a lot of discarded tin cans) and information about battles and strategies.

Down a few kilometers south of the fort the Valparaola road ends at the summit of east-west Passo Falzarego which boasts a couple of restaurants, a cable car to a neighboring peak, and a statue of an Italian World War I hero.

To the east, the Falzarego descends in hairpins past magnificent vertical formations toward Cortina. The figure eight goes the other way, westerly, in a series of hairpins and tunnels. But not too far down. It hangs high on the edge of the mountain back toward Arabba, villages and fields a thousand meters below on one side, snow capped massifs on the other, a thousand meters up.

The area is known as the Col de Lana, a World War I battleground. Look way down in the valley below at a sacrario, cemetery, in the shape of a cross.

Along the edge of a tight hairpin is a World War I stone fort. It would seem to command the entire valley. Now it's a restaurant.

The southern legs of the figure eight, the Passo di Falzarego and the Passo Pordoi, make up part of the Great Dolomite Road which goes east from the Brenner road to Cortina. This is the most touristy part of the Dolomites and the oldest pavement. Still, it's so exciting as to be a must. An occasional tour bus may require every inch of the road to get around a hairpin. Remember, when tempted to duck past a bus, that the rear wheels will track inside of the front. In the Alps when the going gets tight, the descending vehicle is supposed to back up. Tourists are early risers, and are usually off the roads by 4 p.m. The roads and colors are good through the long summer evenings.

Each of the passes on the figure eight has tourist facilities. There are several cable cars to the peaks.

Giro d'Italia bicyclists climb this side of Passo Campolongo, coming out of Corvara. It's easier on a motorcycle.

As soon as the road was plowed after an early fall snow, the bikes were riding the Great Dolomite road past the Evaldo Hotel in Arabba.

At Arabba, the Falzarego joins the Passo di Campolongo heading north, and the Passo Pordoi, still the Great Dolomite Road, climbing west. Passo Pordoi has 33 numbered hairpins on the east side out of Arabba, and 27 down the west side to Canazei.

Before the west base of the Passo Pordoi at Canazei, the Passo di Sella starts heading north on the figure eight. All of the massifs are famous for mountain climbing, but the Sella is probably the best known. Usually there will be climbers hundreds of meters overhead and hikers with binoculars watching them from below.

The Sella comes down a bit on the north, only to intersect the Passo di Gardena heading east on the figure eight. The passes intersect at a road heading west to the Brenner through the Val Gardena, a valley very popular with German tourists, who call it Grodner Tal. The valley is loaded with Germanic hotels, and shops selling copper and leather goods.

About halfway up the west side of the Passo di Gardena is Restaurant Gerard with a view terrace. It also rents rooms. It's much nicer than the tourist traps atop the pass.

The Passo di Gardena's east end is downtown Corvara, where one fork in the Y intersection is the Passo di Campolongo climbing south to Arabba, ten kilometers away.

Trip 51 Dolomites: Giau and Marmolada

Distance About 50 kilometers from Canazei to Pocol
Terrain Steep mountain roads with hairpins
Highlights Almost as fantastic as Trip 50, plus a narrow gorge, all with a lot less traffic. Includes: The Marmolada (Passo di Fedaia) (2,057 meters), and ★Passo di Giau (say JOW, rhymes with how) (2,233 meters)

Ride across the dam atop Passo di Fedaia to one of the restaurants on the far side, the base of the huge granite massif known as Marmolada. World War I battles were fought on the Marmolada. Apparently, many troops froze to death.

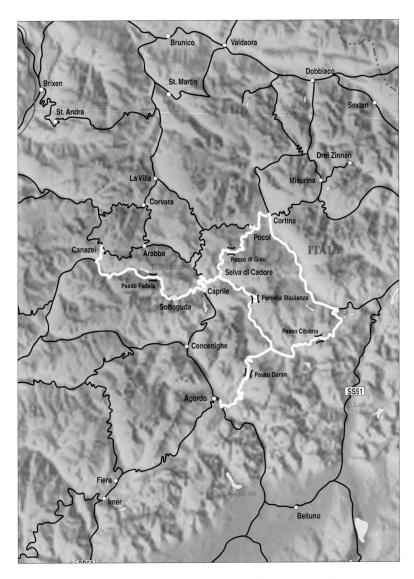

These passes are east-west connections south of the Great Dolomite Road. They're all Italian, from Canazei at the bottom of the Pordoi on the west, to Pocol on the east, just above Cortina on the Falzarego.

Starting east from Canazei, the Passo di Fedaia is off the normal tourist route. It climbs the flank of the Marmolada, the largest massif of the Dolomites and the site of some of the bloodiest fighting of World War I. There's a lake at the top of the Fedaia and a ristorante across the dam on the south side of the lake, with views of the massif.

The east side of the Fedaia goes down on a new alignment of very tight but open sweepers on concrete pavement. A couple of tunnels at the tree line go around a famous gorge, now closed to vehicles. Between the tunnels, a bridge crosses the gorge. Stop and look over from the bridge to see if it might be worth walking into it from below in the village of Sottoguda. There are picnic tables and a small chapel from World War I in the gorge which is so narrow that hardly any sky is visible. The old road went through the gorge.

The area is noted for hand wrought iron work. Some interesting, some weird creations are displayed on buildings in the valley.

Down east below the Sottoguda gorge is the village Caprile. There are two twisty roads from Caprile, back north to the figure eight loop. But go past them and through Caprile, and start climbing the wonders of Passo di Giau, following signs to Selva di Cadore. First comes a spectacular view area known as Colle Santa Lucia looking to Dolomite peaks and down over feathery forests and a blue lake. Just before Selva, the Passo di Giau road turns up. It's a motorcyclist's dream: continuous curves on an alignment laid out in the 1980s. There are a couple of rifugios on Giau, including a handsome new one at the top, the Cima Passo Giau.

A lot of Italians ride Italian motorcycles atop Passo Giau.

Passo di Giau in the Dolomites has a new rifugio and gorgeous views with lots of examples from local wood carvers. An old Moto Guzzi caps the post to the right of the rifugio.

Going into Selva instead of turning up the Giau leads you to Passo Forcella Staulanza (1,773 meters) and either Passo Duran (1,601 meters) or Passo di Cibiana (1,530 meters). From either, main valley roads lead back to the figure eight. The east side of the Giau has some delightful picnic spots.

The Giau comes out on the Falzarego pass road just above Cortina at a small village called Pocol. Here is one of the most impressive World War I monuments and mausoleums in the Alps, and the best view of Cortina. Neither the monument nor the view are visible from the road, and they are not well-marked. To find them, turn up a little driveway just below a big old hotel, usually closed. There's a little sign, SACRARIO. It's just a hundred meters up the drive to the monument entry gates. They may have an international DO NOT ENTER sign, but the keepers have usually let motorcyclists with respectful attitudes ride in. The monument itself is a church, with the stations of the cross set on each side of a stair cut through the mountain leading to it. The cut frames the monument against the Cortina valley.

The best view of Cortina is from a *Belvedere* (a terrace with a view) just a few meters past the gate to the monument.

Trip 52   I Dare You; 17 Passes in One Day

Distance *About 400 kilometers*
Terrain *Every kind of Dolomite pass road, all paved*
Highlights *Each pass on this route is described elsewhere in shorter trips*

This is just a pass-bagging trip. No discussion of lunch or hotels or views. Probably there's nowhere but the Dolomites where seventeen passes can be ridden, bagged, in one long day. Most places, it's a major undertaking to cross seven passes in a day.

Here's the suggested route, starting at Arabba or Corvara, listing the passes in a sort of clockwise order, wasting as few kilometers as possible between one and the next. This circuit is all west of Cortina. If your day is long enough, you could bag more by adding passes east of Cortina.

1. Valparola
2. Falzarego
3. Giau
4. Staulanza
5. Duran
6. Aurine
7. Cereda

That's Corvara down below the curves and hairpins of Passo di Gardena.

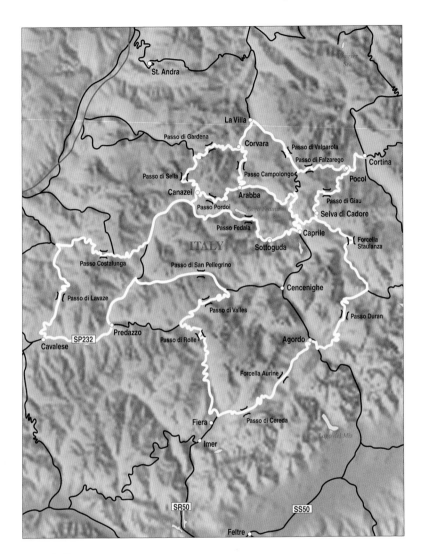

8. Rolle
9. Valles
10. San Pellegrino
11. Lavaze
12. Costalunga
13. Fedaia
14. Pordoi
15. Sella
16. Gardena
17. Campolongo

Trip 53 Southern Dolomites

Distance *About 130 kilometers from Arabba (add another 100 to San Boldo)*

Terrain *Paved mountain roads, some steep tight turns*

A view point near Selva di Cadore on the Passo Staulanza road affords spectacular vistas to the west of the road up Passo Fedaia toward the Marmolada, all highlighted here by sun and cloud shadow. The town immediately below is Caprile. Other roads to the right snake up the mountains toward the Passo Falzarego Pass.

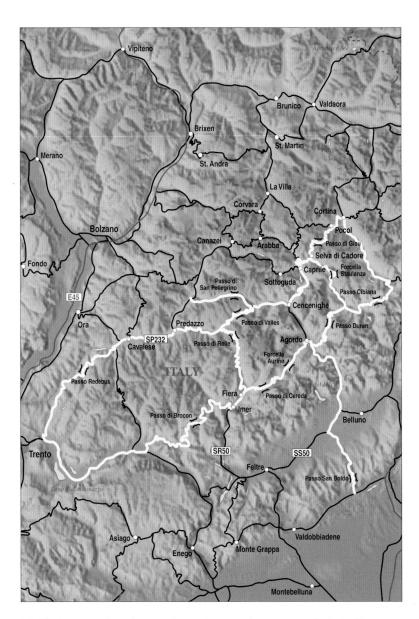

Highlights *Feathery forests, dramatic vertical mountains, little traffic, several rifugios. Includes: Passo Forcella Staulanza (1,773 meters), ★Passo Duran (1,601 meters), Passo Cibiana (1,530 meters), Passo di Valles (2,033 meters), Passo di San Pellegrino (1,918 meters), Passo di San Boldo (703 meters), Passo di Rolle (1,955 meters), Passo di Cereda (1,378 meters), Passo di Brocon (1,616 meters)*

A 15-kilometer jaunt down the valley south from Caprile, away from the figure eight, leads to Cencenighe, the gateway to Passo di Valles and Passo di San Pellegrino. Both go west.

Passo di Valles has a comfortable rifugio at the top with good lasagna. The western slope of Passo di Valles is velvety green. It looks like a park, and it is. Both passes descend deep into the Valle di Fassa, the west extension of the Great Dolomite Road.

The westerly end of the Passo di Valles road is at a T intersection with the Passo di Rolle road. Head north at the T to go back to the Great Dolomite Road. Or head south, up and over Passo di Rolle to Fiera, where a northeast turn leads over Passo di Cereda. Passo di Cereda has two humps, the lower of which is called Forcella Aurine that come down onto the brick paved plaza of Agordo. Turn south a kilometer or so, then east onto the Passo Duran road which climbs to 1,601 meters where there's a small rifugio and a sort-of Disneyesqe chapel. The chapel walls are out of square and the roof tilts crazily. Down easterly from the rifugio and chapel, Passo Duran is very narrow—one lane wide—as it dances between walls and houses and forests.

Passo Duran daylights at an intersection with the Passo Staulanza road. North, the road goes over Staulanza with some sweeping Dolomite views, toward Caprile and the Great Dolomite Road. Southerly, it snakes and dances through a tight gorge onto a main road to Venezia. Before that, there's a possible turn easterly over Passo Cibiana in the direction of Cortina.

Way down south is a pass of amazing audacity: Passo di San Boldo. Each end of each traverse is a hairpin in a tunnel! The tunnels are stacked five or six deep. Now they are controlled by traffic lights so that traffic enters them one-way at a time.

Motorcycles coming down off the north side of Passo Valles are approaching the "T" intersection with Passo Rolle.

To explore farther or to head toward Trento, go south five kilometers from Fiera on the Passo di Rolle road to Imer. At Imer, take a road up and west to Passo di Brocon, where a rifugio awaits you at the top.

These passes mark the southern edge of the Dolomites. There are some good twisties farther south, and one more pass worth a detour because of the audacity of its construction. Called Passo di San Boldo, it crosses a ridge at only 706 meters, not high enough to note otherwise. It's about 15 kilometers southwest of Belluno, one of the major cities south of Cortina, and was the high water mark of the Austrian advance during World War I. The Austrians got down over the ridge in one place, but there was no supply road. So they had to build one. This road is carved out of the cliff face back and forth. But there was no room for a hairpin at the end of each traverse. So the road goes into the mountain in a tunnel, makes a hairpin, and comes out going the other direction. Then it does the same thing in reverse. The hairpin tunnels are stacked five or six deep, one on top of the other, at each end. The tunnels have recently been lighted and equipped with traffic signals.

Once, pulling into Pocol at the east end of Passo di Giau, a rider at the side of the road was studying a map. He was on a Munch, that massive, in-line, four-cylinder machine made in Germany before the Japanese made such a layout their own. "Hey, wait while I get a picture of you and the bike." "Sure, but if you wait a minute there will be a hundred Munchs." And there were.

Trip 54 Adige Canyon

Distance *From Arabba via Wurz Joch, about 60 kilometers to Brixen; via Passo Nigra, about 60 kilometers to Bozen; via Passo di Lavaze and Passo Manghen, about 140 kilometers to Trento*

Terrain *Often narrow, occasionally challenging pass roads. Wurz Joch and Passo Manghen have practically no traffic*

Highlights *A sense of exploring on traffic-free routes to the Brennero Autostrada; ★Wurz Joch (2,002 meters) and ★Passo Manghen (2,047 meters) have attractive rifugios. Includes: the Brenner Pass, the canyon of the Adige River, Passo di Costalunga (Karer Pass) (1,745 meters), Passo Nigra (Niger Pass) (1,688 meters), Passo di Lavaze (1,805 meters), Monte Bondone (1,537 meters), Passo di Pinei (Panider Sattel) (1,437 meters), Passo Redebus (1,449 meters), Petersberg (1,399 meters)*

On the great Dolomite passes, even the bottoms of the passes are high. Cortina at the east end is over 1,200 meters, and Canazei at the west end is over 1,400, so there's still a lot of mountain riding to get to the bottom of things. The great divide, the canyon of the Adige River, home to the Brennero Autostrada, is close to bottom at about 250 meters.

No matter how many mountains you've seen, the first glimpse of the Dolomites takes your breath away. It's almost a religious experience. This first view is from Wurz Joch, a pass that climbs out of the great canyon of the Adige River.

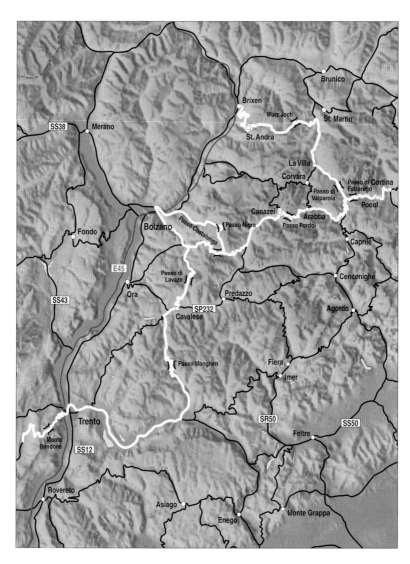

In the Adige Canyon and on the Brennero Autostrada are several cities. Way south down by Lago di Garda is Rovereto. Next, north, is Trento, then Bolzano, then Bressalone (Brixen). A lot of exciting roads lead out of the Dolomites down to them. All here.

Much of the west end of the Great Dolomite Road has been realigned using tunnels. Then a descent sweeping back and forth through orchards and vineyards with great views of the Adige Canyon and all. It finally gets down to the Adige River and the non-toll national road and the toll Brennero Autostrada at Ora (Auer in German).

Many alternate roads go up and over mountain passes on the way to the Adige River Canyon. All of them finally find a tributary gorge to follow down. It's more fun to take one of the up and over and down routes than the Great Dolomite Road.

The most beautiful and most fun motorcycle road between the Dolomites and the Adige Canyon is the Wurz Joch, known in Italian as Passo di Erbe. Find it downstream (north) of Covara, about 15 kilometers north of La Villa. A brown sign points west to Wurz Joch, and a blue sign points west to St. Martin. The road dips across a river and climbs up through St. Martin and then goes around a private little castle before climbing through open fields and forest to the summit where there's an attractive rifugio called Utia de Borz. The rifugio's deck is a great place to contemplate a first or last view of the Dolomites.

West from Utia de Borz, the road is a bouncing one lane affair. About five kilometers from the rifugio, the road splits.

The right, more northerly fork goes down past several attractive hotels like the Edith to St. Andra and Milan and Brixen (Bressanone in Italian). Brixen, on the Brennero Autostrada, is a handsome city with shaded streets and motorcycle shops and a famous hotel/restaurant called Elefant. Seems some eastern potentate of the Middle Ages was shipping a prize elephant to the German emperor across the Brenner Pass. The elephant expired in Brixen. The hotel restaurant named after the expired gift is attractive and has many dining rooms, all different and interesting.

The left, more southerly fork goes through Tirolean farms to a tight squeeze between buildings at St. Peter (see Trip 44) and Hotel Kabis. From St. Peter in a valley called Villnos in German and Funes in Italian, two lanes sweep down to the autostrada with new connections through tunnels.

Going east toward the Dolomites from Brixen, the Wurz Joch is not marked. Follow signs to Millan, a neighboring village, and then to St. Andra. From St. Andra the one-lane road seemingly going downhill is the Wurz Joch road.

Another major access route into the Dolomites from the Brennero Autostrada is the Val Gardena. Unlike the Wurz Joch, the Val Gardena route is well marked from the autostrada. It leads through a popular resort area known to the Germanics as St. Ulrich, and to the Italians as Ortisei. The area is full of hotels. The Val Gardena road ties into the figure eight trip between the Passo di Sella and the Passo di Gardena. A variation is the Passo di Pinei (Panider Sattel) south from Ortisei in the Val Gardena.

About 11 kilometers west of Canazei is the turnoff to the north for the Passo di Costalunga road. Then, just past the top of the Costalunga, the Passo Nigra goes up again, north and west. Both continue down to the Adige Canyon at Bozen (Bolzano) on the Brennero Autostrada. The Costalunga (Karer in German) goes down by a small lake, the Karer See, that's famous for its special colors. It's easy to find the lake because of the tour buses. Bozen has all services

The author enjoying a cappuccino at Utia de Borz, the rifugio atop the Wurz Joch.
Dolomite peaks are reflected in the window glass behind him.

expected of a major city, including traffic. It's home to Iveco trucks and buses (Trip 43.)

Finding the Costalunga and/or the Passo Nigra from the bottom at Bolzano requires careful attention. Both take off just north of the city from the old highway that parallels the Brennero Autostrada. There's no connection or marking from the autostrada. The signs are easy to miss among the traffic and commercial activity of the highway, even though the highway seems to be hugging the edge of high cliffs. It's worth the effort, though, because either of two roads will provide both instant relief from the congestion and some fun riding. The crowds will not be going this way.

Passo di Lavaze is a north-south mountain connection roughly parallel to and east of the Adige Canyon and the Brennero Autostrada. It starts up and south from Passo di Costalunga (Karer Pass) at a country intersection downstream from the village Nova Levante (Welschnofen in German). Signs point south to Nova Ponente (Deutschnofen). In a couple of kilometers, Nova Ponente signs call for a turn to the west. The pass is straight ahead. Turning to climb the mountain to Nova Ponente it's possible to cross Petersberg to Aldino (Aldein) and on down the Adige River at Ora.

But Passo di Lavaze climbs further south. At the top, an unpaved private pass called Passo di Occlini (Grimm Joch) goes westerly. Down south across Lavaze is the town Cavalese on the Great Dolomite Road. (Cavalese is the town where an American military jet accidentally cut a cable car wire). Cross the Great Dolomite Road and ride down into the valley below Cavalese through a village

The vertical massifs of the Dolomite range never fail to inspire. Dolomite pass roads play among feathery green forests, massive vertical peaks, and occasional flowering meadows.

called Molina where the road forks. Straight ahead skirts a lake to Brusago where brown signs point to Passo di Redebus then down to the main highway toward Trento and the Adige. (Trento is Trent in German and English).

The best road from the fork at Molina follows the brown sign to Passo Manghen up a finger canyon. It's about 20 kilometers through forested hairpins to the top. Most Dolomite hands don't know Passo Manghen, even though it's great riding: one lane wide with two-way traffic. The top is just above the tree line. Near the top is a little rifugio and twisting south there's a rustic rifugio called Bar Trattoria Malga-Voltrighetta, and further south, one just above the road called Ristorante Malga Baessa (Malga is an Italian word for a mountain barn). The south end of the Manghen is in a village called Telve where several routes lead to the main valley road and on west to Trento. Coming the other way, from Trento, the Manghen is signed through several twists and turns off the main road which is sort of a freeway, into the town Borgo, and then to Telve where a sharp uphill right turn starts the pass road.

Maps show Passo Cinque Croci just east of the Manghen. It's not open to the public. Just a bit farther east is the south end of Passo Brocon (Trip 53).

The main valley road to Trento goes west into a tight gorge with tunnels and then traverses down and around Trento without ever going into it, crossing the Brennero Autostrada and the Adige River and the railroad tracks. Finally, there are signs for Riva del Garda that seem to be pointing in the wrong direction, but work. (In order to make the Riva exit, you have to go around more than 360 degrees.) The signed route to Riva climbs a new road west out of the Adige Canyon. Go all the way west to Ponte Arche and then south for Riva.

Or, just a few kilometers up west of Trento, an exciting road into Riva turns sharply uphill, signed MONTE BONDONE. With too many hairpins to count, it climbs to over 1,500 meters, passes Hotel Montana, and then swoops and sweeps down to Riva.

If you can't bring your own bike, borrow or rent one. But you simply must experience the Dolomites.

Trip 55 Monte Grappa

Distance *180 kilometers from San Boldo to the Brennero Autostrada at Rovereto, gateway to Lago di Garda*

Terrain *All kinds of rural road, some very remote, some rough, some twisted, and some banked like a race track*

Highlights *From the tunnels of San Boldo to a spumante center, to the top of Monte Grappa (1,775 meters), Passo di Vezzena (1,402 meters), Passo di Sommo (1,343 meters)*

Narrow Passo Duran (Trip 52) comes down in an Alpine Valley at Agordo, and downstream from Agordo is Passo San Boldo.

After the hairpin tunnels of Passo San Boldo, head southwesterly along pleasant rural roads to Valdobbiadene, a town famous for its spumante (champagne) which can be sipped in the town's pleasant plaza. Then cross westerly over the Piave River to the town, Alano, and follow signs for Monte Grappa, but maybe not as many signs as needed. The road becomes very narrow at points as it climbs into several valleys, some of which are lovely. Further up, it barely hangs on the edge of a cliff before becoming a sweeping smooth road to the summit of Monte Grappa, where there are some military installations, and a parking lot offering views to the east and north. The road down to the south is

Not a pass, but a mountain top, Monte Grappa has several fun roads to its peak. This one comes up from the east.

fine, well defined and banked. Before getting into the traffic of Bassano, turn west to the main, mostly four lane valley highway and head north in the direction of Trento for about twenty kilometers, exiting up and over into Enego. This is the same road to Trento that's at the south end of Passo Manghen (Trip 54) and Passo di Brocon (Trip 53).

From Enego, the road to Asiago climbs steeply, through switchbacks and hairpins, then sweeps 30 kilometers through pleasant high valleys and towns to Asiago where a good quality road swoops and switchbacks down to an autostrada. But the mountain way is northwest over Passo di Vezzena. At Lavaronne, it connects with a road west over Passo di Sommo to Folgaria, then down past a fine castle, Castel Pietra, to the Brennero Autostrada near Rovereto.

Trip 56 **Cortina**

Distance *About 40 kilometers to Drei Zinnen; about 120 over Kreuzberg and back*

Terrain *Irregular sweeping mountain pass roads*

Highlights *Mind-boggling views from Drei Zinnen (2,320 meters) (toll); forests, vertical massifs, restaurants and hotels. The trip includes: Passo Tre Croce (1,805 meters), ★Misurina and Drei Zinnen (Tre Cime di Lavaredo) (2,320 meters), Passo del Zovo (1,476 meters), Passo di Monte Croce (Kreuzberg Pass) (1,636 meters), Furkel Sattel (1,759 meters), Passo Cimabanche (1,529 meters)*

Like many European cities, Cortina has a one-way loop street system. Some of the core inside the loop is pedestrian zone. If you miss a stop or turn, the only solution is to go around again. Cortina's loop isn't round—there are some switchbacks and some hairpins—but by the third or fourth circuit, it becomes familiar. In the course of circling Cortina, you'll see brown signs pointing the way to the Passo di Falzarego and to Passo Tre Croce. Both start climbing right in the village, the Falzarego westerly, and the Tre Croce easterly.

The Tre Croce is pleasant enough. The prize is Lake Misurina just east of the pass. Its exquisite blue reflects the surrounding Dolomite massifs. There is a bit of entrepreneurial clutter. On the north side of Lake Misurina, still just minutes

This best of all views of Cortina is from the Passo Falzarego.

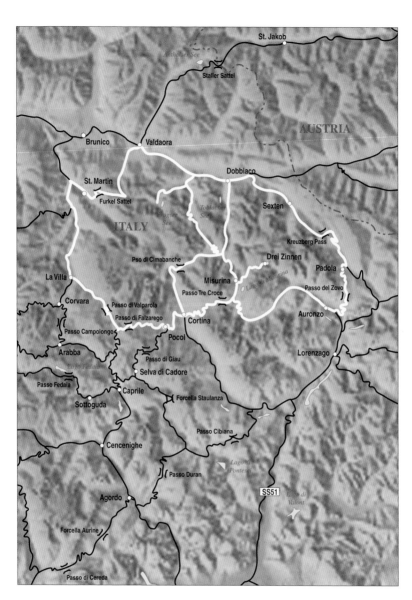

out of Cortina, there's a sunny view restaurant with tables on the lakeside, and a little road marked *Drei Zinnen* and/or *Tre Cime* takes off to the east. It's a dead-end, private toll road that climbs up several hundred meters in a seies of hairpins and sweepers that reveal dramatic views of Dolomite crags, the very best view of the Dolomites possible with wheels still on the ground. The cameras will be out. Traffic is encouraged to park below the rifugio at the top, but bikes should ride right on up. There's room to park.

A one-way loop road on the north side of Lago di Misurina has the restaurant with the best views. The best seats are out over the lake, under the umbrellas.

Seven kilometers north of Misurina, it's possible to turn west over Passo Cimabanche back to Cortina. North, it's all downhill to Dobbiaco (Toblach) and the main roads into Austria, unless you'd like to check out another jewel lake set amidst towering Dolomite peaks, Pragser Wildsee (Lago di Braies in Italian). It's up a dead end road that can be found about seven kilometers west of Dobbiaco. Turn south, under the railroad tracks, and climb the west fork. At the end of the road, there's an old time hotel by the lake. (The east fork climbs higher to a rifugio. No lake.)

The roads east of Misurina are not Dolomite dramatic. At Auronzo it's possible to go back behind the big domed church and get out of the valley traffic on the Passo del Zovo. It heads north and connects with the Kreuzberg Pass in the direction of Austria.

The Kreuzberg Pass (Passo di Monte Croce in Italian) has nice hotels and good views of the Dolomites. Hotel Kreuzberg Pass has many facilities including an indoor pool. The turn off for the Kreuzberg from Austria is at Sexten (Sesto in Italian).

An audacious piece of road that seems without purpose except that it exists can be found east of Auronzo and San Stefano heading south from

Campolongo. It's a rough gravel trail up a canyon. Alas, about eight kilometers up, it turns to marvelously engineered asphalt so tightly lapping its hairpins that it looks like a piece of ribbon candy. Turn after tight turn scales the mountain, to end in more rock trail.

North of Corvara, a little-known pass called Furkel Sattel cuts across some pleasant mountains. Its chief interest is that it cuts out a bunch of congested valley traffic and makes a direct connection with Staller Sattel, one of the best ways into or out of Austria. From the road north of Corvara, five kilometers downstream from the turnoff to the Wurz Joch at St. Martin, is the village Longega, squeezed in the gorge. That's where the Furkel Sattel road heads up a finger valley. Then at St. Viglio, the pass road goes north. The road straight ahead through St. Viglio dead-ends, but the Furkel Sattel passes some minor ski resorts and some lovely vistas over Tiroler countryside, then comes out on the north at the village Valdaora (Olang in German) on the main road into Austria, and at the south end of the Staller Sattel (for another way to use the Furkel and Staller Sattels, see Trips 56, 57, and 66).

Bikes usually fill the parking lot at the rifugio atop Drei Zinnen. The view is down the valley toward Auronzo and Lago di Santa Caterina.

Trip 57 Austrian Connections

Distance   *About 70 kilometers from Cortina to Austria at Staller Sattel; about 150 kilometers to Austria at Plocken Pass; about 175 to Austria at Nassfeld Pass*

Terrain   *Exciting climbs by forests and lakes*

Highlights   *Green lake, one-lane road on ★Staller Sattel (2,052 meters); populated valley roads wind to Plocken and Nassfeld Pass (1,557 meters). Interesting switchbacks on Plocken Pass (1,362 meters), Sella Ciampigotto (1,790 meters), Forcella di Lavardet (1,542 meters), Sella di Razza (1,760 meters), Passo Zovello (963 meters), Passo della Mauria (1,298 meters), Passo del Pura (1,425 meters), Passo Carson di Lanza (1,552 meters), Forcella di Luis (1,010 meters), Sella de Cereschiatis (1,066 meters), Cima di Sappada (1,286 meters)*

North of Cortina and about ten kilometers east of Brunico (Bruneck) at Valdaora (Olang), the Staller Sattel takes off toward Austria. The intersection is

There are a lot of hairpins on the climb up the Italian side of the Plocken Pass, heading for Austria.

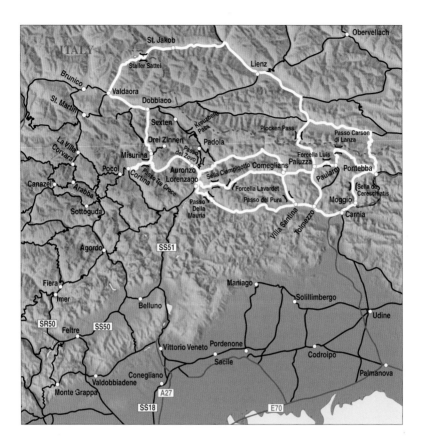

right beside a lumber yard. The pass road winds through lovely Tiroler fields, past a glacier blue-green lake, and climbs to the pass in a fun-and-games, one-way road through the forest. The one-way part is controlled, so there's 15 minutes for up traffic and 15 for down, with 15 minutes to clear each way. So there's only 15 minutes an hour to start up or down.

About 75 kilometers east of Misurina, through moderately interesting countryside and the town of Cima di Sappada, the Plocken Pass makes a dramatic climb into Austria. The Plocken Pass (Passo di Monte Croce Carnico) isn't high, but the switchbacks are dramatic. It's a good gateway to the south end of the Grossglockner via the Gailberg Sattel (see Trip 66). Another 30 kilometers farther east, the Nassfeld Pass road climbs quickly into Austria from the autostrada at Pontebba (see Trip 66).

There's an interesting, occasionally rough little road parallel to the east-west road through Sappada, and just south of it, known as Forcella di Lavardet. There are two ways to it, starting in the main valley just downstream from Auronzo. (Auronzo has to be one of the longest villages in the Alps. It goes on and on.) The main route goes by the village Larenzago, made famous by the visits of Pope John Paul II. The turnoff is marked "Casera Razzo." (Casera is an Italian army installation). The road climbs ruggedly over a pass called Sella Ciampigotto, wends past the usually unoccupied military base at Sella Razzo, then goes over the Forcella di Lavardet. (At this point it meets the other connection.) It's good pavement with lots of markers on down east through forests to Comeglians. From there, a road east crosses a low pass (Passo Zovello, 963 meters) to Sutrio, where the Plocken Pass road heads north into Austria.

The other connection from the area of Auronzo is through St. Stefano. At Campolongo this connection heads south, up a rocky valley. Parts are not paved. Then, wonder of wonders, it climbs the mountain side in a stacked series of perfectly matched and paved hairpins, looking something like that hard ribbon Christmas candy. Then it joins the Lavardet road.

The more traveled commercial route climbs east from Larenzago topping Passo di Mauria in about 12 kilometers. On east toward Tolmezzo about 27 kilometers, it's possible to turn north and climb over a little road called Passo del Pura. It comes down and crosses a dam to an intersection with an all new road. Turn north on all new alignment and paving, climbing up to join the east-west Forcella di Lavardet road. Or back at the dam, south from the intersection leads

Hairpins are stacked like Christmas ribbon candy on the climb north from St. Stefano.

Atop narrow Passo Carson de Lanza is a modest rifugio. Just behind it is the Austrian border.

through a series of tunnels down to the main east-west road toward Tolmezzo.

All of these pass roads get to the road leading north over the Plocken Pass into Austria. Wait. Heading for the Plocken or coming from it heading south, there's some more exploring to do in Italy. Turn into Paluzza on the east side of the main road, and and climb on east over the Forcella di Luis to Paularo, then north on the little forest road along the Austrian border over Passo Carson di Lanza. There's a rifugio atop Carson di Lanza. Down east, the pass road follows the westerly bank of a stream. Would you believe, the Nassfeld Pass road into Austria is on the east bank? Finally, the two roads merge at a bridge just short of a town, Pontebba.

If Carson di Lanza should be closed, head south from Paularo and loop east of Tolmezzo to Moggio, where a remote little road climbs north over Sella di Cereschiatis, to daylight at Pontebba right where the Carson de Lanza and Nassfeld roads meet.

(Note: Pontebba is on the autostrada route into Villach in Austria).

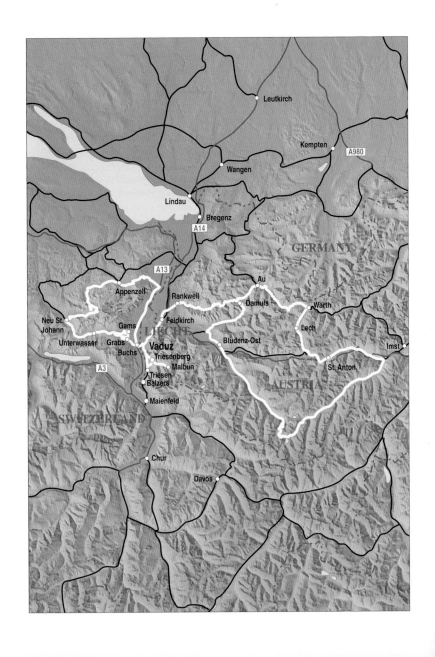

Liechtenstein

Liechtenstein is that little, rich country where the prince lives in the castle on the hill and every once in a while they have a skier in the Olympics. About 30 kilometers long and 15 wide, it's sort of in the Alps, using Swiss money, German language, but its own stamps. Switzerland is to the south and west; Austria is to the north and east. The Rhein, flowing north now, marks much of the boundary with Switzerland. This is downstream from the Vorderrhein and the Hinterrhein and the Via Mala and Chur (see Trips 36, 37, 38). Just across the Rhein is the Swiss Autobahn. You can get anywhere from Liechtenstein.

Vaduz, the capital, and several other villages in Liechtenstein are pleased to accommodate motorcyclists as well as sell stamps.

From the castle-topped village in the south called Balzers, an interesting road runs through the woods, over a little pass, and through a stone military gate into Switzerland and the cute Swiss village called Maienfeld, leading to Landquart and Wolfgang Pass (see Trip 38).

In the middle of the country, starting at Vaduz or the village of Triesen, a Liechtenstein mountain road climbs to the villages of Triesenberg and Malbun. Triesenberg hangs high on the mountainside and has gorgeous views of the valley of the Rhein and Schwagalp. Malbun, on through a tunnel from Triesenberg, is in a high ski bowl at about 1,600 meters.

The secret way up to Triesenberg and Malbun is the narrow, cliff-hanging, one-way (up only) road that starts at the prince's castle.

At Triesenberg a good hotel is the Martha Buhler (named after the skier). Farther up is Rizlina Berg Gasthaus, hung on the edge of the mountain. One of many hotels in Malbun is the Montana. Hotel Landgasthof Schatzman is on the main road in Triesen.

About that (FL)? Furst is a German word for prince. So the Principality of Liechtenstein becomes Furstentum Liechtenstein.

Across the Rhein, right on the main drag in Buchs, Switzerland, is a Honda dealer, Stricker Motos, that has been very helpful to foreign bikers.

Trip 58   Liechtenstein

Distance   *About 60 kilometers explores the whole country*
Terrain   *A few narrow, one-way roads, some sweeping climbs, a slippery tunnel*
Highlights   *Good views of the Rhein Valley, castles, hotels, restaurants*

THE main road in Liechtenstein, almost all of it but two lanes wide, runs south in the Rhein Valley from Feldkirch in Austria to Switzerland. There is a border crossing check at Austria as it's in the European Union and Liechtenstein, along with Switzerland, is not. No guards or stops between Liechtenstein and Switzerland. The gas stations just inside Liechtenstein sell Swiss Autobahn vignettes, and Swiss police have been noted checking for them on the on-ramps just across the Rhein. It's best to mind the posted limits as well as the automatic limit of 50 kilometers per hour in villages. Fines are high and payable on the spot. (One story quotes a Liechtenstein policeman, "Your passport please." Pocketing the passport, he said, "That'll be 100 Francs. If you don't have it, go get it.") There is one brief spot where the posted speed limit is up to 80 kilometers per hour (about 48 mph).

In the north, Liechtenstein is mostly flat valley farm land. About 14 kilometers south of the Austrian border, just south of the village, Schaan, there's a sign for the Prince's castle, Schloss, indicating a turn up and east. You can ride right by the front gate of the castle. Continuing on, the road becomes narrow, one-way, climbing up through forests to the village, Triesenberg, where it joins the main road from the valley. Hanging on the mountain with vistas westerly over the Rhein to Alps in Switzerland, the road climbs up to an abrupt ninety degree turn into a narrow tunnel through the mountain. The tunnel daylights on the east in a high Alpine valley. Then the road sweeps on up to about 1,600 meters at the village called Malbun, where the road ends amid a cluster of hotels and shops and ski lifts.

Coming down, watch the slick pavement in the tunnel and the sharp ninety degree right turn at it's west end. Straight ahead is an Armco barrier, and beyond the barrier is a long straight drop down.

Sweep back down through Triesenberg to the main valley road at Triesen. Vaduz (say fah DUTZ), the small capital village, is back north a few kilometers. Balzers with its castled peak, and Switzerland are south.

There is a stone arch gate at the Swiss border amid concrete hulks that were placed there to deter tanks, standing in a field.

Just westerly from all this a few kilometers is the Rhein River, the border with Switzerland, and immediately across the river is the Swiss Autobahn, with on-ramps located near each of the several river bridges.

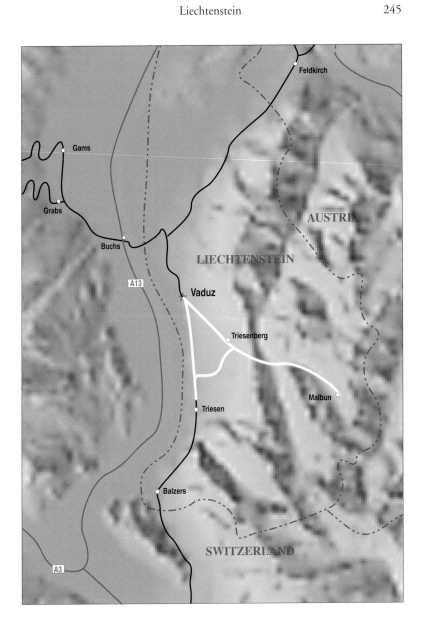

Trip 59 Santis and Schwagalp

Distance *About 100 kilometers round trip from Liechtenstein*
Terrain *Gently climbing and sweeping mountain roads*
Highlights *Less-traveled Switzerland, Schwagalp Pass (1,278 meters),
Wildhaus (1,090 meters)*

A loop climbs through the lower Swiss Alps just across the Rhein from
Liechtenstein into the remote little canton of Appenzell. Appenzell has been
most famous recently for its method of voting in public meetings, from which
voting, women have historically been excluded. Still, it's sort of romantically
quaint, with buildings and people that look the way Swiss buildings and people
should.

Across the Rhein from Liechtenstein, past the sizable Swiss town of Buchs, at
the village of Gams, a road climbs west across the south side of Santis Mountain. This road with little traffic crosses a minor pass of about 1,000 meters at
Wildhaus, and comes in about 25 kilometers to the village Neu St. Johann.

For more fun, go south of Gams to Grabs and take the little one lane road to
Grabser Berg and on to Wildhaus. Then at Wildhaus, take the little road south
to Schwendi, where there's the Alpenrose Hotel. The road wanders across the
mountain, finally rejoining the main road at Unterwasser, right at the fine
Hotel Santis.

From Neu St. Johann, a mountain road heads east toward Appenzell over
Schwagalp Pass. This is no Furka nor Susten Pass, but a forest and meadow
road, with some imposing granite peaks around. At the top of the pass, a turnoff
leads to the base station of a cable car that goes up the mountain, Santis. For
some reason, the parking lot and restaurant at the cable car is a *Töfftreffpunkt*
(motorcycle meeting place). The road goes on down to Urnasch, then to the
town of Appenzell, where a small road heads back over a mountain toward the
Rhein Valley at Oberriet.

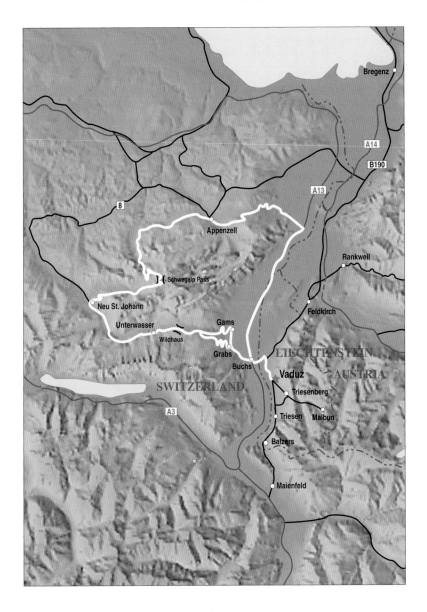

Trip 60 Western Austria

Distance *About 260 kilometers*

Terrain *Some sweeping, some twisting climbs and descents; narrow road on Furka Joch*

Highlights *Lovely farms, forests, glacier views at ★Silvretta (2,036 meters), hotels, restaurants, ski resorts. Includes: Arlberg Pass (1,793 meters), Flexen Pass (1,773 meters), Hochtannberg Pass (1,679 meters), Faschina Joch (1,487 meters), Furka Joch (1,761 meters) (Vignettes, stickers, are required to drive on Austrian Autobahns. They can be purchased at most gas stations and borders).*

Austria knows how to take care of tourists. Practically every corner has an attractive Gasthaus or hotel, with "Zimmer freis" in between. Zimmer frei means "room available," and is the Germanic equivalent of "bed and breakfast." Invariably, they're good and reasonably priced.

The most western state of Austria, called Vorarlberg, and its capital, Feldkirch, are right at Liechtenstein, but separated by high Alps from the rest of the country. So it takes some pretty good pass roads to tie Austria together. Since most Alpine pass roads run north-south, these Austrian roads going mostly east-west can be entertaining as well as useful.

Once past the toll taker on the west side of the Silveretta Strasse, the climb becomes a wondrous and varied challenge.

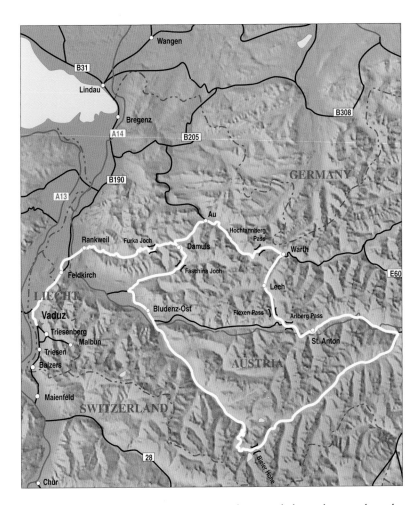

The main one is the Arlberg Pass, now with an autobahn and a tunnel to take the trucks and buses off the good mountain road. It starts at Feldkirch, which is really on the north border of Liechtenstein. Might as well take the autobahn from Feldkirch as far as Bludenz-Ost. (Don't confuse Bludenz on the Arlberg road with Bregenz, north of Feldkirch on the Boden See, the site of popular summer music festivals.)

At Bludenz-Ost, one of the best roads in Austria heads south. Called the Silvretta Strasse, it roughly parallels the Arlberg, but takes a rollicking time getting there, so it has only enthusiasts on it. And, welcome to Austria, there's a toll. Austria has a lot of toll roads.

After a short run up a valley past sturdy Austrian farm houses and neatly manicured pastures, and 50 kilometer speed limits seriously enforced, the road has an exciting steep climb with switchbacks and hairpins and views of the

Austrian restaurants and hotels often fly this flag, Motorradfahrer Willkommen, "Motorcyclists Welcome." This one is at a hotel restaurant atop Silveretta Strasse, also known as Bieler Hohe.

same, up to a lake. This is a *Stau See,* a good German word meaning a lake created by a dam. Then there's more climb to a higher lake and the pass, Bieler Hohe, where there's a delightful restaurant terrace with views over the lake reflecting snowy peaks.

A refreshing non-alcoholic drink available nowhere but Austria and Bayern (Bavaria) is Spezi (spait zee). It's an orange flavored cola. A big one, a *grosse Spezi,* usually comes in a half-liter beer glass.

From the top, the pass road works down eastward through a valley, pleasant enough in the summer, but the site of deadly avalanches in recent winters. About six kilometers down, there's a side road that climbs up north to another Stau See with a restaurant. On down east, the valley road connects again with the Arlberg road. Just before the junction, there's a good view of a castle and an often photographed high bridge called Trisannabrucke that carries the railroad up the Arlberg.

Heading west, back up the Arlberg from the junction, the old road is a good climb that also avoids the toll tunnel under the pass. Watch for the beautiful Austrian farm houses showing considerable pride of ownership. With elaborate corner bay windows, deep arched doors, balconies, and wide, overhanging roofs, they are often decorated with pictures and maybe poems or historical names in Gothic script. Contemporary ones are of block construction with light beige stucco and dark brown trim. The gable end almost always faces the road. On a pole over the front gable end is a lantern-like bell tower. Some of the lanterns are pretty ornate.

The old road up the pass is okay because the traffic is taking the autobahn tunnel. Along it are a bunch of saintly towns: St. Jakob, St. Anton, St. Christoph, all of them labeled *am Arlberg* to distinguish them from saintly towns of the same name scattered all over Austria.

Just west of its summit, the Arlberg intersects the Flexen Pass. The Flexen heads north in a series of fairly tight sweeps covered by wooden snow sheds hung on the mountain. Just over its top are the famous ski resorts of Zurs and Lech, in the valley of the Lech River (Lech Tal) and the Austrian state of Tirol. Both towns have noteworthy buildings decorated with pictures of saints and local heroes, or maybe the building's first owner. The Hotel Post in Lech is particularly nice. (Every town in the Alps has a Hotel Post.) Lech has attractive outdoor restaurant facilities. If tablecloths and umbrellas are out, the place is in operation.

Seven kilometers below Lech, at Warth, there's an intersection where the Hochtannberg Pass heads northwest. East is the Lech Tal and roads described in Trip 62. Just west of the intersection on the Hochtannberg road is Hotel Warther Hof: large, handsome, and well known to Edelweiss Tour folk. Its brochures show bikes and bikers.

It's about 23 kilometers westerly over the Hochtannberg to the village of Au, where the Furka Joch road heads back to Rankweil and Feldkirch. (This is Furka *Joch*. Furka *Pass* is at Andermatt, Switzerland, and Furkel Sattel is in the Dolomites.) Above Au, at a village called Damuls, a new road heads back to Feldkirch over the pass Faschina Joch, 1,487 meters. It's completely roofed with grass growing on top. From above, it looks like a long line of windows.

The Furka Joch, a remote, nobody-takes-it-on-purpose road, goes through Damuls.

Damuls has a couple of nice hotels. One, Hotel Adler, in a crook of the Furka Joch road, has a good baker as well as a cook. The hotel dates from before Columbus, but has every modern convenience.

Above Damuls, the Furka has some one lane parts. Just east of the summit is a restaurant with a sweeping mountain view, Jagerstuble, advertising good "burger" food (not ham-burger food) as well as deer specialties.

Heading the other way, looking for the Furka Joch and Damuls roads from Feldkirch, follow signs first to Rankweil. Here's the best, and almost secret way.

In downtown Feldkirch, just east of the tunnel that takes the main road around the old town is a plaza, platz, with motorcycle parking yet. On the edge of the platz, right where the cobblestoned street is marked for pedestrians only, there's a sign for GOFIS. It points up a steep cobbled road. Take it. In a minute you're high above Feldkirch, in fields crossing over everything, including the autobahn, all down in tunnels below. Gofis is a village on the mountain. From it, more signs point to Rankweil, gateway to the Furka Joch.

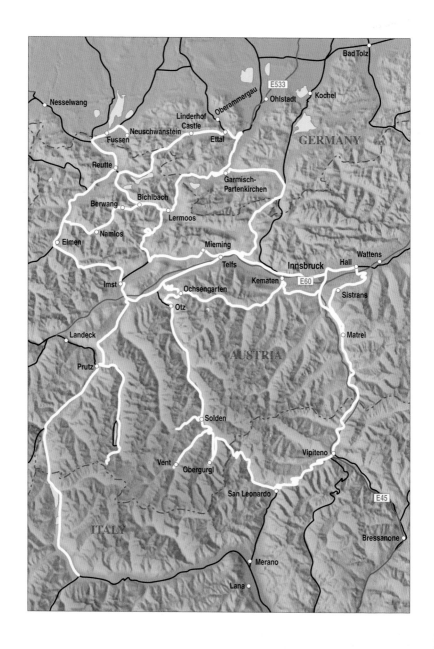

Austrian Tirol

Tirol is the mountainous narrow waist of Austria with Bavaria to the north and Italian Sud Tirol to the south. Tirol has beautiful mountains and exotic valleys and delightful villages and lots of good roads to play on. Innsbruck is the historic capital of the state of Tirol. It's a good-sized city strategically located where the relatively low Brenner Pass from Italy comes down into the Inn Tal (valley). The east-west autobahn in the Inn Tal goes by Innsbruck hung on the edge of the mountains. It's free (with a vignette) and it's the recommended route around Innsbruck. The Brenner Autobahn from Italy makes a T with the one in the Inn Tal at Innsbruck.

Check out the baroque details in the Rottenbuch church, just a few kilometers north of Oberammergau. Here, some "putti" (cupids) help frame the distant altar.

The Inn River flows easterly from St. Moritz in Switzerland (see Trips 36–40) and heads easterly through Innsbruck where there is indeed a brucke, a bridge, and finally north to Germany were it flows into what we call the Danube (in German it's the Donau). The autobahn follows the Inn around to Germany so while Munchen lies straight north of Innsbruck, the autobahn connection loops around to the east. It's the fastest way to get to Munchen.

To add to the general geographic confusion, the only autobahn route from the Tirol in Austria to Salzburg and Wien (Vienna), both also in Austria, follows the Inn through Germany.

The Tirol is packed with hotels, some beautifully elaborate, comfortable in every respect including value.

Hotel Boeglerhof is up a lovely finger valley of the Inn Tal east of Innsbruck in a village called Alpbach. Hotel Muttererhof is on the mountain above Innsbruck at Mutters. In the Sellrain Tal (Trip 64), coming down from Kuhtai, is Hotel Antonie. With a lovely view of the Inn Tal, the Ferienschlossl is at Haimingerberg on the Haiming Joch road west of Innsbruck (Trip 63).

Imst is a town about 70 kilometers west (upstream) of Innsbruck in the Inn Tal where several good pass roads come together. Just up the Hahntenn Joch road out of Imst is Hotel Linserhof and near it, Hotel Belmont, both set back from the road, but well signed.

If you've time for one church, try this one at Rottenbuch, just meters off the main road from Oberammergau. It's a baroque riot featuring the birth of Mary. You can park at the door, and they have rest rooms.

At European gas stations, air comes from a canister which hangs from a filer valve. It can be removed to a convenient spot near the tire being checked. Atop the canister, a dial reads both metric and pounds per square inch, and there are buttons marked plus and minus.

Across the Hahntenn Joch is a charming and very reasonable Gasthof-Pension that is a motorcycle favorite, Zur Gemuetlichkeit, in the village of Bschlabs.

Closer to Germany is a village called Berwang on the Namlos road, with several hotels including the large Kaiserhof.

Or check the hotels listed in Trip 62 at Damuls and Warth, or the ones listed in Trip 63 along the Timmels Joch road.

Up the Lech Tal in Steeg is another Hotel Post.

Trip 61 Innsbruck Passes

Distance *Via Brenner Pass, about 30 kilometers to Italy; via Timmels Joch, about 100 kilometers to Italy; via Reschen Pass, about 100 kilometers to Italy; about 100 kilometers via Piller Hohe up Kauner Tal*

Terrain *Brenner: low pass, major autobahn; Timmels Joch: long, sweeping valley to high exotic pass; Reschen: long valley run, low pass; Kauner Tal: steep mountain climb*

Highlights *Brenner Pass (1,374 meters) quick route to Italy (toll), fantastic bridges; Timmels Joch (2,509 meters) nice valley villages, sweeping climb to high mountains (toll); Piller Hohe (1,558 meters), Kauner Tal (2,750 meters), Reschen Pass (1,504 meters) (no toll) leads to Passo dello Stelvio*

A view spot atop Piller Hohe gives a glimpse of mountain villages way down below and the road in the Inn Tal. Switzerland is upstream to the left and the Reschen Pass to Italy, more to the left.

It's a short, quick run, less than 50 kilometers, over the Brenner Pass from Innsbruck to the area of the Italian passes around Merano (see Trips 41–45) and the Dolomites (Trips 50–57). That's the Brenner's chief merit. But it's so low and so congested that it hardly deserves other comment.

There is a *Bundesstrasse*, a non-freeway, non-toll, federal road, across the Brenner alongside the autobahn. It has usually been the choice for motorcyclists. From it, the gigantic structures of the autobahn, including the famous Europabrucke Bridge, look awesome. But the road goes through a picturesque town called Matrei am Brenner with one narrow street that has tried to outlaw motorcycles. Various courts are hearing appeals of the arbitrary decision. The only way around Matrei is the toll autobahn. So far, motorcycles are legal.

It's one way at a time on the Staller Sattel. All await the hour (the 1/4 of the clock face above the car that's green). Some of the bikes are planning to jump ahead of the car.

Investing a little time, many motorcyclists avoid the autobahn by using mountain roads south of Innsbruck: not spectacular, but not a freeway either. From Hall in Tirol, about 15 kilometers east of Innsbruck, the route crosses the mountain to Matrei on the Brenner. Exit at Hall, cross under the autobahn, and climb up through Sistrans and on south to Matrei.

Approaching the Innsbruck area from the west, like from Kuhtai or Garmisch, follow the signs to Axams, then to Mutters (site of Hotel Mutterershof) and on to the Brenner Autobahn. The same route can be used approaching Innsbruck eastbound on the autobahn. Just take the Zirl exit (ausfahrt). Heading west off the Brenner, exit Innsbruck Sud and follow the signs for Mutters or Natters.

About 13 kilometers up Stubai Tal, a dead-end finger valley, west off the autobahn at the famous Europabrucke, is the motorcycle friendly Hotel Capella.

If there's time, it's more fun to take the Timmels Joch rather than the Brenner Pass, or even the Reschen Pass. The Timmels Joch (its other end is described in Trip 41) parallels the Brenner starting about 45 kilometers west of Innsbruck, near Kuhtai and Haiming (Trip 62). It climbs south up the Otz Tal, through the town, Otz, where there's the large comfortable old time Hotel Post (of course). Farther up the Otz Tal, just upstream, south of Solden, there's a dead-end valley road to the west, Rettenbach Tal, the top of which claims to be one of the highest paved roads in the Alps. It's called Otz Taler Gletscherstrasse, and there is a toll. Then, a couple of kilometers further up the Otz Tal, at Zwieselstein, a finger valley called Vent Tal climbs up west. At the end is another Hotel Post. It's at almost 1,900 meters and sports a small indoor pool looking out at glaciers.

The Reschen Pass (see Trip 44) starts up out of the Inn Tal just east of Landeck about 75 kilometers west of Innsbruck. The first several kilometers are in a new tunnel. Another good way to get to the Reschen is to head south, up and out of the Inn Tal from Imst following signs for Pitzer Tal. Up Pitzer Tal at Wenns, turn up over Piller Hohe and come out on the Reschen Pass at Fliess or Prutz. Little Piller Hohe allows the rider to sail along the high mountain, occasionally looking down on the traffic in the Inn Tal. Piller Hohe is a narrow road. From Prutz, a road up the dead end Kauner Tal is one of the highest roads in Austria. It ends at a Stau See where there's a restaurant. There's a toll on the Kauner Tal.

Got all those Tals straight? The dead end road off the Brenner is the Stubai Tal. The main valley is the Inn Tal. Just west of Innsbruck the Kuhtai road follows Sellrain Tal (Trip 64). Further west the Oetz Tal climbs up to the Timmels Joch (Trip 63). Next comes the Pitzer Tal. It connects to the Piller Hohe (Trip 63). Kauner Tal is one of the highest roads in Austria from Prutz. East of Innsbruck is the Ziller Tal (Trip 65). Just east of that is the Alpbach Tal.

Snow in September, like this on the north side of the Timmels Joch, is always a possibility. Usually it doesn't stick on the roads.

Trip 62   Obscure Tiroler Roads

Distance   *About 250 kilometers*

Terrain   *Some sweeping, some tight, narrow mountain roads*

Highlights   *Famous castles, churches, little-used mountain roads, nice restaurants and hotels. Includes: Ammer Sattel (1,118 meters), Berwang (1,336 meters), ★Hahntenn Joch (1,894 meters), ★Haiming Joch (1,685 meters), ★Kuhtai (2,017 meters), Seefeld in Tirol, Telfs, Holzleitner Sattel (1,126 meters), Fern Pass (1,209 meters)*

The village church in Gries in Sellrain Tal just above Innsbruck has an onion dome, more typical of Bavarian churches.

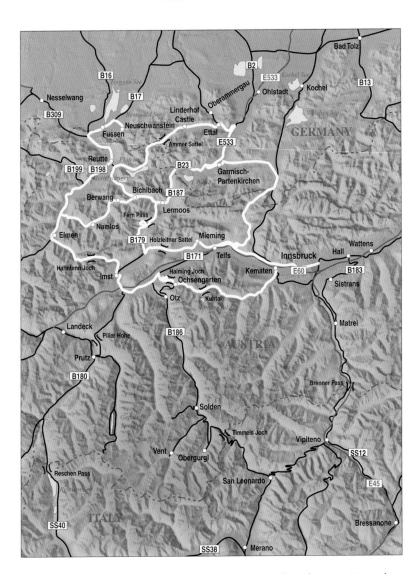

In Ober Bayern (southern Bavaria), the mountains and roads are exciting when compared to the Great Plains, but the real riding is readily available in the high Alps of the Austrian Tirol just across the border. This trip is easily accessible from Munchen as well as Oberammergau and Garmisch, and anywhere in the Tirol.

Starting from the town of Ettal, just outside Oberammergau and just north of Garmisch, escape the traffic and tourists by turning south over the Ammer Sattel. Ettal has a huge domed baroque monastery church right near the intersection. Apparently the monks make good brandy, and the handsome

Mad King Ludwig's fantasy castle, Neuschwanstein, crowns a mountain knob across from his childhood home, the yellow castle called Hohenschwangau. The castles are just outside of Fussen in Germany and Reutte in the Austrian Tirol.

interior of the church has consumed some of the profits. The interior is spectacular in gilt and white with plenty of baroque cupids (artists call them "putti") hanging around the pillars and over pictures, and with a celestial dome, all in the style of the mid-1700s. Some exterior traces of the original Gothic building (like the front doorway) are still visible. Worth a visit, and it's free. Park close, at the east end of the lot, in front of the shops.

The turn for the Ammer Sattel is marked with signs for the Konigschloss Linderhof, one of Mad King Ludwig's castles which is ten kilometers up the road. The German noun *Schloss* is almost always translated to the English word "castle." This can be misleading, because Schloss can also mean "palace." (No walls or battlements on a palace; a castle may have a moat and other fortifications.) This Konigschloss, royal castle, is Ludwig's small baroque jewel of a palace, with a jet fountain and an underground lake for Wagnerian opera, built in the late 19th century. It can't be seen from the road. Tours take a couple of hours.

Ludwig was king of Bayern in the days that Bismarck was uniting Germany under a German, rather than an Austrian Kaiser. Ludwig's sympathies were with the Austrians, which as it turned out, was unfortunate. Meantime, he built two other castles besides Linderhof to play in: Neuschwanstein is the turreted wonder on every travel poster, near Fussen and Reutte; and Herrenchiem See, on an island in a lake named Chiem See, between Munchen and Salzburg. Of course, he had inherited other castles and palaces. Neuschwanstein was the inspiration for Disney's Magic Kingdom castle. Herrenchiem See on the island is supposed to look like the French Chateau of Versailles. It's necessary to take a ferry to Herrenchiem See.

Past Linderhof, the Ammer Sattel road goes through a forest and climbs to the low Sattel which happens to be the Austrian border. Into Austria a few kilometers, the road winds around an Alpine lake called Plan See, with a nice hotel at the end of the lake closest to the border and several serviceable restaurants. Then it makes a quick descent into Reutte (say Roy tuh), a bustling Tiroler town.

Reutte has a two-lane autobahn around it which can seem confusing. Follow signs south toward Lermoos and Fern Pass, away from Germany (D), and exit in a couple of kilometers at Bichlbach and head for Berwang and Namlos. This is delightful rural Tirol. Some of the road is barely one lane, dancing around high Alpine meadows. Berwang has nice-looking hotels.

The road comes down in the Lech Tal (the valley mentioned in Trip 60). Five kilometers west up the Lech Tal at Elmen is the obscure turnoff for a great, usually ignored pass, the Hahntenn Joch. The narrow road crosses a little field and then starts climbing the rock face in a long steep traverse before turning into a high valley for some more twisting fun. There are no facilities at the top, which has a huge slope of sliding alluvial granite, but short of the top is a cute Gasthaus named Zur Gemutlichkeit in the town of Bschlabs. (How many other towns start with five consonants?) It faces an equally cute onion-domed church. Prices at Zur Gemutlichkeit are very reasonable.

The narrow road comes down through the woods, past the Hotel Linserhof, into Imst, another prosperous Tiroler town with a typical Austrian church. Bavarian churches usually have onion domes on the tower. Austrian churches, like that at Imst, have a square tower with a clock face on each side, then an open belfry topped with four gables finished off with a tall pointed steeple.

Imst, like Reutte, has a two-lane bypass autobahn around it, connecting with the major east-west autobahn in the Inn Tal between the Arlberg and Innsbruck.

Head toward Innsbruck about ten kilometers to a small village named Haiming. Haiming is a marked autobahn ausfahrt (exit). Opposite the village, heading south up the mountainside, is the Haiming Joch road. It's hardly more than a driveway. The signing is to Ochsengarten. This narrow, one-lane road climbs past fields with little haystacks and occasional Zimmer Frei signs, a Gasthaus, and a delightful hotel with a view of the whole valley named Hotel Ferienschlossl. Past the hotel, the road climbs into a high forest, and then comes down just a bit to the Kuhtai road at the intersection called Ochsengarten.

Kuhtai is a high pass, but for some reason it's never called a pass, just Kuhtai. It goes east-west, roughly parallel to the Arlberg-Innsbruck Autobahn down in the Inn Tal, but higher in the Alps. Even though it's close to such traveled ways and to Innsbruck, it never has traffic. At Ochsengarten, it seems hardly more prominent than the tiny Haiming Joch road.

West from Ochsengarten, the Kuhtai road makes a steep descent to Otz, on the Timmels Joch road. Kuhtai, the pass, is the other way, east and up over the tree line past a massive earth dam and its lake. There are a couple of ski hotels at the top. And a "Bike Stop," called Kuhtaier Dorfstadl on the north side of the road. You have to go in. The interior is a delight, and so is the staff. Nothing wrong with the outdoor view terrace, either.

Atop Kuhtai, this interestingly decorated restaurant advertises itself as a "Bikers Stop."

Then a fairly modern road sweeps down east in a long valley called the Sellrain Tal. Some straights end in rather abrupt tight corners through villages, including Gries, with attractive Hotel Antonie. Then the road enters a tight gorge shared with a raging mountain torrent, exiting without further ado in the Inn Tal, at a village named Kematen. From there you can stay above the crowd following signs to Axams and the Brenner Pass, all just a couple of kilometers above Innsbruck.

Here, the secret is to go straight ahead through Kematen and under the autobahn, and sweep up the mountain on the north side of the Inn Tal. This is the main Bundesstrasse (federal road) toward Garmisch in Germany. But up the mountainside a few kilometers, still in Austria, is the exit for Seefeld. Seefeld is famous for cross-country skiing. Guess that means it's flat on top. West of Seefeld, a delightful little road hung on the mountainside heads for the Tiroler town of Telfs. Straight on through Telfs toward Holzleitner Sattel, the road passes through Mieming, known to many motorcycle tour-takers as the home of Edelweiss Bike Travel.

The west side of the Holzleitner has wonderful, wide sweepers down to the picturesque village of Nassereith. But first, on the way down, pause to view the lush green Tiroler valley below. Often there's a vendor selling *heiss Wurst und Brot,* the Tiroler equivalent of a hot dog, only better. A good munch helps you contemplate the view. (Sometimes "heiss wurstl" gets translated, "hot sausage." In this instance, it's hot, cooked, not HOT HOT.

North from Nassereith is the Fern Pass, a nice road, with too much traffic and too many anxious drivers, that fortunately isn't too long. There's a Gasthaus at each side of the top, both with elaborate painted scenes on the exterior walls. The southern one has historical pictures, including the arrival of American tanks near the end of World War II, with the building in flames.

Even though it's pretty low by Alpine standards, the Fern Pass is the closest mountain pass for many Germans, and always has a lot of tour bus traffic. To accommodate all the traffic, the north side has new tunnel work that leads quickly toward Lermoos and back to Germany at Garmisch, or on to Reutte.

Just across the German border from Reutte is Fussen, and Ludwig's castle Neuschwanstein, alongside the older castle, Hohenschwangau.

If there's time for one Bayrisch baroque church, choose the one at Rottenbuch, just a few kilometers north of Oberammergau. It's just off the main road through a low arch gate. Typically, baroque churches are very plain on the outside with no stained glass. But the inside of Rottenbuch is astonishing. Elaborate carving and plaster detail have run riot. It's delightfully flamboyant. The frescoes cast a rosy glow, much cozier than the famous Wies Kirche only ten kilometers away. Tours never go to Rottenbuch, probably because buses can't get through the village gate.

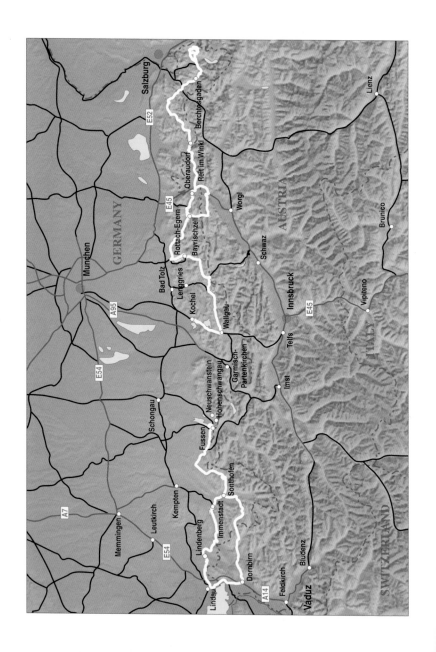

Deutsche Alpenstrasse

The southern border of Germany, and of Bayern, is where the Alps begin. The big stuff is all south of Germany. In fact, the Zugspitze, the highest point in Germany, is on the Austrian border.

In fits and starts, Germany has been constructing a road along the border, called the Deutsche Alpenstrasse. Little of it bears comparison with the high Alps. But a few parts are interesting and are popular with German motorcyclists. The best part by far is a little loop, the Rossfeldringstrasse on the mountain above Salzburg and Berchtesgaden.

As a well-promoted vacation area, the Bayern region is full of hotels and restaurants. One less-trafficked village is Lenggries, northeast of the town of Garmisch-Partenkirchen, and just a few kilometers from Austria. From Lenggries, a hardly used one-lane road goes west along the Alp foothills past sturdy Bayrisch farmhouses, the kind with the barn attached to the house. It's signed to Jachenau, and on to Wallgau (see below) and Garmisch.

South of Lenggries is the low Achen Pass leading directly to the Inn Tal in Austria and across to the Ziller Tal and Gerlos Pass.

A large, multi-storied, full-service hotel in Lenggries is the Brauneck. Nearby, a smaller Gasthof is the Lenggrieser Hof.

Closer to Munchen is the Waldgasthof Buchenhain. It's in the woods, as its name implies, all by itself. Very Bayerisch in style, it has a beer garden out front. And it has its own train station, so that it's only a few minutes from the city by train, and right on the highway heading for the Alps.

Trip 63 Deutsche Alpenstrasse West

Distance *About 110 kilometers from Lindau to Fussen*
Terrain *Gently sweeping asphalt, one tight climb*
Highlights *Bucolic countryside, some traffic, photogenic towns, Oberjoch Pass (1,180 meters), Riedberg Pass (1,430 meters), Gaichtberg Pass (1,093 meters)*

Lindau is a picturesque island town on Boden See, the very large lake called Lake Constance in English, which is really part of the Rhein River, downstream from all those good passes in Switzerland (see Trips 36, 37) and just west of Bayern. There's a causeway onto Lindau for trains and vehicles. The trains come in frontward, and exit backward, or vice versa. Other vehicles have to park and turn around to leave. The town is all foot traffic. There is marked motorcycle parking.

East from Lindau, the Deutsche Alpenstrasse makes a pleasant sweeping run along the Austrian border. Green meadows and farms. No big mountains.

At Immenstadt a dead-end valley cuts south into the Alps and toward Austria. A part of it, called Klein Walser Tal, actually is in Austria, but you can't get to the rest of Austria from it.

A parallel and more interesting route starts just south in Austria by Dornbirn. It climbs up a valley called Balderschwang into Germany, where it crosses over Riedberg Pass, then down toward Sonthofen and Klein Walser Tal at a village called Fischen. Riedberg is sort of gnarly. Be warned, crossing into Austria along Lake Constance, if you take the tunnel, you are automatically on an autobahn requiring a vignette, and the Austrian police are waiting.

Heading east, the road climbs up the only really good twisties, the Oberjoch Pass, only to run into the Austrian border at 1,180 meters elevation. Straight ahead, another small pass, Gaichtberg (1,093 meters), leads down to Lech Tal and Reutte in Austria (see Trip 62).

Meanwhile, the Deutsche Alpenstrasse detours north in Germany to Fussen, site of Ludwig's Neuschwanstein castle, where it sort of ends, to resume farther east beyond Garmisch-Partenkirchen.

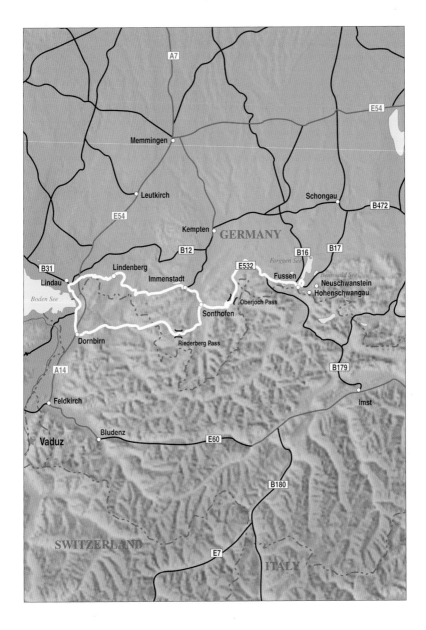

Trip 64 Deutsche Alpenstrasse East

Distance *About 200 kilometers*

Terrain *Some rough and narrow, some sweeping*

Highlights *Cute villages (like Wallgau), popular biking roads like Kesselberg (858 meters), Sudelfeld (1,097 meters), Ursprung Pass (849 meters), and ★Rossfeldringstrasse (1,536 meters)*

Spring snow remains on the mountains surrounding the Rossfeldringstrasse in Germany above Salzburg, the east end of the Deutsche Alpenstrasse.

About 12 kilometers east of Garmisch-Partenkirchen on the road toward Innsbruck, a fork goes north to some interesting riding and a delightful picture-perfect Bayrisch village, Wallgau. It's close to all the tourists in Garmisch, but hardly touched by them. Several buildings are elaborately painted, including the Post Hotel. The inside of the hotel is as interesting as the outside, and so is the food. In the morning, locals have *Weiss Wurst,* a sausage made of white meats. Try *Grill Teller,* on the menu at most Bayrisch and Austrian restaurants. *Grill Teller* means a plate of grilled meats, usually five or six kinds, garnished with interesting vegetables.

Before heading on east, a German rider would suggest going north from Wallgau a few kilometers around a lake, Walchen See, famous for windsurfing, to climb a little mountain called Kesselberg. The tight sweepers of Kesselberg attract motorcyclists from all of Bayern. So many, in fact, that the road has been closed to southbound motorcycles on weekends and holidays. There's a rest area turnout on the inside of a long sweeper that's a *Tofftreffpunkt.* The village of Kochel, at the north base of Kesselberg, has attractive country hotels.

A motorcycle favorite on the Deutsche Alpenstrasse is this part called the Tatzelwurm. It's just east of the favorite stretch over Sudelfeld.

Back to the Deutsche Alpenstrasse. From the north edge of Wallgau, a tiny, rough, one-lane toll road heads east along the border toward Achen Pass (941 meters). Before it gets to the pass, it becomes a sweeping modern highway.

Once again, straight ahead leads into Austria, a wonderful way to get to the Inn Tal below Innsbruck and the Ziller Tal without any traffic. (Into Austria, the Achen Pass road skirts an Alpine lake with many hotels, then makes a sweeping descent into the Inn Tal. A hairpin on the descent, called the Kanzel curve, has a restaurant with a magnificent view of the Inn Tal and the Ziller Tal).

From the Achen Pass, the Deutsche Alpenstrasse goes north again toward a lake, Tegern See, which has too much traffic. The old, one lane section east from Rottach-Egern has been closed to motor vehicles, so it's necessary to detour north around Schlier See. (Schlier See is known in history as the site of the "Night of the Long Knives," when, in the mid-thirties, Hitler turned on the brownshirts after they helped him rise to power, and had them killed.)

East from Schlier See toward Bayrischzell, the Alpenstrasse again becomes a modern road—for a while. And from Bayrischzell, another road heads south into Austria and the Inn Tal over another little pass, Ursprung (849 meters). Ursprung has two parallel legs descending to Kufstein in the Inn Tal. The southern one is the most fun.

But the best is yet to come: Sudelfeld.

East from Bayrischzell, the road climbs and sweeps in a fashion so delightful that it attracts motorcyclists by the hundreds. On weekends, every corner and the little restaurant at the top is full of motorcyclists watching friends sweep back and forth. So much sweeping, in fact, that the local authorities got the road closed to motorcycles. Court cases got it opened again, but with a speed limit.

Funny thing. The great sweeping road just *ends,* or almost does, at a little, narrow toll tunnel that leads down into the Inn Tal. It's possible to turn off east just before the tunnel and head down another narrow, winding road called Tatzelwurm, past a Gasthaus of the same name with a pleasant terrace. Tatzelwurm gets down to the Inn Tal town of Oberaudorf on the German side of the Austrian border. Another end of the Deutsche Alpenstrasse.

From Oberaudorf, the best bet is to head straight on east into Austria, over the Inn River (which is the border). About 25 kilometers into Austria, cross back into Germany at Reit im Winkl, a village with many cute buildings decorated in Bavarian style. Here the Deutsche Alpenstrasse takes off again in good sweeping style toward Berchtesgaden. (South of Reit im Winkl, a wide, smooth Austrian road winds easily through mountains to Lofer and the roads of Trip 67.) Berchtesgaden is touristy.

On the mountain above Berchtesgaden is the best part of the whole Deutsche Alpenstrasse, the Rossfeldringstrasse. This trip (about 25 km) is high dancing along the Austrian border, with gorgeous views across Salzburg and its valley to the high Tannengebirge Mountains in Austria and in the other direction, over Berchtesgaden. There are several restaurants on the ring road. To get up on the ring from Berchtesgaden, follow the signs to Obersalzberg, a steep climb in the direction of Hitler's Eagles Nest. The Rossfeldringstrasse turns off, and then there's a toll booth! In fact, there are two toll booths, one at each end of the toll part of the ring road (see Trip 68).

From the ring road there's a well-kept secret way down into Austria with easy access to the Austrian Autobahn. It's pretty and fun and hardly ever used by anyone. Just below the northerly toll booth, a small road heads north. That's it. It has no significant marking, but it goes to a tiny border crossing, and then down to the Austrian mountain town, Durrnberg, site of the famous Salzburg salt mines, then on down to come out in the valley of the Salzach River at the Austrian village of Hallein. It's much easier to get to the Rossfeldringstrasse on this road from Hallein, just south of Salzburg, than from Germany through Berchtesgaden. From Hallein, Austria, look for the new bridge looping over the main street and up the mountainside just north of the old town. The new bridge is the road (see Trip 68).

Hordes of tourists visit the salt mines at Durrnberg, but they come up a little cable car from Hallein, not the road.

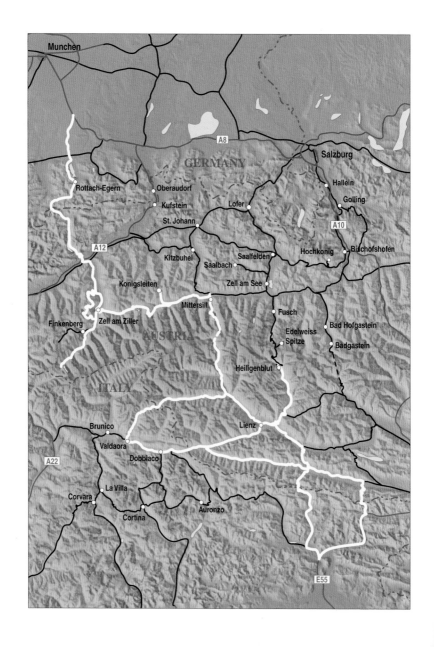

Eastern Tirol

Central Austria south of Salzburg is the very narrow waist of the country, just over 100 kilometers across, from Berchtesgaden in Germany to Italy. Innsbruck, Tirol, and Vorarlberg are in the west, and Wien (Vienna) is to the east. Since the narrow waist area is all high mountains with many good north-south pass roads, there's a lot of good riding.

There are millions of Germans on one side and millions of Italians on the other side of Austria's narrow waist, all busy going back and forth across little Austria, such a short distance across that they need not stop even for a WC, let alone gas. Except that prudent Austria has concluded that most of this north-south traffic should pay a toll. A couple of the roads are actually private enterprise endeavors.

Heiligenblut, Austria, at the south end of the Grossglockner Hochalpenstrasse, has a picturesque village church with typical Austrian pointed steeple. The Glocknerhof Hotel on the right is a MoHo, one that specializes in serving motorcyclists.

On the south side of the Grossglockner Hochalpenstrasse, right in the hairpin above the village of Heiligenblut, this small road takes off weaving south staying high on the side of the mountain with views of the valley and far mountains.

Austrian private enterprise has also provided a plethora of tourist accommodations. In the first two trips described here, there's a Gasthaus on practically every corner, with Zimmer Freis in between. Most hotels are attractive Austrian mountain style, with huge roofs, balconies garlanded with flower boxes, and interesting illustrations painted on exterior walls. They almost guarantee good food, attentive service, and spotless, attractive accommodations. Many have elaborate carved wood and wrought iron detailing. There are so many establishments, all so inviting, that any traveler with an economic bent must wonder how they can possibly produce a return on what has to be a very large investment. To an American mind they just don't make economic sense, but they surely are nice.

Most of the hotels spend as much on cooking as on decoration. Area sweet specialties besides *Apfel Strudel* include *Toffel Strudel* (more of a custard base), both with vanilla sauce or the more standard whipped cream. *Kaiser Schmarrn* is a crepe-like concoction smothered in fruit. Practically every menu will have a *Grill Teller,* or mixed grill platter. Sometimes it's good to ask for recommendations. Find out what is just out of the oven, or is specially prepared.

The Hotel Glocknerhof is spectacularly set in the high mountain village of Heiligenblut on the south side of the Grossglockner. It hangs on the mountain edge at the entrance to the village with views of the very Austrian village church (tall steeple) and craggy mountains across the green *Moll Tal* (valley) below. Even the indoor swimming pool has sweeping mountain views. The interior is spacious and charming modern mountain design. Hotel Glocknerhof is a MoHo, one of several hotels in Austria that advertise themselves as Motorrad Hotels. They specialize in serving motorcyclists. Each is different. By contrast, MoHo Landhaus Jausern is modest, high in a dead-end valley just north of Zell am See and south of Salzburg. From the main road into Saalbach, turn south. It's behind and above a larger hotel. Another is Hotel Iselsbergerhof on the low pass road of the same name south of the Grossglockner and just north of Lienz. There's Hotel Solaria south of Salzburg atop Radstadter Tauern Pass, and Hotel Capella in Stubai Tal off the Brenner Pass.

The Boglerhof up the dead end Alpbach Tal is in a cute village.

The water in European swimming pools, like this one in the Glocknerhof in Heiligenblut, Austria, is at floor level, so that swimmers have views of the surrounding mountains and valley. An indoor pool in German is a Hallenbad.

Trip 65 Achen Pass and the Ziller Tal

Distance About 170 kilometers from Germany via Zillertaler Hohenstrasse, Schlegeis, Gerlos Pass, to Grossglockner

Terrain Good sweepers, narrow erratic road on Zillertaler Hohenstrasse, old Gerlos

Highlights Lovely farms and villages, fun roads with some traffic spots, good hotels and cafes. Includes: Achen Pass (941 meters), Zillertaler Hohenstrasse, Schlegeis (1,784 meters), Gerlos Pass (1,507 meters), Konigsleiten, Pass Thurn (1,273 meters)

Still narrow, some parts of the Zillertaler Hohenstrasse open up a bit.

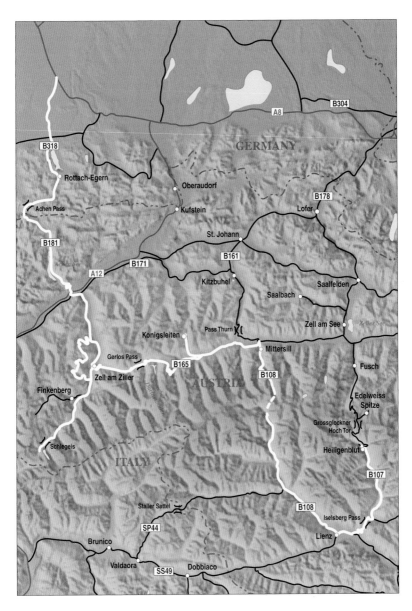

The Achen Pass (see Trip 64, Deutsche Alpenstrasse) sweeps magnificently down into the Inn Tal, and it's possible to proceed across the autobahn and right up the Ziller Tal, a valley with every imaginable shade of green. The Ziller Tal is decorated with a narrow gauge railroad, sometimes sporting a chuffing steam-powered train. At Zell am Ziller, the Gerlos Pass road leaves the Ziller Tal and starts climbing a finger valley to the east.

Just north of Kitzbuhl on the road up Pass Thurn, this restaurant is advertising for motorcycle customers.

But before that, at Ried, the Zillertaler Hohenstrasse climbs the mountain-side to the west, where it hangs and dances in a one-lane game in and out of the tree line, offering dazzling views of the yellow-green, blue-green, and just-green quilt below and the Gerlos Pass road snaking up opposite. It finally comes back down in the Ziller Tal at Ramsberg. There's a toll.

Atop the Zillertaler Hohenstrasse is the Almgasthof Zirmstadl of interesting log construction and sporting a terrace with a fine view.

Head farther south up the Ziller Tal past Mayrhofen through Finkenberg with Sporthotel Stock. Just above Finkenberg, traffic is directed to a new road and tunnel going farther up the valley. The old road, to the right, is the correct choice. It snakes through a gorge with overhanging cliffs.

Farther up, a toll road with a one-way-at-a-time traffic light leads into the high Schlegeis. Near the end of the road, a gravel drive leads up above a lake to the Dominikushutte, a restaurant with a view of Italian mountain peaks. It's a good turnaround spot.

Back down at Zell am Ziller, the Gerlos climbs east through a tourist town of the same name, Gerlos. Near the top there's a toll gate onto a new swooping alignment that supposedly offers views of the Krimmler waterfall. The views are from quite a distance. Turn north and take the old road instead. It bounces and weaves and heaves in great sport down the mountain. Part is narrow. Some bridges are wooden.

Near the top of the Gerlos, just about where the toll road splits off, is an opportunity to climb a bit higher to a ski village called Konigsleiten, with a couple of good hotels like Hotel Gasthof Ursprung.

From the Gerlos Pass, it's straight ahead east to Zell am See and the Grossglockner, skirting the high Tauern Mountain spine of Austria to the south, and the Kitzbuhel Alps to the north. At Mittersill, little Pass Thurn joins from the north, and the big Felbertauern toll tunnel road joins from the south, coming out from under the Hohe Tauern Mountains. The Felbertauern tunnel is the main north-south, all-weather connection across the waist of Austria, parallel to the Grossglockner.

On this trip between Zell am Ziller and Zell am See, there are many villages. Be not deceived by the signs at the entrance to each village indicating the end of the 80 kilometer speed limit. It means the beginning of 50.

The narrow old road above Mayrhofen up to Schlegeis hugs the cliffs under overhanging rocks.

Trip 66 Passes From Italy

Distance *From Italy to Grossglockner, via Staller Sattel, about 65 kilometers; via Plocken Pass, about 50 kilometers; via Nassfeld Pass, about 60 kilometers*

Terrain *Via Staller Sattel, good sweepers; via Plocken Pass, pleasant road; via Nassfeld Pass, pleasant road*

Highlights *Via ★Staller Sattel (2,052 meters), pretty country, hotels in east Tirol; via Plocken Pass (1,362 meters), quick connection over Gailberg Sattel (982 meters) and Iselsberg (1,204 meters) to Grossglockner; via Nassfeld Pass (1,557 meters), good escape from Italian autostrada; ★Kartischer Sattel (1,526 meters)*

Staller Sattel is the fun one-way-at-a-time pass into Austria from the Dolomites in Italy (see Trip 57). It comes down into Austria from the one-way part, past the Tandlerstub'n hotel restaurant in St. Jakob, joining the Felbertauern road south of the tunnel, and goes on into the major city of the Ost (east) Tirol, Lienz. (The Ost Tirol is the part that voted to rejoin Austria in the 1920s after it had been awarded to Italy at Versailles. It is separated from the rest of the Austrian Tirol by the Sud Tirol, still part of Italy.)

The Italian side of the Staller Sattel is one way at a time as it winds down to beautiful Antholzer See (Lago d'Anterselva in Italian).

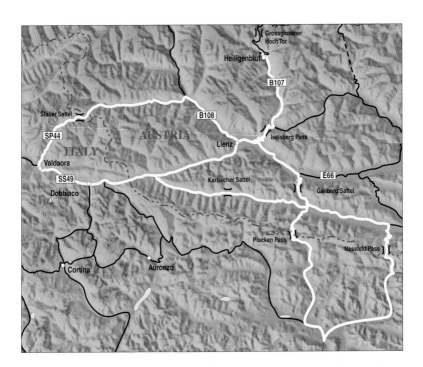

From Lienz, a fine sweeper climbs the Iselsberg Pass (site of one of the motorcycle hotels) toward Heiligenblut and the Grossglockner. The Iselsberg provides the last (or first) glimpses of the Dolomites.

Another route from Lienz is to head back toward Italy about 28 kilometers on the main highway, almost to Sillian in order to catch the dancing Kartischer Sattel road. From its well-marked intersection, the sattel has been improved through several curves and hairpins. Once across the sattel, into Karnten Land, it becomes a tortuous dance down to Kotschach-Mauthen where it meets the Plocken Pass and the Gailberg Sattel roads right by one of the MoHos, the Gailtaler Hof.

East of the Dolomites and east of Cortina, two seldom-used passes (Plocken and Nassfeld) cross from Italy into Austria (they aren't often called by their Italian names, Passo di Monte Croce Carnico and Passo di Pramollo) (see Trip 57).

The Plocken especially has an exciting climb up out of Italy in layered switchbacks through forests, then down north to Kotschach-Mauthen in the Gail Tal where it meets the east end of the Kartischer Sattel. Farther east in the Gail Tal, the Nassfeld Pass comes down into Austria. The top of it is just ten kilometers above Pontebba on the autostrada/autobahn between Venezia and Wein. It's a wonderful way to escape the diesel trucks and buses of the autostrada. From the Gail Tal, passing the MoHo Gailtaler Hof, the Gailberg Sattel connects directly to Lienz in the East Tirol, Iselsberg, and the Grossglockner.

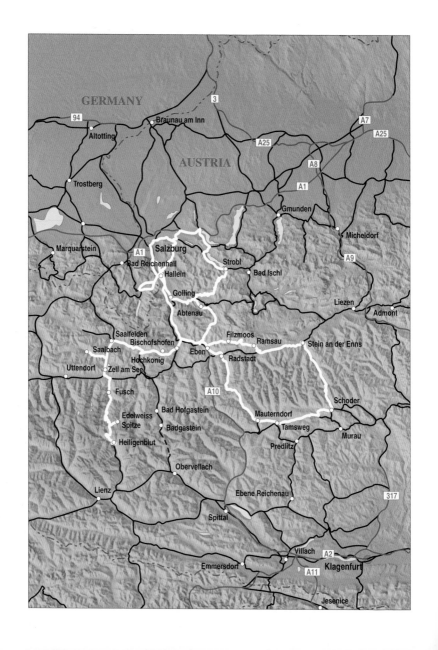

Salzburg Land

Salzburg is the name of a state, Salzburg Land, as well as of the city. It includes the land drained by the Salzach River.

Bookshelves are full of stuff about the romance of Salzburg, the city, what with Mozart and the *Sound of Music*. But are there many about the entertaining roads around it?

There are a couple of easy-to-get-to hotels out on the north fringe of Salzburg's congestion. Find them by going a couple of kilometers north from the Salzburg Nord Autobahn Ausfahrt (Salzburg North exit). Gasthof Brauwirt is off to the left of the highway in a village called Lengfelden. It got its beer license several hundred years ago. Hotel Gmachl is a bit further north in the village called Elixhausen. From both it's possible to take a bus into the center of Salzburg.

One of the MoHos, Hotel Solaria, is in Salzburg Land, down south atop Radstadter Tauern Pass. It's marked on the pass road by an older motorcycle pointing to the hotel.

Several hotels in Austria advertise themselves as MoHo, Motorcycle Hotels. Hotel Solaria, high atop the Obertauern Pass, and set back from the main road, is easy for a biker to find.

Trip 67 Grossglockner

Distance   *About 200 kilometers over Grossglockner (toll) to Salzburg*
Terrain   *Every kind of mountain road: tight, sweeping, narrow hairpins over a major pass and a couple of lesser ones*
Highlights   *Exhilarating riding and scenery. Includes: ★Grossglockner Hoch Tor (2,575 meters), Edelweiss Spitze (2,577 meters), ★Grossglockner Fuscher Tor (2,428 meters), Filzen Sattel (1,291 meters), Dientener Sattel (1,357 meters)*

The Grossglockner Hochalpenstrasse, Grossglockner for short, is one of the major play roads of the Alps. In crossing the highest spine of the Austrian Alps, it combines every test of driving skill: hairpins, sweepers, jig-jags, cobblestones, steep descents, narrow ledges, sometimes ice and snow and hanging clouds of fog, along with spectacular views and plenty of restaurants. It's only a half-day's drive from Munchen and the big cities of northern Italy, and even less from Salzburg, so it is a testing spot for the latest machines and visiting drivers. And it's a private enterprise.

Yes, it's a private toll road. The same company owns the toll part of Gerlos Pass (Trip 65) and the Nockalmstrasse (Trip 71). The Grossglockner toll is fairly expensive, 18 Euros. (If you make reservations for two nights in Heiligenblut,

From Edelweiss Spitze, the last several curves of the main road up the north side to Fuschertorl are in clear view.

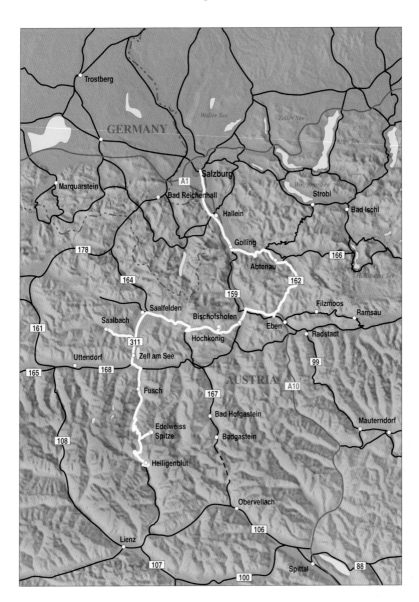

you'll get a pass for the Grossglockner). Typically, Austrians in cute costumes at the toll booths will take any kind of money or credit card. They also record license numbers and put it on your ticket. Then they hand over a decal and an elaborate brochure detailing the wonders available for motorcyclists on the road. There are indeed lockers for jackets and helmets at view spots. It's possible to book a return at reduced rates. There are reduced rates for auto club members.

Once through the toll booths, it's possible to play back and forth and up and down and explore a couple of dead ends and even stay at one of several hotels. The high Edelweiss Hutte atop Edelweiss Spitz has attractive rooms.

(Sorry, Austrians don't know the "Edelweiss" song from *The Sound of Music,* although tour guides in Salzburg are pleased to show where Maria lived and got married.)

The south half of the Grossglockner is in the Land of Karnten which we English speakers call Carinthia. The north part is in Salzburg Land.

The Salzburg approach from the north is up the Fuscher Tal, a lush green valley from Zell am See and Bruck, past the village, Fusch. Then the climb.

There are two short tunnels and two humps across the top. The north hump is called Fuscher Tor (Fusch Gate) and the other Hoch (high) Tor, with a high Alpine valley between the two, where the road often cuts through deep snow banks.

Near the Fuscher Tor, what looks like a restaurant parking lot leads to the snaking little road up to the highest point, Edelweiss Spitze. The road's worth the trip. The view from the restaurant at the top is reward enough. The restaurant, Edelweiss Hutte, is down over the edge from the parking lot. Sometimes it's possible to ride down to it. Above, all around are high peaks, and below, bits of ribbon roads. To the south, the ribbon, not really a ribbon but a string, works across the Alpine meadows. Until August it's just a slit in deep snow banks that disappears into a tunnel. To the north, the road seems to weave to the mountains' edge and then disappear into the Fuscher Tal.

The side of the Hutte at Edelweiss Spitze with its new symbol with Edelweiss blooms as spokes of the idealized motorcycle.

The Heiligenblut town band, mostly brass and drums, leads villagers past the Glocknerhof Hotel to services in the steepled village church. Austrians are very good at marching in step.

Time for hot chocolate.

About halfway down the south, Karnten side, well below the Hoch Tor, a road climbs back up about nine kilometers through concrete snow sheds to a huge parking garage called Franz Josefs Hohe. Outside the garage there is convenient designated motorcycle parking and free lockers and a view of the Grossglockner itself, the big mountain that's supposed to look like a big bell, and a cable car ride down onto the ice of the Pasterze Glacier.

On down south, down below the toll plaza, right in the last hairpin before the village of Heiligenblut, a little one lane road takes off weaving on south staying high on the side of the mountain with views of the valley and far mountains. In ten kilometers, it makes its way down to the main valley road at the village of Dollach.

Just below that last hairpin on the main road is the village of Heiligenblut (Holy Blood), hanging on the mountainside. The Hotel Glocknerhof, right at the entrance to the village, there are several other hotels and Gasthaus possibilities. (Check with your hotel in advance about a complimentary pass over the Grossglockner). In the little town square by a fountain made of huge mountain crystals, there's often an evening brass band concert. The square has motorcycle parking. Heiligenblut's little church with a very tall steeple is a good example of original Austrian Gothic that has not been baroqued ("modernized" with putti and such). The memorials in it illustrate the horrible costs of 20th century wars to families of the village.

The Grossglockner Company is engaged in a serious effort to accommodate motorcyclists. This sign at the parking lot for Fuschertorl invites bikers to ride on up to the top of Edeweiss Spitze. Large vehicles are forbidden.

South from Heiligenblut, down the Moll Tal, past Dollach, is the Iselsberg Pass (site of one of the MoHos) up and westerly toward Italy through Lienz in the East Tirol, or southerly to the Gailberg Sattel and Plocken Pass (Trip 57).

North of the Grossglockner and the Fuscher Tal and north of Zell am See about five kilometers is the turnoff west to Saalbach, site of another MoHo. A few kilometers farther north is Saalfelden and the pleasant Austrian roads to Reit im Winkl on the Deutsche Alpenstrasse (Trip 64).

A new tunnel through the adjacent mountain eases the traffic around Zell am See on the west. But a better route is to head around the east side of the See, then continue on country lanes through Gerling to Maria Alm.

The main road north from Zell am See goes to Saalfelden, then heads east to Maria Alm, a pleasant village pleasantly bypassed by the new road up the Filzen Sattel. Beyond Maria Alm, the Sattel road climbs steeply and irregularly. Parts have been improved, but the old sections are the most fun. All of this is just south of Berchtesgaden and the Rossfeldringstrasse in Germany.

The road dips, then climbs the Dientener Sattel. Over the sattel an interesting road climbs up toward the German border. Signed for Hochkonig, it deadends at a hotel called Arturhaus.

The countryside is rural, remote and tourist free all the way across the Sattels and down a twisting gorge to Bischofshofen. The road bypasses most of Bischofshofen, connecting straight across the Salzach River to the Tauern Autobahn, high on the mountain opposite. The autobahn connects Salzburg with southern Austria and Italy. It's free except for a toll tunnel through the highest part of the Tauern Mountains.

Sail up to the autobahn (with a vignette) and take it about ten kilometers south to the Lammer Tal Ausfahrt, then follow the Lammer Tal north on the Salzburger Dolomitenstrasse along a raging mountain stream through Annaberg, past the turnoff for Pass Gschutt on to Abtenau (and a turn to Post Alm, Trip 68). Then sweep down to the Salzach River at Golling and thence back north toward Salzburg, passing Hallein (Trip 64), the gateway to the Rossfeldringstrasse.

The row of windows climbing the far mountain is the concrete roofed highway to Franz Josefs Hohe and the Pasterze Glacier.

Trip 68 Post Alm

Distance *165 kilometers*
Terrain *Narrow mountain roads and pretty country*
Highlights *Salzkammergut lakes, Post Alm (about 1,500 meters) (toll),
Gaisberg (1,287 meters), bucolic mountains and views*

From Salzburg, take the autobahn in the direction of Wien, east for about 25
kilometers, exiting at Mond See. This is the Salzkammergut, land of lakes and
mountains. South along some lakes, and over a low pass brings you to St. Gilgen
on St. Wolfgang See. Mozart's mother lived here. The main road east from St.
Gilgen follows the south shore of the lake as far as Strobl, where a mini-inter-
change has a sign pointing south to Post Alm. It's a little road that climbs
through the forest with some switchbacks. No tourists. There's a toll.

Near the top, the through road turns sharply left, signed for ABTENAU.
Straight ahead goes to a parking lot for hikers. Climbing up over another hump,
Gasthof Alpenrose can be spotted on the mountainside with a little drive lead-
ing up to it.

After wandering down into a lovely valley, the Post Alm road arrives at a
tee-intersection. Turning east is a real adventure. It seems like driving through
farm driveways. But it connects with the main road back through Abtenau and
down to Golling.

*Hardly anyone bothers to see this lovely view near Salzburg as the Post Alm road sweeps
down through lush green valleys toward Abtenau.*

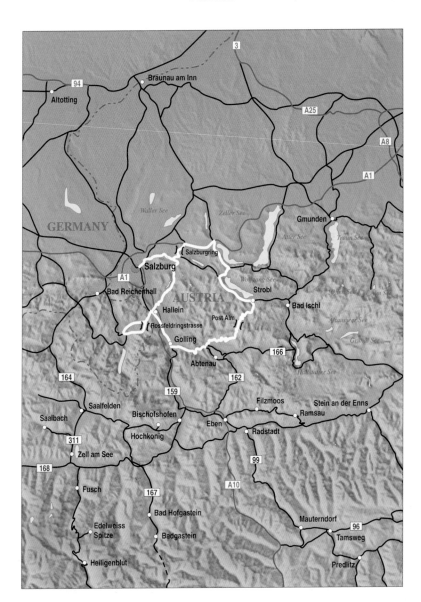

North of Golling, at Hallein, detour up the Durrnberg road to the
Rossfeldringstrasse, if you haven't done it (Trip 64). It affords great views of
Salzburg, Golling, and the mountains of this trip.

From Hallein, a road heads northeast, behind Salzburg, coming out east of
the city right at the Salzburgring, the famous G.P. race track. Back toward
Salzburg five miles, a road climbs Gaisberg Mountain. From it, Salzburg is all
spread out below.

Trip 69 Filzmoos and Tauern Passes

Distance *130 kilometers, plus a turn on the autobahn*

Terrain *Back and forth on the Tauern Mountains, some small roads, steep climbs and switchbacks*

Highlights *Filzmoos (1,056 meters), Ramsau (1,135 meters), Solker Tauern Pass (1,788 meters), Radstadter Tauern Pass (1,739 meters), Seetaler Sattel (1,246 meters)*

Hotel Solaria, one of the MoHos listed at the head of the chapter, Salzburg Land, is atop the Radstadter Tauern Pass on this trip.

Two rivers run roughly parallel, from west to east, south of Salzburg, the Enns and the Mur with the Tauern Mountains in between. This route crosses the Tauern Mountains from one valley to the next, and then back. Trip 70, Turracher and Nockalm, adjoins this trip on the south.

South of Salzburg, on the Tauern Autobahn, exit at the Eben Ausfahrt, just past the Gasthofgut, and head east up the mountain road to Filzmoos, an attractive mountain village with lots of hotels and restaurants. East of Filzmoos, toward Ramsau, the road becomes much less traveled. Keep east and the road eventually comes down in the valley of the Enns River, the Enns Tal. There'll be signs to Stein a.d. Enns, across on the south side of the river. That's the gateway to Solker Pass, a non-commercial north-south crossing of the Tauern Mountains. It's a good road, decorated by many signs, each the silhouette of a

Solk Pass crosses through a park, and motorcyclists are advised to keep the throttle under control. Between the two black motorcycles is the word "Please." Then "Drive slowly and quietly here, or else:" and a motorcycles forbidden sign.

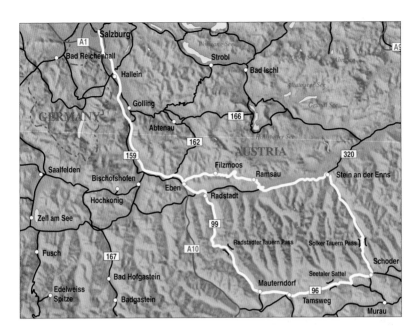

motorcycle with the words "slowly" in many languages, including English. But it's a great climb. On the north side, short of the top, is a gravel driveway leading to a very comfortable restaurant, the Erzherzog Johann Hutte. At the top of the pass is a big sign in German addressed to "Dear Motorcycle Riders" and saying in effect that if you don't watch your playful speed on this road, maybe, and then there's the symbol of "motorcycles forbidden." It's a good ride anyway. The south side is through mostly unoccupied forests.

From Schoder at the south base of the Solker, head west on very lightly traveled roads high above the Mur Tal, playing along the south edges of the Tauern Mountains through Krakaudorf, over Seetaler Sattel, and on west to Tamsweg, a fair sized town, and on to Mauterndorf. At 1,122 meters, with a photo-worthy castle, Mauterndorf is the gateway back north over the Radstadter Tauern Pass to Salzburg. The pass road climbs through high meadowlands, then rather steeply to the top of the pass at the village, Obertauern, site of the MoHo Solaria. (Look for the motorcycle beside the road.)

A short way down the north side of the pass, there's a small monument which recognizes the work of Russian prisoners who built the road during World War I. (Austria was pretty successful in its eastern front battles with Russia in that war. Of course, the Russian Revolution started. Meanwhile, the serfs built this road for us to enjoy.) Below the monument, the road enters a narrow gorge and twists beside a rushing stream before daylighting in some rolling hills with quaint farmhouses leading to the town Radstadt and the autobahn back to Salzburg.

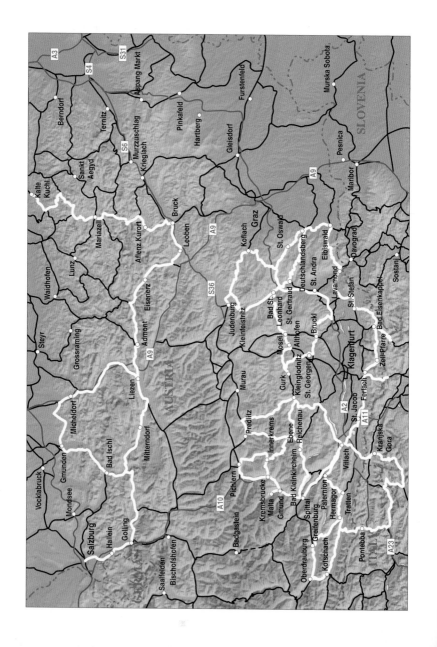

Karnten Land and Steiermark

Austria's southern state, Karnten (which we call Carinthia), borders both Italy and Slovenia. Slovenia is the northwestern part of the former Yugoslavia. Karnten is a land of mountains and lakes which some have called warmer than the rest of Austria. Trip 70 is to the north in Salzburg Land and Trip 59 is southwest along the border with Italy.

Steiermark, the state that we call Styria, is north and east of Karnten.

One possible hotel in Karnten is the Hotel Post (of course) in Villach, a medium size town in the valley of the Drau River that flows out of the Dolomites and across southern Austria into Slovenia. The Post Hotel is almost next door to the cathedral, the Dom, on Hauptplatz (Main Square). Other Karnten hotels are listed in Trip 57.

The Villacher Alpenstrasse climbs west out of Villach to about 1,000 meters where it ends. Faaker See, just east of Villach, is the site of the largest Harley rally in Europe.

About 30 kilometers northwest of Villach, east of Millstatter See, is the mountain village Bad Kleinkirchheim (little church home) with several hotels capitalizing on the mountains and the water. One is the Hotel Pulverer with elaborate pools inside and out, water slides, and huge jacuzzi baths. It boasts bountiful food, heated bathroom floors, and heated towel racks.

In Steiermark, southwest of Graz is Deutschlandsberg, base for some good pass roads, and home to the Burg Hotel. (Notice, the town is "berg" and the hotel is "burg." German ears can hear the difference.) The Burg Hotel is indeed a castle on a hill amid vineyards, just west of the town. Ride on up through the castle gate.

North of Graz is Motorradhotel Hubertushof in Aflenz-Kurort just south of Mariazell and just north of Bruck an de Mur. The owner is the importer for several brands of bikes. Kurort roughly translates as cure village. So Aflenz-kurort is an attractive village nestled in alpine foothills, bypassed by main highways, with public baths and pools.

Some Californians may want to remember that Arnold Schwartzenegger is from a suburb of Graz called Thal.

Trip 70 Turracher and Nockalm

Distance *200 Kilometers*
Terrain *Seldom traveled mountain roads and passes, some narrow*
Highlights *Flattnitz (1,400 meters), Turracher Hohe (1,783 meters),
Nockalmstrasse (toll) with Eisen Tal Hohe (2,042 meters) and Heiligenbach
(1,920 meters), Dr. Josef Mehrl Hutte (1,700 meters), Katchberg Pass (1,641
meters), Hochrindl (1,561 meters), Porsche Museum*

The Mur River and the Drau River are roughly parallel, flowing from west to
east. This route weaves back and forth several times across the mountain that
separates them.

The south part of Trip 69 was across the Mur north of this trip.

Northeast of Villach, and east of Bad Kleinkirchheim is a village called
Ebene Reichenau. Right by the church, a little road starts to climb east over
Hochrindl. At a fork, the unpaved road is the pass. (The paved road goes quite a
ways before it deadends). The unpaved road climbs several kilometers to
Hochrindl where the asphalt begins again and forks. Either fork offers a nice
ride down east to the village, Kleinglodnitz, where the Flatnitz road begins its
climb north. Almost at the top of Flatnitz there's a fork, with the westerly
branch being the pass. It wends down to the Mur River. You know when you get
there because there's a railroad track beside the Mur. Cross the tracks and only
six kilometers west is Predlitz where the Turracher Hohe road heads back south
across the mountain. The climb is sweeping and fun to the top where there are
several restaurants and hotels. Some have found the toilets in one, the
Schlosshotel Seewirt, to be amusing. The descent on the south side is very steep,
a 23% grade, so if it's cold on top, you can warm up fast.

As soon as the road flattens out, there's an intersection with the
Nockalmstrasse, marked by a cute waterwheel. (And you're just two kilometers
north of Ebene Reichenau.) Make the sharp turn, back northwesterly across the
mountain again. Like on the Grossglockner, there's a toll on the Nockalm, and
like on the Grossglockner, there are restaurants and small hotels and you can
play back and forth before exiting. In fact, the same company owns both roads.
There are two high points on the road, which finally makes it down to the valley
of the Kremsbach, at a village called Innerkrems. The other Krems is downstream. But don't go that way. Turn easterly, upstream on a road that doesn't
look very promising. But it crosses the next mountain at a place identified only
as Dr. Josef Mehrl Hutte (known locally as "Bund Shuh"), and comes down in
the Mur side of the mountain in a tee-intersection. Head west through Pichlern
and in six kilometers join the main highway crossing back south over the
Katchberg Pass. The Katchberg is rather steep on both sides. And all of a sudden

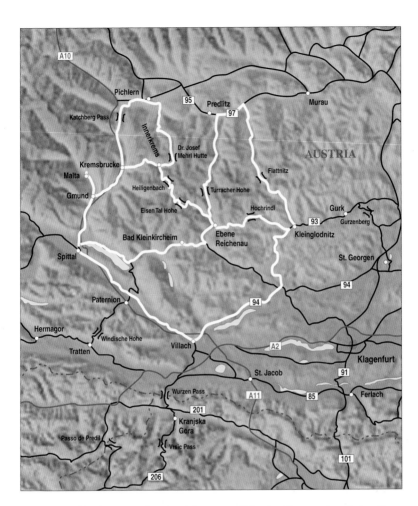

there is traffic, because the Katchberg parallels the Tauern Autobahn from Salzburg, and at this point, the autobahn has a toll. The Katchberg doesn't.

South of the Katchberg, you'll be amazed at the towering concrete structures far overhead, carrying the autobahn down the narrow valley without scarring the mountains, leaving farms and villages underneath it. There is an autobahn connection just at the base of the Katchberg, and there's no toll to go on south. The entrance to the autobahn is called Rennweg . . . raceway. On either road, up on the autobahn or down below on the regular road, head south to Gmund, site of the famous Porsche Museum. It's necessary to loop into and around the village of Gmund to get to the museum. Many collector cars are on display.

Behind Gmund, a dead end road climbs the Malta Tal about 35 kilometers to 1,931 meters. There's a toll, and a hotel restaurant and a Stausee at the top.

Villach, the Drau, and Bad Kleinkirchheim are farther down south.

Trip 71   Klippitztorl and Hochosterwitz

Distance   *150 kilometers*
Terrain   *Small, seldom used pass roads, forested mountains*
Highlights   *Fun pass roads through non-tourist, rural Austria, giant cathedral in a village, and a real castle on a pinnacle all with fun names: Klippitztorl (1,644 meters), Diex Sattel (1,219 meters), Gurzenberg (1,039 meters), Gurk Dom, Hochosterwitz Castle*

North and east of Villach and Bad Kleinkirchheim, just east of Trip 69, is the Gurk Tal with the small village of Gurk just off on the south side of the valley road. Gurk has some attractive tourist facilities and a huge twin-towered cathedral that dominates the area. The cathedral is romanesque in style with small arch windows.

Three kilometers east of Gurk, turn south on a local road that climbs up Gurzenberg and down to a "Y" intersection. Take the left leg of the "y" and straight across the highway, then up by a small lake called Langsee at a village called St. Georgen. In a couple of kilometers Hochosterwitz Castle will dominate the view. It looks as a castle should look, atop a pinnacle with a walled road with many gates circling up to the top dominated by a fortress. It was built in the fifteen hundreds as a defense against Turkish invasions. From a parking lot at the base, a steep incline cable car provides access to the top. Interesting.

All of a sudden, Hochosterwitz Castle and the winding walled road up to it dominate the horizon. It was built four hundred years ago to help protect Vienna from Ottoman Turks.

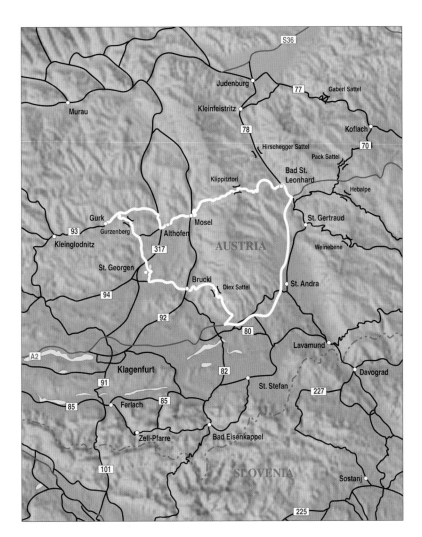

On east ten kilometers from Hochosterwitz cross through the small village Bruckl and on up over the little road to Diex Sattel. When it gets down to the next valley there will be an autobahn. Take it in the direction of Graz from the entrance called "Volkermarkt Ost," or the parallel Bundes Strasse about 40 kilometers, exiting in the direction of Bad St. Leonhard.

Just a couple of kilometers toward Bad St. Leonhard is the obscure turn westerly marked "Klippitztorl." That's the name of the pass. There are several great views of forested mountains with a couple of gasthof restaurants amid the twisty turns in the next 30 kilometers.

At the next intersection, jog south one kilometer and turn west to Althofen and on to Gurk.

Trip 72   Deutschlandberg Figure 8

Distance *206 kilometers*
Terrain *Moderate mountains with demanding pass roads*
Highlights *Five passes, three known only to locals: Weinebene (1,663 meters), Pack Sattel (1,169 meters), Gaberl Pass (1,547 meters), Hirschegger Sattel (1,543 meters), Hebalpe (1,380 meters)*

A moderate mountain known as Koralp is crossed in a northwesterly direction from Deutschlandsberg by two almost unknown pass roads, Weinebene and Hebalpe. At their west end, they are joined by Pack Sattel making sort of a loop. North of Pack Sattel, Gaberl Pass and Hirschegger Sattel make another loop.

Wienebene starts just south of Deutschlandsberg and climbs steadily and smoothly past vineyards and farms before topping in a forest. Without an intersection or village, it daylights in 41 kilometers down at a Bundes Strasse just as the Bundes Strasse starts an exciting climbing north over Pack Sattel. On the Pack Sattel road, passing the turnoff for Bad St. Leonhard (Trip 69,) play the tight sweepers over the top, on past the intersection with the Hebalpe road.

Seven kilometers past the top, take an insignificant-looking left turn to Hirschegg. On through Hirschegg the road may have sections of compacted gravel. It climbs through forests with no sign of civilization over Hirschegger

Coming from Judenburg through the little village of Kleinfreistritz, these bikes are headed for Hirschegger Sattel.

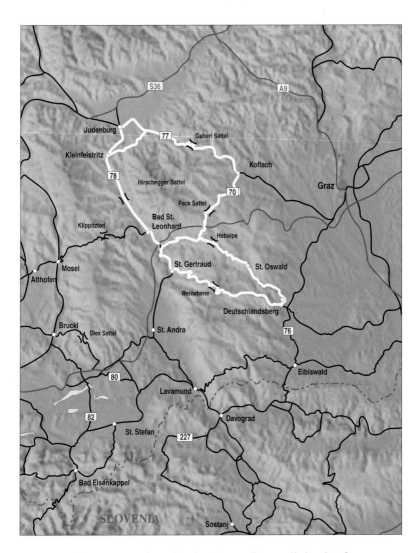

Sattel. Finally on the far side there's a village called Kleinfeistritz. At Kleinfeistritz it's possible to turn north down across a stream and up onto the Gaberl Pass road. Or go on down toward Judenburg and turn right onto the Gaberl Pass road. It'll climb nicely with a couple of tighter turns near the top where there's a hotel/restaurant with views of neighboring forests. On down 22 kilometers to Koflach there's an intersection with old friend Pack Sattel. Twenty-three kilometers back over Pack Sattel (past the turnoff for Hirschegg) is a left turn for Hebalpe. Climbing through forests, Helbalpe comes down easterly 14 kilometers to a fork. Both branches go to Deutschlandsberg. The right hand one, the southerly one, is most scenic and goes right to the Burg Hotel.

Trip 73 **Near Wien**

Distance *About 300 kilometers from Salzburg to Aflenz-Kurort*
Terrain *Gently sweeping over low passes*
Highlights *Popular, scenic lakes and lower mountains, occasional narrow roads, popular motorcycle cafe at Kalte Kuchl. Includes: Pass Gschutt (969 meters), Potschen Hohe (992 meters), Aflenzer Seeberg (1,253 meters), Rottenmanner Hohentauern (1,278 meters), Lahn Sattel (1,015 meters), Prabichl Pass (1,015 meters), Pyhrn Pass (954 meters), Kalte Kuchl*

East of the Solker Pass, almost to Wien, are lovely lakes and low mountains that have captured the hearts of romanticists. Names like Salzkammergut, St. Wolfgang See, Bad Ischl (a favorite of Kaiser Franz Joseph up to World War I), Gesause, Mariazell, and Raxalpe are all famous. Some roads are nice. Some, not so nice. Nothing is exotic. Nothing like the Dolomites, Andermatt, or the Grossglockner. Some of the valleys are rather tedious and industrial.

South of Salzburg on the autobahn, past Hallein where the road climbs up to the Rossfeldringstrasse, at the Golling Ausfahrt, a wonderfully pleasant sweeping road heads up and east through a fine mountain village, Abtenau, and on across low Pass Gschutt, to a popular mountain lake, Hallstatter See. Almost the whole thing is new, sweeping, smooth asphalt. North around the Halstatter See leads to another lowly pass, Potschen Hohe, and to Bad Aussee. South around Halstatter See is a smaller road that takes a tunnel around a village, then makes a steep rough climb to Bad Aussee.

Almost to Wien, the most easterly passes of the Alps attract motorcyclists from the city. The Gasthaus at Kalte Kuchl is right where a couple of good roads intersect.

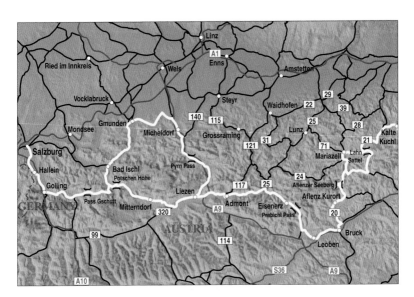

Bad Ischl and St. Wolfgang See are north of this route on the main road east from Salzburg. North of Bad Ischl are some nice roads climbing small passes between lovely lakes. There's one between Bad Ischl and Attersee, and one between Attersee and Gmunden, and one between Gmunden and Micheldorf. Midway on the latter is Scharnstein. South from Scharnstein, an interesting dead-end road up the Alm Tal leads to a tight, twisting climb through the woods on a one-lane paved road to a high restaurant-hotel called the Hochberghaus. The road up is called the Bergstrasse Farrenau.

The main road south from Micheldorf climbs over the low Pyhrn Pass (954 meters) into the Gesause region at Admont. There's a fun little road south from Admont to Trieben where the road south climbs quickly to the top of Rottenmanner Hohentauern Pass, then winds gently down to Judenburg. The Osterreichring race track is just northeast of Judenburg.

Meanwhile, the Gesause road east from Admont is rather uneventful until it climbs Prabichl Pass at Eisenerz. The countryside looks like it has been strip mined, and it has. Eisenerz seems to be the company town that shipped iron ore down stream to the factories of Steyr. Recently the terrible slag heaps have been used for wild dirt bike contests.

The Alps have their last fling about 90 miles short of Wien. The area is easily reached from the Motorradhotel Hubertushof at Aflenz-Kurort, listed above. The meeting point for riders from Wien and eastern Austria who know where the good roads are is an intersection with a Gasthof called Kalte Kuchl. Despite its name, "cold kitchen," it has good hot food and the terraces are full of bikers on weekends. The two passes of note, Lahn Sattel and Aflenzer Seeberg, are between Aflenz-Kurort and Kalte Kuchl.

Trip 74 Three Country Loop

Distance *200 kilometers*
Terrain *Modestly high passes, narrow roads*
Highlights *Loop across Wurzen Pass (1,073 meters) into Slovenia, through Triglavski Narodni, Slovenia's National Park, Vrsic Pass (1,611 meters), World War I fort and monument, Passo de Predil (1,150 meters) into Italy, Passo Sella Nevea (1,190 meters), Nassfeld Pass (1,557 meters) into Austria, Windische Hohe (1,110 meters), Kreuzberg Sattel (1,077 meters), Gailberg Sattel (982 meters)*

Villach is just north of where Slovenia (formerly part of Yugoslavia) borders Italy. This loop south from Villach explores that three country corner.

Wurzen Pass into Slovenia is signed, straight up and south from Villach. It's only 15 kilometers from downtown to the border at the top of the pass.

Insurance for vehicles registered in Europe should be valid in Slovenia, which many consider the most stable of the new republics. Check the green card to be sure SLO, Slovenia, is not crossed out. It probably is crossed out on most vehicles not registered in Europe. If it is crossed out, it will be necessary to buy Slovenian insurance at the border. It's not a bargain. It might be handy to get Slovenian money, too. Remember there will be both Austrian and Slovenian border checks. Slovenia does have moderately priced gasoline at modern stations with handicapped facilities.

Just down off the pass into Slovenia a few kilometers, there's a junction. Jog easterly a couple of kilometers and turn south by Kranjska Gora to climb southerly up the Vrsic Pass. The hairpins climbing the pass are cobblestone, and at one of them is a place to park because there's a very Russian looking church in the woods. It is Russian. It was built by Russian prisoners during World War I while they were working on the road. This is the National Park, Triglavski Narodni, that occupies a large part of northwestern Slovenia.

There's a modest restaurant at the top of the pass, and a good road down in a southwesterly direction with more than thirty numbered hairpins. At the junction at the bottom, head northerly, back up the Passo de Predil. In World War I, this area was all in Austria and the Predil was the border with the Italian enemy. So near the top of the pass is a stone fort much like those in the Dolomites. It's sited to command the valley approaches. There are metal rungs in the cliff opposite the fort, apparently installed like a ladder to some higher observation point. It looks pretty exposed. Nearby, in an arcing curve of the road, is an elaborate monument honoring an Austrian nobleman who apparently came to grief in the area. His name was von Hermann.

Across the border, it's only a couple of kilometers down to an intersection.

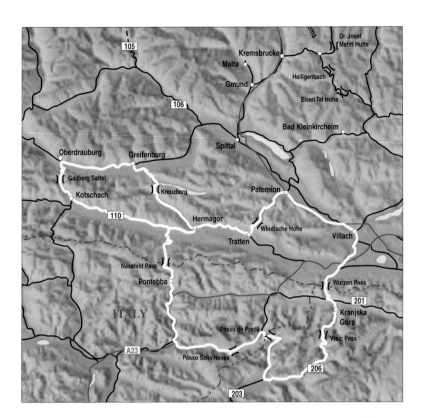

The road southeast is a pleasant and forgotten pass, the Passo Sella Nevea, through the Julian Alps, with a rifugio named Julia. West of the rifugio, the pass snakes down through hairpins and tunnels, then wanders west through relatively unoccupied mountains, finally meeting the main autostrada connecting this part of Italy with Austria. Take the regular road beside the autostrada north only eight kilometers to Pontebba (Trip 55). Cross the ponte (bridge) leaving the autostrada to head east. Go straight north. Actually, not very straight; very twistily. It's only 13 kilometers up to the Austrian border and the Nassfeld Pass (Passo di Promollo in Italian). It's just 12 kilometers down the pass. Head east seven kilometers to Hermagor.

Or get to Hermagor the long way, by heading west to Kotschach, north over the Gailberg Sattel, and east from Oberdrauberg to Greifenburg, then up the Kreuzberg Sattel to Hermagor. Just about 100 kilometers extra.

From Hermagor, head easterly to Tratten, and climb north over the Windische Hohe, down to the valley of the Drau and Villach.

To get to Bad Kleinkirchheim from the north end of the Windische Hohe road, cross under the autobahn to Paternion and then cross the river Drau and turn north.

Trip 75 **Dodging Slovenia**

Distance *160 kilometers from Villach to Deutschlandsberg, 40 more to Loibl Pass and Seeburg Sattel*

Terrain *Nipping at the Slovenian border, using mountain back roads in Austria including Soboth, a motorcycle favorite.*

Highlights *Faaker See site of huge Harley rally, Schaid Sattel (1,068 meters), Loibl Pass (1,367 meters), ★Seeburg Sattel (1,215 meters), ★★Soboth (1,065 meters), Riepl (1,249 meters), all on the Austrian side of the Slovenian border*

The Burg Hotel, Deutschlandsberg, Steiermark, is really a castle on a hill.

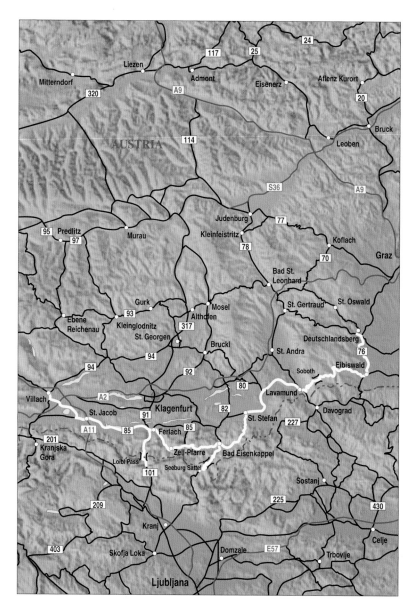

The border between Austria and Slovenia follows the crest of a mountain range. From west to east, there are some entertaining Austrian roads that kind of weave together along the border mountains. Unfortunately, there are no roads doing the same on the Slovenian side, so enjoy the couple of passes climbing to the border, and return (passport checks leaving Austria and entering Slovenia, and vice versa). The best road of all, called Soboth, is all in Austria.

A couple of riders from Wien get checked out as they take off down Soboth from the motorcycle buffet.

Head for Faaker See a few kilometers east of Villach then on east along some lakes through St. Jakob (where an autobahn tunnel heads south for Slovenia) and on to Ferlach. The main road south from Ferlach climbs the Loilbi Tal toward Slovenia. Straight east through Ferlach a little country road climbs up to Zell-Pfarre and on east over Schaid Sattel. A few villagers there. Then down east to Bad Eisenkappel where the Seeburg Sattel road starts a tight sweeping climb to the border. From Bad Eisenkappel, jog on east on another back road that climbs up to Riepl and down to St. Stefan. Then easterly across farmlands to Lavamund.

At Lavamund, cross the Drau River and go a kilometer south. Then the fun begins. Turn up and easterly. Immediately the Soboth road invites a joyous pace, swooping and climbing. Just before the top, there's a turnout that is a favorite motorcycle tire-kicking spot. It has a small stand selling snacks and post cards. On through nice views of forest and field, Soboth ends at Eibiswald. It's only 16 kilometers north to Deutschlandsberg.

Beyond Andermatt

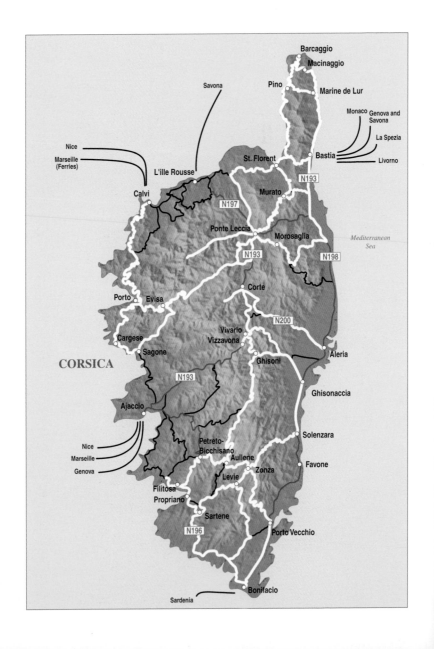

Corsica

Corsica should be on every motorcyclist's must-do list.

Little more than 150 kilometers, north to south, and 80 kilometers wide, it's packed with high rugged mountains—even some skiing—and gorges and canyons and passes with enough tight, twisty roads to exhaust the most ardent enthusiast. It takes a week of all-day riding to cover the roads.

It takes a lot of stones piled on stones to hold up the typical Corsican road.

And it's breathtakingly gorgeous. Exotic rock formations in all colors, rushing streams and waterfalls, pine forests, chestnut forests, deserts, and cliffs down to private little beaches.

Because most Americans might have difficulty finding Corsica on the map (and because most Corsicans have never seen an American) here's a bit about it.

It's an island in the Mediterranean south of Genova, west of Livorno (and Pisa), and north of Sardinia (Sardegna in Italian). For 200 years it's been French. For a thousand before that it was Italian, under Genova or Pisa, with a bit of Spain thrown in. To Italians it was Corsica. That's what we call it. Germans use "k"s, Korsika. But in French, it's Corse, or le Corse. There's Italian food and French food. But the stamps, the phone, and the police are all French (they use the Euro now). Le Corse is a department of metropolitan France. And there's the rub. Some locals would rather not be.

The difference need not affect motorcyclists. Surely not the thousands of bikers that fill most every ferry to and from the island. The ferries to Corsica often look like those to the Isle of Man during TT time, packed with every kind of motorcycle imaginable. There's play room for all.

You don't have to worry too much about high brow culture on Corsica. Some prehistoric types—like 20,000 years ago—carved figures on the southwest coast. The Romans tried unsuccessfully to farm the few level parts on the east coast. Since then various city states and kings fought with scant success to control the island. There were lots of places to hide in those mountains and canyons that we love today.

Several coastal towns, notably Calvi on the northwest coast and Bonifacio on the south tip, remain walled fortresses left over from the battles of the Middle Ages. Then there's the fortress of independent Corsica in the middle of the mountains at Corte.

The proud symbol of Corsica is a black head with a white headband. (Sardinia's symbol is a black head with a blindfold.) The island has two administrative departments: the southwestern part is Corse du Sud (southern Corsica), while the northeastern part is Haute Corse (high Corsica). The license plate of all vehicles registered on Corsica has a final digit "2," with an "A" or "B" after it.

There are only a couple of kilometers of more or less straight road, just south of Bastia on the northeast coast. The main road across the island and mountains from Bastia to Ajaccio on the opposite coast swoops and sweeps in daringly inviting asphalt—and the locals dare—to 1,163 meters at the Col de Vizzavona. Most other roads are so gnarly and/or so precipitous as to require constant attention while providing exciting riding pleasures. They climb through such wild landscapes that it seems you're exploring some strange planet, not a small European island. Ride in the mountains all day. Sleep by the seashore.

Tourist offices: Offices de Tourisme; 1 Place Foch; F-21076 Ajaccio; 495 21 4087.

The Corsica ferries always have a lot of motorcycle traffic. Somehow, the word is out among European motorcyclists that Corsica is a great place to ride.

Offices de Tourisme de la Haute; Corse; F-20200 Bastia; 495 31 0204. Or, check their web sites.

HOW TO GET THERE

Fly. Sail. Bikers will probably ferry to Corsica from the continent. There are multiple ways.

Three companies do most of the ferrying. One French. Two Italian.

The French one, S.N.C.M. Ferryterranee, sails from French ports like Marseille and Nice and Toulon. (You want to know what those letters stand for? Societe Nationale Maritime Corse Mediterranee.)

Corsica Ferries, an Italian company, sails from Nice and Toulon in France, and from Savona and Livorno in Italy. Both of these two lines have introduced fast boats, capable of about 40 knots that make the crossing from France or Savona in three or four hours. The fast boats have special facilities for securing motorcycles. Trouble is, they can't operate in heavy seas, so the crossings are subject to cancellation. The shortest crossing by standard ferry is from Livorno, the port near Pisa, a long way south of the Alps. Savona and Nice are the ports of embarkation closest to the Alps.

Navarma (Moby Lines) sails from Livorno.

A sweet night has been enjoyed by these riders at Hotel Dolce Notte, right on the banks of the Mediterranean at St. Florent.

An Italian company, Happy Lines runs boats from the Italian Riviera at La Spezia during summer months.

The standard ferries are large ships carrying several decks of trucks and busses and cars towing boats and trailers and lots of motorcycles. They're equipped with restaurants and lounges and maybe movies and pools. Overnight ferries have cabins with a private bath available for much less than most hotel rooms—a good choice. Ferries run on multiple schedules serving multiple ports on Corsica. Not all ports are served every day.

Bastia on the northeast coast of Corsica is the closest to Italy. Calvi on the northwest coast is the closest to France. Ajaccio, the only city on Corsica, is on the southwest coast.

Ferries ply regularly between Bonifacio on the south tip and Sardinia, about an hour boat ride, but a world away.

Savona is but a half day's ride from most any place in the Alps. Its port, called Porto Vado, has nice terminal facilities and the most sailings. Play in the Alps all morning, then cut to the coast. Terminals are signed from the autostrada.

Recommended is the overnight ferry from Savona. Just get there in time for the evening sailing. The crew secures the bike along the bulkhead of one of the garage decks. Head up to your cabin, clean up, have a nice dinner, and sleep in a cosy bunk. Get off the ferry in the morning for a great riding day on Corsica.

Ferry companies take credit cards and the Italian ones speak English.

Addresses, e-mail listings, FAX, and phone numbers for them are in the Hotel Appendix at the back of this book under Corsica.

WHERE TO STAY

Like western Austria, Corsica is packed with hotels in exotic spots.

Take Porto, for instance, on the west coast. It's a tiny village that's a must see and stay, wedged in a crevice between towering pink mountains with surf crashing on pink rocks and good hotels and restaurants and three roads in (and out). Each of the three roads in (and out) rates three stars from Michelin. That's their top rating, and they're right. Mind, it's the roads that get the stars, not some building or other wonder. Each of the three roads is an exhilarating adventure.

At Hotel Les Flots Bleus (the blue waves) each room has a deck facing across water to mountains and the tumble-down watch tower built by the Genovese hundreds of years ago.

On the rocks beyond the watch tower is Hotel Belvedere. In complete contrast is the Grand Hotel du Monte d'Oro. It's in the forest, all by itself at about 1,000 meters elevation just off the main trans-island highway at the Col de Vizzavona. There's nothing grand about the hotel except its name. It faces the peak it's named after. And they do have snow. There's an old part to the hotel and a newer part. Neither would rate high on the amenities scale, but the lounge has a huge fireplace and lots of overstuffed chairs. Meals are family style. It's fun.

Twenty-five kilometers west and across a pass from Bastia is St. Florent, one of the few Corsican villages with a French name. It has a yacht basin, waterfront restaurants, and several hotels. One is the Hotel Dolce Notte (sweet night) directly on the beach (a bit rocky) at the edge of the village. The hotel has no restaurant, but serves breakfast on your patio, directly on the water.

Porto Vecchio is on the southeast coast, with a medieval town on the hill and newer stuff around its yacht basin. There's the Hotel Shegara.

Hotel Solemare is down at the southern point of Corsica at Bonifacio. The hotel faces the massive ancient walled city across the fjord-like harbor.

A few kilometers north of Porto Vecchio is a small village named Favona. Right on its curving white sand beach is Hotel U Dragulinu. The Mediterranean is crystal clear and the lounges on the sand have umbrellas and soft pads. Dinner and breakfast diners can look out on the waves. Maybe the first course for dinner will be some wonderful mussels.

Each of the hotels listed has a web site. Most hotel operators will insist that bikes be parked in a locked garage at night. A good idea.

The first Corsica trip, below, starts as if you had just arrived on Corsica. The trips following are from the base communities listed above.

Trip 76   Col de Vergio to Porto

Distance   *190 kilometers*
Terrain   *Mountain roads, some very narrow*
Highlights   *Delightful villages, some asleep; a couple of medieval relics; pine and chestnut forests, exotic gorges; ★Col de Vergio (1,477 meters), Col de Bigorno (885 meters)*

Leave Bastia or Calvi following the signs for St. Florent. It's only 25 kilometers and a pass (Col de Teghime, D81) away from Bastia. Just a little farther from Calvi. From Bastia, the road climbs aggressively and tight even while still in town. Toward St. Florent it passes through vineyards. If you're coming from an overnight ferry, St. Florent is a great firt stop. Right on the little main square is a patisserie serving fresh croissants and other breakfast fare. There's a short one-way loop from the square into the old city and back by the yacht harbor lined with restaurants.

Take the tiny road going south from the little square (not the main one west of town). Very rural. In about five kilometers it passes a 12th century church, still a cathedral, called Nebbio. Nobody's there, but it's worth a look. A perfectly preserved Romanesque style building, it was built by the best artisans Pisa could send.

Porto looks exotic as the sun rises over the mountains behind it.

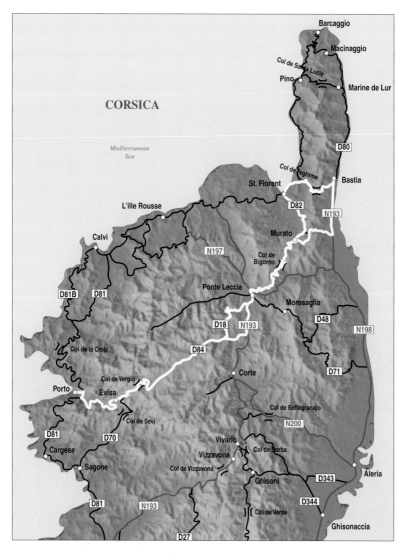

Past Nebbio, climb on up the mountain road through open countryside to Oletta and on to Murato. Murato sits upon the crest of the island with views to the Mediterranean on the east and west. And there is a little black and white stone church (they couldn't decide whether to make it black and white stripes, or black and white checkerboard) built about the same time as the cathedral below, and a delightful contrast in craftsmanship. (It helps to remember that Pisa was building its cathedral and leaning tower about the same time in black and white, and seems to have been more ambitious, although Murato's tower doesn't lean quite enough to be famous.)

The road south from Murato (D50) to Ponte Leccia has just been paved—one narrow lane with a center strip. Over the Col de Bigorno there are views of the oft-snow-capped Monte d'Oro and down through little villages below. Just before Ponte Leccia, there's a railroad crossing with electric signals and a junction with a main road. It's a left turn into Ponte Leccia where there are a couple of shady restaurants.

To stay on a wider road, backtrack a couple of kilometers from Murato and take the wild ride down the Defile de Lancone to the east coast road, and then follow signs south and west in the direction of Corte and Ajaccio. At Ponte Leccia there is a bridge, and a traffic circle merge with the road from Murato.

South of Ponte Leccia just two kilometers, turn west on little D18 twisting through remote countryside, then on west toward Porto on D84. First comes the awesome Scala de Santa Regina (steps of the holy queen), a gorge with the road hung on the edge of giant cliffs with overhanging rocks. Then the road opens onto a ride around a lake, Calacuccia, and sweep up into a dark pine forest with a couple of view spots to the Col de Vergio and a monument figure of a beardless Christ. Across the col, the forest turns to chestnut, the Forest d'Aitone. Pigs like chestnuts. There may be some of both.

A typical Corsican village with beige stuccoed houses and tile roofs hangs on the mountainside below the Col de Vergio.

Coming down toward Porto from the Col de Vergio, the road enters the Gorges de Spelunca.

Below the forest, the road enters the Gorges de Spelunca, majestic walls and formations in pink. Somehow, the road has to get to the bottom of the gorge.

On the way down is a little village, Evisa, with a hotel restaurant called Scopa Rossa. There are several pull-out view sites.

At the bottom and mouth of the gorge is Porto. Everything is still pink, except the eucalyptus trees.

Some American bikers came upon some German bikers climbing the Col de Vergio. All but one of the Germans took the bait and played across the pass, stopping at a pull-out view spot. Finally, the holdout rode up and immediately fell over. Rushing to assist, the Americans noted the rider's leg alarmingly crumpled under the bike. "Not to worry," said the German, in English, "it isn't mine." It was a prosthesis.

Trip 77 Calvi

Distance *160 kilometers (it'll take all day)*
Terrain *Very, very tight, twisting roads (No highway speed possible.)*
Highlights *Wild mountains and coast to Calvi, a medieval walled city with busy waterfront cafes and promenades*

The corniche road north from Porto (D81), climbs the cliffs with one magnificent view after another; views down over the village and gulf; views of red mountains. The whole gulf is a UNESCO designated preserve. There will be

Red granite cliffs and blue Mediterranean waters are the view from the Corniche road north of Porto.

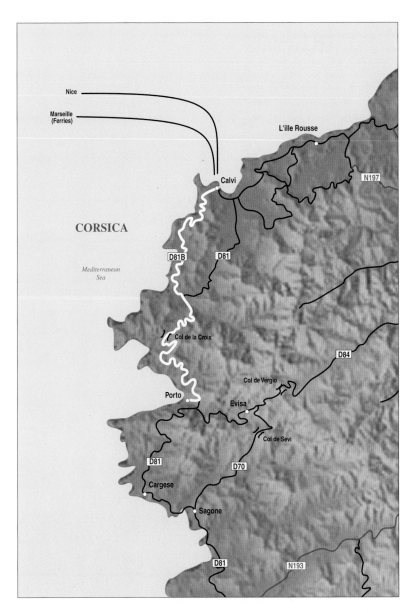

stops for pictures of the giant red cliffs and blue, blue Mediterranean. There has been steady progress in replacing the old patched and rough pavement with new smooth asphalt. Cutting across the Col de la Croix, the road keeps twisting toward Calvi. Calvi is a busy town with a medieval citadel and waterfront cafes. Even though the views are equally exciting heading back along the coast south to Porto, some may opt for the faster inland road.

Trip 78 Les Calanche

Distance *100 kilometers*
Terrain *Some tight, narrow roads, but mostly more open two lane*
Highlights *More exotic pink rock formations and rocky coastline; beautiful beaches and forested mountain pass; Col de Sevi (1,094 meters)*

A rider crosses a stone bridge and a small waterfall along the Les Calancehe road south of Porto.

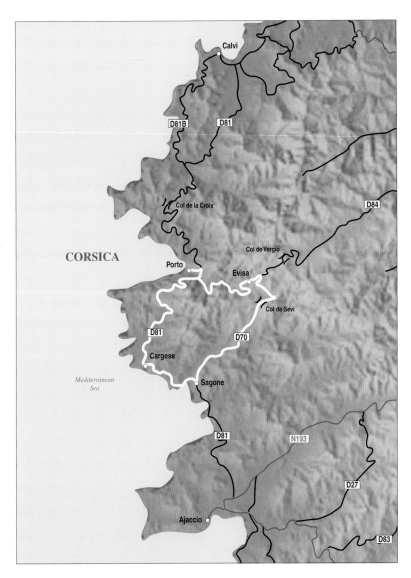

Follow the Les Calanche road (D81) south from Porto. The formations and the road will require some stopping and picture taking. Unbelievable. Through Cargese and down to the coast at Sagone there is a lovely, broad, white sand beach. At the south end of the beach, just as the road turns inland, is a tiny hotel restaurant, La Marine, with shaded tables overlooking the sublimely white beach and blue water.

Back in Sagone, an inland road (D7) climbs over the Col de Sevi and connects with the Gorges de Spelunca road back to Porto.

Trip 79 Bonifacio

Distance *220 kilometers*

Terrain *Fairly open, smooth, two lane coastal roads, then some tight mountain stuff*

Highlights *The walled city of Bonifacio, fjord-like harbor, clifftop view of Sardinia, yacht-filled waterfront at Propriano, prehistoric carvings at Filitosa, mountain roads and villages, Col de St. Eustache (995 meters)*

Don't be tempted by the parking lots as you ride into Bonifacio. Go by them and drive right on up the steep road and in through the arched gate in the massive walls of the Bonifacio citadel. On through the village and out atop the cliff (past the cemetery) it's possible to see crashing waves far below and Sardinia in the distance. Note the tiny stairway up the massive cliff that was supposed to give besieged defenders access to the sea.

Emerging from the citadel, take the road down by the very narrow harbor sheltered by cliffs. It usually sports an international collection of yachts. The little road along the harbor is lined with restaurants and souvenir shops and the ferry to Sardinia. Usually there's a place to park a bike or two.

The back (south) side of Bonifacio rests high on these cliffs facing Sardinia across the "Bouches de Bonifacio."

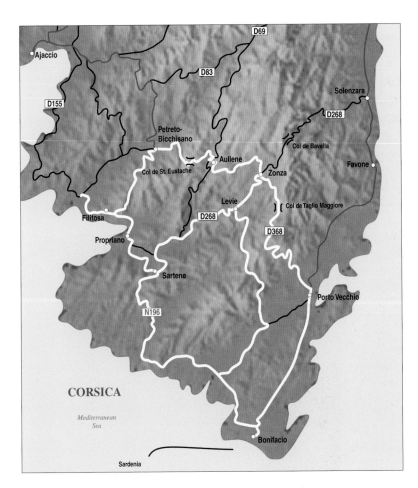

It's open sweeping road north along the west coast (N196) for about 16 kilometers to a turn, easterly, marked for the airport (D859). Go 11 kilometers, on past the airport, to a turn north (D59). There begins a really fun, deserted road twisting over moutains, through a tunnel, for 40 kilometers to Levie. At Levie turn west (D268) to Propriano, a town with an active yacht harbor. On the north side of the harbor is the shoreline road toward Filitosa, the site of pre-historic carvings.

From Propriano, twist north on the main road (N196) to Petreto-Bicchisano, where another fun, twisting road (D420) climbs over several passes including the Col de St. Eustache. Parts of the road are modern, swooping and smooth. Parts aren't. Pass through Allene and Quenza to Zonza where there's sort of an x-shaped intersection. Follow the sign for Porto Vecchio (D368) around a lake through the forests of l'Ospedale, over the Col de Taglia Maggiore with views of the east coast, then sweep on down to Porto Vecchio.

Trip 80 Vizzavona and Restonica

Distance *About 150 kilometers one way from Ajaccio*
Terrain *Some very tight, twisty roads*
Highlights *Climb through forests alongside rushing mountain streams to a high mountain bowl at 1,300 meters; ★Col de Vizzavona (1,163 meters)*
From the south, cross the Col de Vizzavona (N193), a well-maintained sweeping highway, through forests and past the Grand Hotel du Monte d'Oro as far north as Corte, the historic capital of independent Corsica, noted for its citadel on a high rock outcropping. The highway loops east around Corte.

Through the Gorges de la Restonica is one of the high mountain roads on the little Mediterranean island of Corsica. Corsica has more roads than a good rider can cover in a week, including passes through mountains like this.

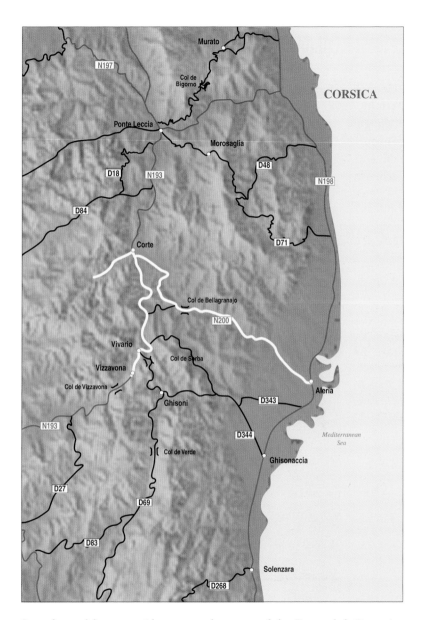

Several roundabouts provide access to the town and the Gorges de la Restonica road (D623). Most of Restonica is a narrow, one-lane wide, rough road. It deadends at a peak-rimmed mountain bowl.

From Corte back to Vizzavona, try going a few kilometers down the main road southeast (through a grove of cork trees) and then climb back over the Col de Bellagranajo.

Trip 81 Col de Verde and Col de Bavella

Distance _225 kilometers (a long day)_
Terrain _Mostly rough paved, narrow, tight mountain roads_
Highlights _Wandering mountain roads with remote villages and a couple of good passes, especially the Col de Verde (1,289 meters) and the ★Col de Bavella (1,218 meters), Col de Sorba (1,311 meters)_

From Vizzavona, ride north (N193) about 12 kilometers and then turn east (D69) over the Col de Sorba, through lovely forests to the mountain village of Ghisoni. Ghisoni has a few commercial establishments, and each will be pleased to see customers. The road works (that's the right term) its way on south through woods and past small waterfalls over the Col de Verde, finally reaching Aullene, a mountain crossroad village with restaurants and services (see Trip

Not much traffic is crossing this one lane wide bridge on the north side of Col de Bavella. "Look! There are trout down there."

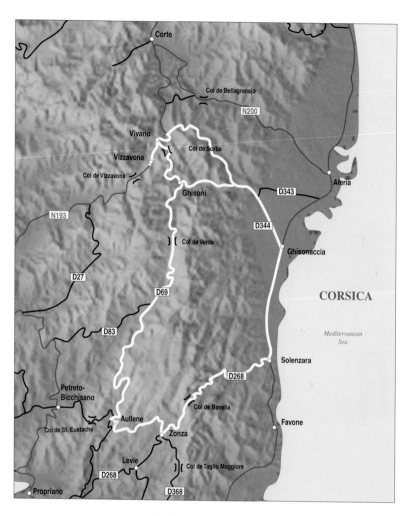

79). On east from Aullene (D420), cross a canyon to Zonza where all of a sudden, and inexplicably, there's a fine sweeping highway northerly up the Col de Bavella (D268). The top of the col, in a pine forest, has several rustic restaurants and views across miles of island peaks and the sea. The road down the northeast side of the col to the coast is being rebuilt. It had been notoriously rough, narrow, and potholed. It traverses wild forests with views of Dolomite-like peaks, bridges, trout streams, and passes spots popular for stream-side bathing, before reaching the east coast at Solenzara. (Favone with the beachfront Hotel U Dragulinu is 12 kilometers south.) From there, follow the coast road (N198) north 17 kilometers to Ghisonaccia. Then turn inland (D344), westerly through the exotic gorges called the Defile de l'Inzecca and Stretta to Ghisoni, the Col de Sorba and Vizzavona.

Trip 82 St. Florent

Distance *180 kilometers*
Terrain *Mountains and desert and forest*
Highlights *Ski bowl at 1,450 meters, desert that looks like southern California (but just a few kilometers of it) with more twisty mountain roads*

The main road southwest from St. Florent (D81) crosses the Desert des Agriates that seems like the desert mountains of southern California, except that there's that sea out there. The road is sort of tortured for about 25 kilometers. Then it joins the main road (N1197) heading inland (southeasterly). Make time, maybe speed, toward Ponte Leccia, just before which there's a small road that follows the Gorges de l'Asco southwesterly into a high mountain bowl (D147). It's about 30 kilometers one way to the bowl where there is a bar restaurant.

Back at Ponte Leccia, cross the main Bastia-Ajaccio highway and head southeasterly up the small mountain road to Morosaglia (D71), climbing over some minor cols and finally wending down to the main road on the east coast. Then it's probably best to head north to Bastia and across to St. Florent.

Over the top, this view is south from the Col du Bigorno. Ponte Leccia is way down there.

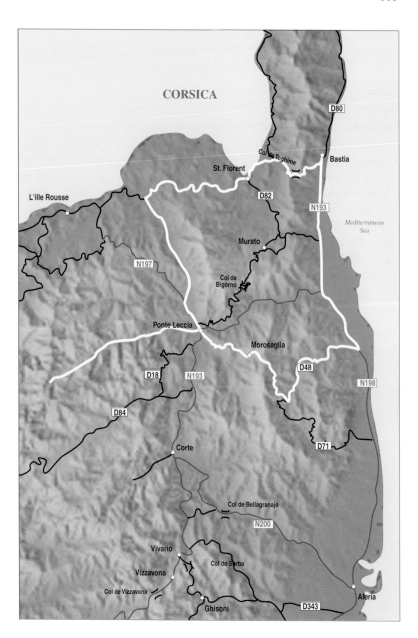

CORSICA

D80

Col de Teghime
Bastia

St. Florent
D82

L'ille Rousse

N193

Mediterranean
Sea

Murato

N197

Col de
Bigorno

Ponte Leccia

Morosaglia

D18   N193

D48

N198

D84

D71

Corte

Col de Bellagranajo

N200

Vivario
Col de Sorba

Vizzavona

Col de Vizzavona

Ghisoni   D343   Aleria

Trip 83 Cap Corse

Distance *170 kilometers*
Terrain *Tight, twisting roads along rugged coast*
Highlights *Similar to California Highway One north of San Francisco, except more precipitous*

Cap Corse is the name usually given to the whole mountainous finger that projects about 50 kilometers north from Bastia and St. Florent. There's nothing flat on the finger. One road (D80) circles it following the coastal cliffs as best it can. Sometimes there are little clusters of houses along the road. Sometimes they are far below on the beach with minimal trails down to them. Start out on the road north from St. Florent. The only recommended detour down to the water is at the north end. A windy loop road goes right down to the water at the northernmost point of Corsica with a cluster of buildings known as Barcaggio.

Then the main loop road around Cap Corse actually gets down to the beach on the east coast at Macinaggio which happens to have a nice row of waterfront restaurants.

This is as far north as you can get on Corsica, on the point called Cap Corse. Over the horizon (beyond that island) are Italy and France.

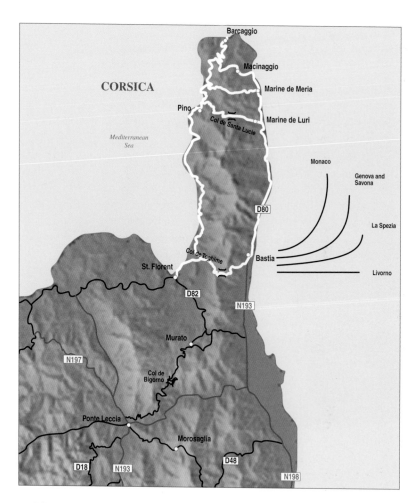

There are two transpeninsular roads that climb across the mountains from coast to coast. They're roughly parallel. So it's possible to take one, and come back on the other. The more northerly one (D36) is just four kilometers south of Macinaggio at Marine de Meria. The second (D180) climbs back over the Col de Santa Lucie and gets back to the east coast at Marine de Luri.

Then follow south along the east coast, which is a pleasantly sweeping highway, to Bastia, and home to St. Florent.

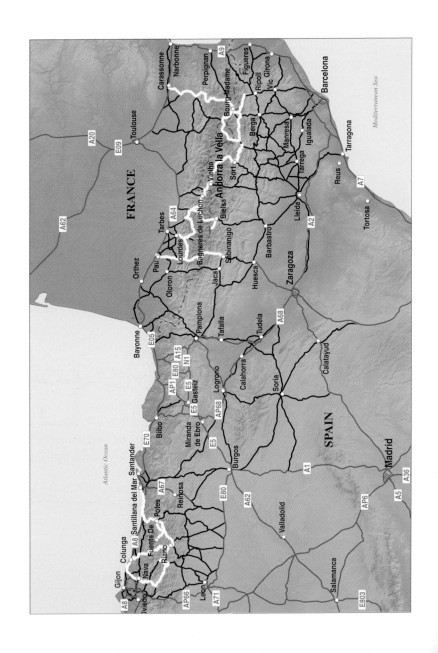

Pyrenees and Picos

The Pyrenees Mountains that separate France from Spain (Espana) stretch about 400 crow-fly kilometers east to west between the Mediterranean and the Atlantic. In both countries the shortest freeway between the coasts is about 600 kilometers. That's from Narbonne to Biaritz in France where it's an autoroute, and from Barcelona to San Sebastian in Spain where it's an autopista. It's about 150 crow-fly kilometers across the Pyrenees between those freeways.

The highest peaks and the most exotic roads start about 100 kilometers from the Mediterranean, and taper off about 100 kilometers from the Atlantic. At the east end of the high stuff is tiny Andorra, an independent and tax free principality with two co-princes, the bishop of Le Seu just south in Spain and the president of France. The international symbol for Spain (Espana) is (E). Andorra is (AND). On the north side of the Pyrenees, things are French. On the south side, things are not always Spanish. The east is Catalonian and the west is Basque, each with a language that sounds sort of clipped, at least to English speaker's ears. In each language, some town names are different. But, Spanish works anywhere in Spain and dinner hours are definitely Spanish (like 9 p.m.). Motorcycle enthusiasts will recognize Spanish gasoline stations, Repsol. Gas is usually cheaper in Spain.

The Spanish side of the Pyrenees will have wonderful smooth asphalt through beautifully banked sweepers.

From Biaritz, which is the southwest corner of France, Spain extends almost 800 more kilometers west into the Atlantic; almost as far out in the Atlantic as Ireland. It's almost as green as Ireland, so it's called the Costa Verde. That whole coast, facing north on the Atlantic is fairly rugged. Out about a third of the way west, right on the coast, is a range of high mountains known as the Picos de Europa. Reportedly, the first land sailors saw returning to Spain from the New World was the snow covered peaks of the Picos. The rain in Spain stays mainly on the coast. So the inland slopes of the Picos are dry. On the coastal side of the Picos, there are two states, Asturias and Cantabria. The inland sides are in Castilla y Leon.

The Picos, like the Pyrenees, are snow-capped and full of twisty exciting roads. In France, passes are still called "cols." In Spain, they are usually called "ports."

Both France and Spain use the Euro. Both are in the EU, so that while language and pavement quality change at border crossings, there are no guards or customs inspectors. There are customs inspectors leaving tax-free Andorra. In Spain, count on wonderful smooth asphalt even on small narrow mountain roads.

Food and drink—always, but only in Andorra do they haul gas to the top of the pass.

There are shops selling most every kind of motorcycle at La Villa.

Do check out Paradores in Spain. They are government sponsored hotels located in out-of-the-way places and/or in ancient palaces or castles. They vary in quality and cost (three, four, and five stars—www.parador.es). Spanish tourist offices in major cities will steer you to special deals and help with reservations. Mentioned here are the Paradores in the Pyrenees at La Seu d'Urgell (Trip 84); Arties and Vielha (Trip 86); Bielsa (Trip 87); and in the Picos de Europa at Fuente De, Santillana Gil Blas, Santillana, and Cangas de Onis.

Trip 84 Andorra

Distance *150 kilometers*

Terrain *High mountain passes, tight, twisting roads followed by urban congestion*

Highlights *Collado de Toses (1,800 meters), Col du Puymorens (1,920 meters), ★Port d'Envalira (2,408 meters), Andorra la Vella, prosperous capital of Andorra with a traffic-jammed street passing every shop and financial center*

Andorra is on the Spanish side of the crest of the Pyrenees. Everywhere where there isn't a building, one is being built. In La Vella, the capital, the main road starts climbing north toward France across the highest pass in the Pyrenees, Port d'Envalira. The climb up the pass from the town is not difficult, passing a couple of turnoffs northwesterly into a dead-end valley. The French border is across the pass on the north side, marked by many gas stations as French cars loop in to fill up on tax free gas. Down into France the road is tighter and quite twisty. There's a car tunnel under the pass. Just five kilometers below the French-side exit of the tunnel is a turn back east (N20E) up and over the Col de Puymorens. There's another tunnel under this pass. Across Puymorens in a more level valley, the road passes between two pieces of Spain, separated by the

In Andorra, riders round the last curve to the Port d'Envalira, the highest pass in the Pyrenees, and one of the highest in all of Europe.

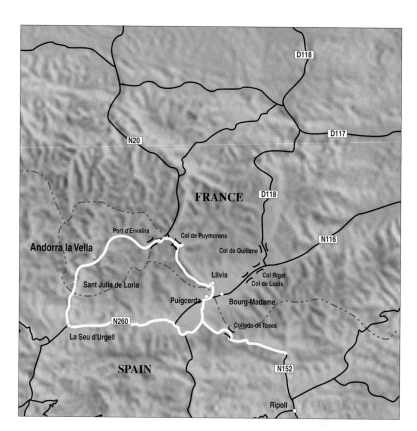

French road. The little cut-off piece of Spain has a town, Llivia. In Bourg-Madame a turn south brings you back across the border into Spain at Puigcerda
which has a nice village square on a hill above the highway. On south into
Spain, N152 is a lovely climb up the Collado de Toses over the Sierra del Cadi
Mountain Range. There's a comfortable restaurant at the top. Most traffic is
going to Barcelona under the Sierra del Cadi in a tunnel.

On back toward Puigcerda, avoiding the Sierra del Cadi tunnel, N260 skirts
the north flank of the Sierra west to Le Seu d'Urgell, also called Seo de Urgel,
seat of the bishop, who's one of the co-princes of Andorra. Seu has a tree shaded
promenade and a Parador in a fomer cloister.

From Seo, it's only 26 kilometers north on N145 across the Andorra border
to Sant Julia where one road scales easterly up the mountainside, and another
westerly. La Vella is just a couple of kilometers further.

Everything is up to date in La Vella, and it seems like everything is for sale.
Roads are full of trucks hauling stuff in so tourists can buy and haul it out. In
addition to clothing and jewelry, there are stores selling every brand of motorcycle with some specializing in motorcycle accessories.

Trip 85 Carcassonne

Distance *125 kilometers, one way north into France*
Terrain *Lower mountain passes, twisting roads*
Highlights *Col de Louis (1,345 meters), Col Rigat (1,480 meters), Col de Quillane (1,713 meters), Carcassone, perhaps the most exotic and most famous walled city in Europe*

Carcassone is a double-walled fortress from the Middle Ages with lots of towers and a moat with a drawbridge. There are two hotels inside the walls of "la Cite." One is expensive. The other is Best Western Hotel le Donjon. Ride across the drawbridge to le Donjon. It has enclosed parking.

From Puigcerda and Bourg-Madame east of Andorra on the Spanish-French border, high in the Pyrenees, ride north on N116 over the lower Col de Louis and Col Rigat, then turn north on D118 over the Col de Quillane. From there, it's all twisty, tight little roads downhill into open country toward Carcassone.

Viewed from approaches in the Pyrenees, la Cite is forbiddingly impressive. All grey walls and grey towers and grey roofs. Circle it to the drawbridge and

To get into "la Cite," take this formidable drawbridge across the moat at Carcassonne.

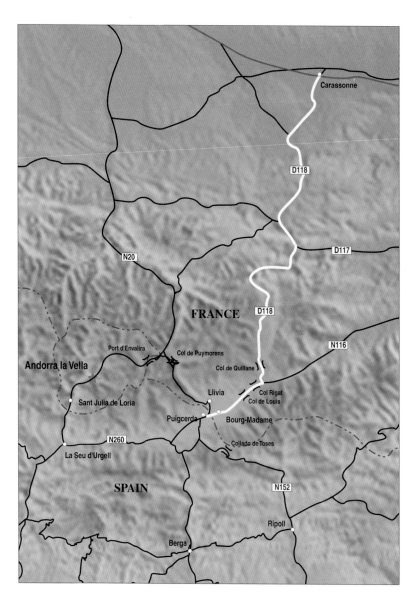

ride on across through the narrow gates into the narrow streets. It is said that la Cite was besieged in the Middle Ages by an opposing religious faction. Starved into submission, the conquering bishop ordered the slaughter of all remaining alive. His general is supposed to have objected, noting that some survivors might be true believers, to which the bishop replied, "Good. Then the Lord will recognize them."

Trip 86 Val d'Aran

Distance *160 kilometers, in Spain, one way west of Andorra*
Terrain *Winding roads over lonely mountains, skirting the south edge of the Pyrenees to a hidden forest*
Highlights *Collada del Canto (1,725 meters), Port de la Bonaigua (2,072 meters), Collada del Portillon (1,320 meters), passes leading to lush forests of the Val d'Aran, the home of Gaspar de Portola who lead the first Spanish expedition into California*

It's about 100 crow-fly kilometers west of Andorra to the next opportunity to cross the Pyrenees between Spain and France at Vielha. The best and practically only route west to Vielha crosses wide open and lonely spaces on the Spanish

From the heights of the Port de la Bonaigua the green of the Val d'Aran comes into view.

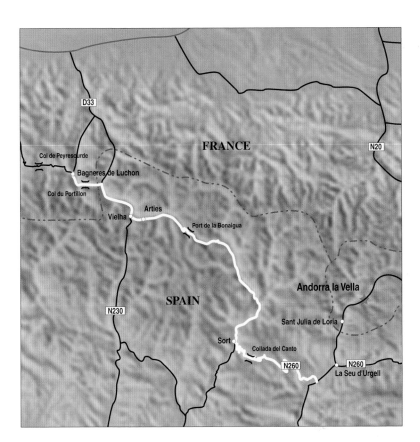

side. This route starts south of Andorra and six kilometers on south of La Seu at a country intersection where N260 starts up and west over the Collada del Canto to a village, Sort, in the next valley. Then, north from Sort, the route climbs higher in the Pyrenees through seemingly empty country before crossing the Port de la Bonaigua where a small restaurant will grill you a fine lunch with a view. From the port, the road descends into the beautiful Val d'Aran on the north side of the Pyrenees, still in Spain, covered with dense coniferous forests.

Down at Arties in the Val d'Aran, the road passes the home of Gaspar de Portola, now a Parador. At Vielha there's an intersection with a main road, N230, heading north through the valley down into France or back to the south side of the Pyrenees through a tunnel toward Lleida. Before the tunnel, Parador Vielha is handsomely sited just a couple of hairpins above the town with views of the densely forested valley and the peaks of the Pyrenees.

France is 26 kilometers down and north from Vielha. But before the border, there's a turn west for a steep climb up the Col du Portillon into France at Bagneres de Luchon.

Trip 87 Lourdes Highs

Distance *160 kilometers, one way*
Terrain *High twisting mountain roads in France, westerly across the north flank of the Pyrenees*
Highlights *The major pilgrimage center of Lourdes, Tour de France favorites ★Col d'Aubisque (1,709 meters), ★★Col du Tourmalet (2,115 meters), Col du Soulor (1,474 meters), Col d'Aspin (1,304 meters), Col de Peyresourde (1,569 meters), Port del Portelet (1,794 meters)*

Lourdes, in the foothills of the Pyrenees, is where the girl, Bernadette, reported that she saw the Virgin, back in the mid-19th century. Since then, it has become a major destination for pilgrims by the hundreds of thousands, so there are all kinds of facilities in the area. It's northwest of the border crossing from the Val d'Aran at Bagneres de Luchon, Trip 86.

This route follows the highest possible passes west from Bagneres de Luchon crossing above Lourdes and several routes down to it.

Close to the north side of the town, Bagneres de Luchon, is the turn west on D618 up over the Col de Peyresourde. The intersection is not well marked, but the road is interestingly twisty across into the next valley where it intersects a road coming down out of Spain. The road from Spain crosses the Pyrenees

It's spring snow in the high Pyrenees as seen from the Col d'Aspin in France.

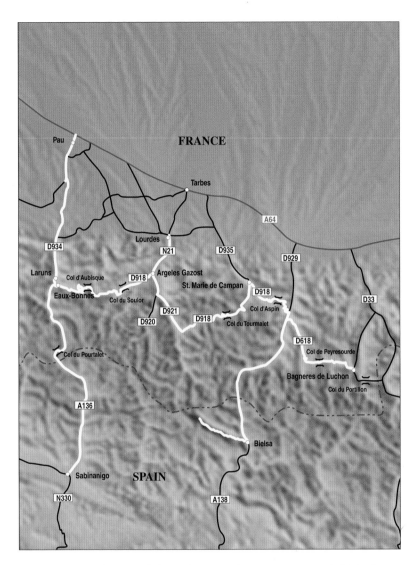

through the Bielsa tunnel from the Spanish Parque Nacional de Ordesa y Monte Perdido. Just through the tunnel, on the Spanish side, in the park, there's a road west up the Valle de Pineta into a spectacular bowl of vertical cliffs and little waterfalls tumbling off of peaks towering to 3,300 meters. At the end of the road, practically in the center of the bowl, is Parador Bielsa.

But straight across that road from Spain, D918 is beginning its climb further west over the Col d'Aspin. It traverses up the mountainside, crosses a higher plain, and comes down to a small village called Sainte Marie de Campan which is important because it's the easterly base of the mighty Col du Tourmalet.

What do you do when the fence across the pass road says "Route Barree?"

Turn south following D918 at Sainte Marie and start the climb up the Col du Tourmalet. At the top are wondrous views of snow capped mountains. Then on down west, the road is more difficult. As it opens into vast green fields, there are usually vendors selling food in open cafes. On down the road through the Gorge de Luz at Argeles Gazost, it's only thirteen kilometers to Lourdes.

On the French side of the Pyrenees, atop the Col du Tourmalet, it really seems like the Alps.

Here's a view of some of the cliffs and waterfalls coming off them in the bowl of granite above the Parador Bielsa.

But at Argeles, D918 turns west again toward the Col du Soulor. The road is fairly open, until it turns up at the pass. Just over it is the turn west to the famous Col d'Aubisque. This col is quite narrow, a corniche, barely hanging on the mountain edge, twisting around the base of cliffs on one side with deep drop-offs on the other. Then it comes down in a pleasant town, Eaux-Bonnes, and then to a major north-south road at Laruns. North, on downstream, is the large city Pau and the autoroute to the Atlantic. South over the Col du Pourtalet is Spain and Huesca and Zaragoza and the autopista to the Atlantic.

Once a group of American riders sporting German license plates was stymied at Sainte Marie by a fence across with the sign, ROUTE BARREE. Just then, a Gold Wing rider came down off the pass, rode around the fence and shouted in English, "You may do the Tourmelet." So they did, riding around the fence on the other side of the pass, too.

Trip 88 Fuente De in the Picos de Europa

Distance *About 250 kilometers*
Terrain *Twisty gorge roads and mountain passes*
Highlights *Central bowl of the Picos, twisting gorges, pre-historic caves, preserved village, Puerto de San Glorio (1,609 meters}, Puerto del Ponton (1,280 meters)*

Santillana del Mar is not del Mar. It's about five kilometers from the Mar, about 20 kilometers west of Santander and about 200 kilometers west of the French border. It's a preserved 17th century village that's about five kilometers from the 18,000 year old pre-historic cave of Altamira. The cave was uncovered about 1880. It has painted pictures of bison, horses, deer, hands, and mysterious signs. Both the village and the cave are worth a visit. There are two Paradores in the

Up in a high dead-end valley in the center of the Picos is the Parador Fuente De.

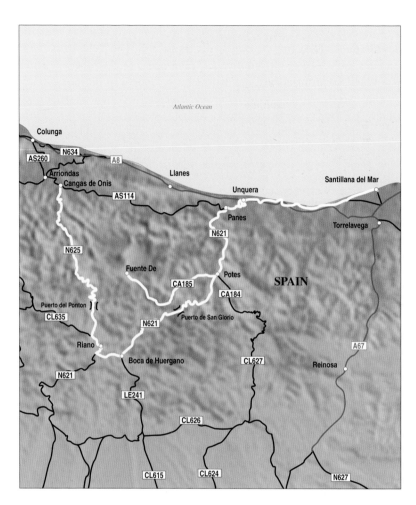

village, and the only way to legally ride on slippery cobblestones into the handsome and lovely village is to visit the Paradores. Otherwise park outside. The cave is world famous with a museum and a walk-in tour of a carbon-copy cave. People breathing in the real cave were destroying the old paintings.

From Santillana there's a scenic and pleasant coastal road about 50 kilometers west to Unquera and a south turn up the Val de San Vicente on N62 which becomes N621. Soon, the Val becomes a gorge and the road gets to twist excitingly alongside the stream that made the gorge through the Desfiladero de la Hermida up to Potes. A road west from Potes climbs 25 kilometers up to about 1,200 meters into a bowl surrounded by peaks over 2,000 meters high. At the end of the road is a village called Fuente De with a Parador and a hotel and a cable car ride up to one of the peaks. The Parador is built with shutters enclosing balconies, so the facade is all shutters.

Back down at Potes, turn south on N621 up the mountain to the Puerto de San Glorio, with exciting views in all directions. Down westerly, off the pass, now in Castilla y Leon, the countryside is more open around a reservoir with a new town, Riano, apparently built to replace one flooded by the reservoir. Just six kilometers further northwest around the reservoir from Riano is a wide open country intersection and a turn north on N625. An easy climb leads to Puerto del Ponton. Then the fun begins with fine asphalt and banked curves, some tight, down through the Desfiladero de los Beyos, daylighting at Cangas de Onis about fifteen kilometers from the Atlantic. Cangas has most facilities, including a Parador.

A wonderful sweeping ride awaits through the Desfiladero de los Bayos.

Santillana del Mar is "near" the Atlantic, on the east edge of the Picos de Europa. It's a preserved village with no traffic allowed on its cobblestone streets except for those visiting the Paradores.

There are two Paradores in the village, this one is just called Santillana.

Trip 89 Mirador del Fito

Distance *About 250 kilometers*
Terrain *Fine mountain and coastal roads*
Highlights *Ocean views to die for, mountain passes on the dry side of the Picos, Mirador del Fito, Puerto San Isidro (1,520 meters), Las Senales (1,625 meters), Puerto de Tarna (1,490 meters), Puerto del Ponton (1,280 meters)*

A couple of kilometers downstream from Cangas is Arriondas. Most traffic goes right or left. Don't. Jog through the village and out the far side on AS260. It's a wonderful climb over the Cordillera de Fito. Perfect pavement, perfectly banked up through a beautiful forest to the Mirador del Fito at about 630 meters. There's a small refreshment stand. Park and climb up and around to the top of the peak, and then up the spectacular cantilevered platform for sweeping views down over lush farms and tile roofed houses, the blue Atlantic on one side, and the granite mountain peaks of the Picos on the other.

Across the Fito, the road down is more open in long traverses. Just short of the ocean, the road crosses under an autopista to a minor coastal road. The coastal road wanders almost aimlessly in a westerly direction without many chances to view the coast. Take it or the autopista about 25 kilometers west and inland to an exit for Nava and N634. East five kilomteters, at Nava, find tiny

These riders are heading down the north (Atlantic) side of the Mirador del Fito.

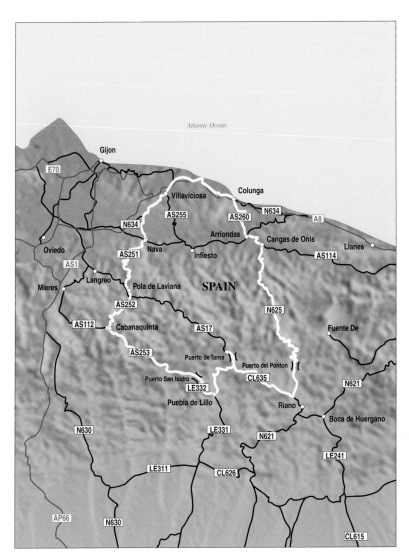

AS251 which climbs in a snakey fashion over the next mountain range to Pola, and then on south on AS252 to Cabanaquinta. East on AS253 climbs easily with just a couple of tight corners to the Puerto San Isidro. Across the puerto, the descent into Castilla y Leon is quicker. In only 16 kilometers, a sharp left turn, out in the country, on LE333 keeps to the heights on a tiny little road over Las Senales. Just a couple of kilometers over Las Senales is Puerto de Tarna. Turn southeast at the puerto, and in 20 kilometers come upon the reservoir of Trip 88. At the wide open country intersection, turn north over the Puerto del Ponton and down through the Desfiladero de los Beyos to Cangas.

From the cantilevered view platform atop Mirador del Fito, you can note the proximity of the peaks of the Picos de Europa to the Atlantic Ocean.

A rider is enjoying the sweepers through the forests of the south side of the Mirador del Fito road.

Appendices

Good Stuff to Know

OF SHOWER CURTAINS, WINDOW SCREENS, SEALING WAX, AND HAIR DRYERS

Okay, if the Alps are so great, how come:

1. There aren't any window screens?
2. Or wash cloths?
3. The shower curtains are too small or non-existent?
4. My hair dryer fries?
5. Double beds aren't?
6. The feather bed is too hot and too small?
7. The steak is tough?
8. Water's rationed?
9. There aren't any laundromats?
10. There's that extra appliance in the bathroom?
11. They can't count?

1.   It's true. The Alps are full of cows and all. They tinkle their bells and so forth everywhere. And there are no window screens in the Alps. Mechanically, there isn't a double-hung window in the Alps. All windows are on hinges, so screens aren't handy, and the finest establishment may have flies. Almost all hotel rooms have a sheer curtain that can serve as a screen at night.

2.   In the Alps, only branches of American hotel chains have wash cloths. Others may have a tray of toiletries, needle and thread, a razor, and an assortment of towels of all sizes, but no wash cloths. If a wash cloth is important to your lifestyle, bring one from the New World.

3.   For some reason, you're expected to sit down in the tub to shower with a hand-held shower on a flexible hose. So, why would you need a shower curtain? Some suggest that you are expected to wash before you shower. Maybe because Americans have flooded too many bathrooms, shower curtains are gaining a foothold in the Alps.

4.   American appliances will not fit European plugs, voltage, or cycles. European plugs are round, and the prongs are too. Adapters are available, but their use usually burns up the appliance and trips the circuit breaker, leaving everybody unshaven, undried, and in the dark. Some electric razors will switch to 220, and will work with an adapter. Some hotels have outlets in the bath good for 110 SHAVERS ONLY. They will not work with hair dryers. Hair

dryers of modest price are available in Europe. Better to buy one there if it's absolutely needed. But they take up so much room! To save them and us the hassle, many hotels now have built-in hair dryers.

5.   Almost all double beds are two singles pushed together. Sometimes, expressing a desire for a *grand lit* (a big bed, say grahn lee), or a "matrimonial bed," will help.

6.   Everywhere that the Alps speak German—in Germany, Austria, north and west Switzerland, and the Sud Tirol part of Italy—beds have feather beds. A feather bed is like a giant pillow, or maybe a fat comforter. It rests in a big hump on the bed, which otherwise is more or less similar to a bed anywhere. That means there's a sheet on the mattress, but no blankets, no cover sheet, and no bedspread. Just a luxurious feather bed stuffed inside a washable cover. Feather beds vary in size and quilting. Without quilting, all the feathers may end up in one spot. Hardly ever will the thing cover the shoulders and feet at the same time. Some, in frustration, have been known to take the cover off the feather bed and crawl inside the cover. Better to curl up with the feather bed. It can be wonderful. If hot, leave a leg out, or more.

7.   Steak is not an Alpine specialty. The hills are alive with music . . . it's cow bells. *Cow bells.* Not bull bells or steer bells. Boy cows become veal. The Alps have wonderful veal in all kinds of creative ways. But steak is very likely a mature cow. Schnitzel is a cutlet, usually veal, but sometimes pork. Wiener Schnitzel can be either. Pork is usually cheaper.

8.   Drinking tap water is very American. It's not customary in Europe. There's absolutely nothing wrong with drinking tap water in the Alps. It is always safe. But Europeans don't think it's a nice thing to do in public. Most hotel operators know that Americans have the uncouth habit of drinking water, even with meals, and they probably will make a modest carafe available upon request, but don't be surprised if the cook objects. It's reassuring to note that in the interest of safe driving, even the French have cut wine consumption dramatically in recent years, and Oktoberfest tents in Munchen are required to have alcohol-free drinks available. If it becomes an issue, get mineral water, with or without "gas." Some presumptuous hotels with stocked refrigerators in the room may have a little sign in the bathroom advising against drinking the tap water. It's a ruse.

9.   There are hardly any self-laundries in Europe. For whatever reason, entrepreneurs don't deem them worthy. Be prepared to hand-wash whatever needs washing. Detergent works better than soap. Finer hotels will have pricey laundry service.

10.   Hotel baths in Italy and France very often have bidets. They're for washing what's hard to wash in a basin. And for rinsing socks. (Don't be confused by the European use of the word "dusche." It means shower.)

11.   In Europe, the ground floor of a building is just that, the ground, the earth, terra firma. So the next floor up must be the first floor. And what Americans would call the third floor is clearly labeled "2," etc.

REST STOPS

A roadside Gasthaus, hotel, or restaurant is a logical rest stop in the Alps. It's diplomatic to order something from the bar before using the facilities. Coffee, tea, and hot chocolate come from the bar in Europe, and each is made one cup at a time. No refills. In the home of Swiss chocolate, hot chocolate is a cup of hot milk and a package of powder (the real thing is in Italy). A hot fudge sundae is always good in Switzerland and is called a Coupe Danemark. In Switzerland, Sinalco is a carbonated grapefruit drink, and Rivella tastes something like ginger ale. If you like the fizz, stop the waiter before the drink is dumped in a glass. There's always beer and wine, though most Euro restaurants feature only one local brew and few bars have hard liquor. Since the waiter will be charged for your order, pay and tip the waiter directly. In the Swiss countryside, the only currency is the Swiss Franc (a credit card slip signed in Swiss Francs will come home in dollars). If the bill is hand-written, remember that a European numeral "1" looks like an American "7," while Euro sevens have a horizontal line through them, and Europeans use a comma where Americans use a decimal point.

Spezi (say SPAIT zee) is a cola drink available in Bavaria and Austria. Soft drinks are a little less varied in France and Italy, so mineral water should be a safe bet.

Cold drinks hardly ever have ice. Ice cubes (*Eiswurfel* in German) are a rarity. Some warmer climes have started serving ice water.

WHEN

When is the best time to ride the Alps? Spring? Summer? Fall? The best time is as soon as possible, of course.

Late spring, May, and June, are spectacular. Eighteen hours of daylight illuminate meadows carpeted with new yellow and blue flowers. Flower boxes have new geraniums. High mountains, still snow capped, are awesome backdrops to larch trees, just showing new green needles. Gorges are gorged with white water. Temperatures are moderate, yet the high passes cut through deep canyons of snow. Even the southernmost reaches of the Alps should be temperate. The only problem is that some passes may still be snowed in. Any pass needed for access or commerce will be open, but those just for playing on, the more remote ones, may be awaiting sun and snow plows.

Come summer, all the passes open, and the south warms up. Seldom are the Alps really hot by American standards, but Italy and the south of France can be. August is vacation time in Europe, so major areas can be peopled, and prices may reflect "high season." Flower boxes are masses of pink, red, purple, and yellow. Whole families rake and mow steep mountain meadows. Cow bells tinkle until dark.

Fall can turn the meadows pink. Mountain ash trees are loaded with orange berries. Near the tree line, larch needles are turning yellow. Last winter's deep snows are long gone and the mountains show rocky faces. Streams are drier. Days are shorter. Most of the tourists go home. Sometimes a passing weather front can dust the mountains with new snow, perfectly etching each formation and crevice. Fields of brilliant yellow-gold are "rape," a plant whose seed produces vegetable oil and biodegradable plastic.

Each Alpine country has special holidays. Sometimes, only one part of a country has a holiday. On one side of a pass, everything is closed. Across the pass, everything is open. Like in the U.S., holidays are arranged to make a three day weekend. Then everything closes and everybody goes someplace. In order to avoid arriving for a big trip only to find everything locked up, it's wise to check ahead. Many family run hotels and restaurants close for one day a week. In Germanic areas you may be greeted by locked doors and a little sign, RUHETAG, quiet day.

Some claim that there is less rain in the fall but any season in the Alps is a good season.

WHAT TO WEAR

Europeans *expect* motorcyclists to be fully dressed in motorcycle gear, probably full leathers. A motorcyclist in full gear will be welcome anywhere in the Alps.

Ideally, wear full leathers as the primary article of attire all the time. They're lightweight, versatile, protective, not too bulky, and good in most Alpine weather conditions. All that you need under them is easily washed and dried underwear, and possibly a turtle neck.

A rain suit should go on easily over the leathers. The simplest is a hip-length jacket over elastic-waisted pants. (The jacket goes on first, so you don't get soaked pulling on the pants and so either top or bottom can be entered easily for keys or passport or whatever, without removing the other part.) One-piece rain suits work fine at keeping water out, but they sometimes are hard to get into and out of, especially dancing on the edge of the traveled lane, or in a small WC (water closet; toilet—the term "rest room" is meaningless in Europe). Soleless, snap-on rain booties are effective and easy to use. Some Gortex boots really are waterproof. Most rain boots are very hard to get on, and won't last if walked in. Remember, the boots go under the pants. Stores selling safety equipment have cheap and effective rain gloves to wear *over* leather gloves.

For cold, there should be a jacket to wear *over*, not under, the leathers. American softies have been known to enjoy an electric vest.

Leathers can be wiped off and debugged at the end of the day, and underwear washed in the basin if necessary, but jeans draped over the flower boxes on the balcony probably won't dry overnight.

Sport clothing, maybe just a colorful warmup suit, will last a long time between washings if it's worn only a couple of hours in the evening.

TWO-NIGHT STANDS: A HOME BASE

When you're reading a tour brochure at home, it does seem exciting to actually contemplate 12 exotic hotels in two weeks. But that takes a lot of packing and unpacking and hotel adjustment to move lineally along the road. Instead, how about establishing a base camp in an interesting smaller town like Andermatt? That means at least a couple of days of baggage-free riding; convenient, almost familiar, stores and shops; and a knowable home base at the end of each great riding day.

GAS AND OIL AND SERVICE AND TIRES

Some Alpine roads seem otherworldly, like a wild moonscape. But the Alps are not Siberia, or even Alaska. Even the most remote mountain pass is just a few kilometers from civilization. Europe has a well-motorcycled population. There are services and probably motorcyclists in every town and village, down at the bottom of the pass. And if you're at the top of the pass, everything is downhill.

Gas stations are plentiful, but not on mountain tops. Since they weren't in any medieval town plan, most are located outside the historical old parts of cities and towns and near the edge of smaller communities. Everything about a gas station looks familiar, with pumps and islands—everything, that is, but the price, which will be three or four times the U.S. price. Both gas and oil are sold by the liter. Leaded gas is being phased out, but both leaded and unleaded have higher octane than is available in the U.S.

In many smaller localities, stations close for a two-hour lunch at noon. Some stations announce that they are open (little signs, APERTO, or OUVERT), but only for drivers paying via automated credit card or cash machines.

Air is most likely available from a portable canister with a dial on the top. The canister hangs from a filler valve. Usually, the dial has pressure readings in both metric and pounds. Take the canister over to your tire. It should have a plus and a minus button for pressure regulation. The metric unit of pressure is kilograms per square centimeter (usually called "bar"). One pound per square inch equals 0.07 bar; 33 pounds per square inch is about 2.33 bar. Finicky tire adjusters might want to carry a pocket gauge.

Most communities of any size have at least one motorcycle shop. At many the staff may appear busy even if they are not, so scheduling service in advance is wise. Store hours and days vary. Most depend on overnight delivery of parts from some central warehouse. Best way to find a shop is in the phone book, the yellow pages, or in motorcycle magazines, or by asking another biker. Smiles and pointing always help in an emergency. Pointing at a worn tire or a brake pad or a headlamp, etc., will register with most riders, dealers, and mechanics. They've probably been on the wrong side of a language barrier themselves.

This gas station in the Dolomites is Geoffenet, aperto, with an attendant who will take credit cards.

An American on the Italian island of Sardinia once cracked a wheel hub on a BMW ST, not a very common bike. Calling around and using all possible translators, he learned about an overnight ferry from Sardinia to Genova on the mainland. The broken BMW was to take the ferry to Genova. Meantime, the BMW dealer in Genova would order a new hub from the BMW importer in Verona, Italy, and the hub would get to Genova overnight, too. The bike made it on the ferry. Other bikers on the ferry helped find the dealer in Genova. The hub arrived from Verona as scheduled, delivered by a 3-wheeled Lambretta truck. The wheel was laced and the American was off and running for the Alps that day (Italian headquarters for BMW bikes are now in Milano).

Accelerating and braking and leaning on twisty roads all day long may wear tires faster than normal. Nothing spoils the enjoyment of a good road like worrying about a tire. Many motorcycle shops do not sell motorcycle tires. Tire stores do and usually they will mount them for you. A motorcycle dealer may send out to the tire store for the needed tire and then mount it for you. Dealers will want to follow the law, which requires them to mount only matching, factory approved tires.

CALLING AMERICA

Most U.S. telephone companies have a "USA Direct" service. In each foreign country there's a toll-free number to call and the U.S. operator answers. It's cheaper and it's easier than dialing direct. The charge goes on your credit card or phone bill. A call from a hotel room using the USA Direct number should not record on a hotel's billing machines. Before you leave, get the toll free numbers for each country you plan to visit from your company (AT&T, MCI, Sprint).

CALLING EUROPE

It's really cheap during low-rate hours. Mid-day in Europe is early morning in the U.S.—the cheapest time to call.

In the U.S. dial 011 to get the international circuit. Then dial the country code (43 for Austria, 33 for France, 49 for Germany, 39 for Italy, 34 for Spain, or 41 for Liechtenstein and Switzerland), then the area code (for example, the area code for Andermatt is 41) and the desired number.

Most Europeans list their phone with the area code first, and a zero in front of the area code. The zero is like a "1" in America. Use it the same way. Dial it first to call out of the local area from within the same country. It isn't necessary if the call is originating inside that area, or if calling from another country. When calling to a European country from America or any other country, just use the country code and the area code. No zero. Except Italy. Italy has changed to require the zero on international calls.

Of course, the answering party may speak very fast in German or Italian or some other language. If uncertain, ask for "English, please."

Except for big city hotels, hotel staffs in Europe go to bed, so there may not be any answer in the middle of the night.

Almost every European business has a fax.

CELL PHONES

Cell phones are big in the Alps. The street sweeper has one. Everybody has one. They're usually called "Handys."

Most North American cell phones use CDMA technology. Europe uses GSM. And European GSM uses a different frequency than GSM phones in North America.

Most cellular phone companies offer a program to make your North American phone compatible. With some you can keep the North American number. Check before you go.

DEMI-PENSION

All the hotels listed in this book have been enjoyed. All will serve well. All rooms have private baths. Some are exceptionally attractive, worth a special journey just to stay in them. Please note, none are in cities, none are expensive by American standards. Most will seem reasonably priced, especially if meals are considered in the total. The few that are a bit more expensive will have clues here, like "exceptionally attractive," and "pampering service." Keep in mind that French hotels are likely to expend more resources on dining than on accommodations. Prices will vary by season and the exchange rate. Policies in Washington, or New York, or Zurich will affect what you pay more than what the hotel actually charges, so it doesn't seem practical here to quote prices.

Almost every hotel in Europe will make a special price for "demi-pension," half pension, which is room, dinner, and breakfast. Full pension includes lunch. Quite often demi-pension is a good deal, and may be a necessity in remote locations. Sometimes there will be a choice available at dinner, sometimes not. Most of the time, breakfast is a buffet with a variety of wonderful fresh breads (no breakfast until the bakery has delivered), cold cuts, cheese, and possibly nowadays, juice and fruit, but hardly ever eggs.

Demi-pension prices are per-person. Often a hotel is listed as a "garni," or "pension," usually meaning it has no public restaurant, although it should serve breakfast.

Bread and rolls are delicious in Europe and are served at all meals. Most Europeans visiting the U.S. say what they miss most is good bread. Good beer is a distant second. In Europe, butter comes only at breakfast.

Campgrounds abound in the Alps and usually have fine facilities.

Addresses, phone, fax, and e-mail addresses for hotels listed in the text are in the Appendices.

CASH MONEY

It's best to have cash money for small purchases like coffee or cappuccino. One side of a border may have cappuccino and the other side not, but it can be bought with the same currency, the Euro. No more lire (one lira, two lire) with columns of zeros. No more Deutsche Marks, no more French francs, no more Austrian schillings. Money is the Euro. Except in Switzerland. Swiss Francs still rule in Switzerland.

So, away with little baggies to keep currencies and coins separate. No more of those little purses, no more billfolds with multiple pockets. No more long division or multiplication problems trying to figure out just how much 43,000 lire is going to cost in dollars.

It's never advantageous to change twice, for example, to get Euros for dollars in Switzerland. There'll be a fee for changing to Swiss francs, then another for changing to Euros. (In some languages "Eu" is pronounced "oy" like in boy or toy, so the money is called "oy row" not "you row").

The Euro has paper bills varying in size and color in accordance with the denomination, each decorated with pictures of different epochs in European history. Each epoch has a bridge on one side (the Pont du Gard in France, for the Roman period), and a window on the other side. Coins are all the same on the front, with the back side varying with the country of origin. Presumably, they're good everywhere. Except, of course, in Switzerland and Slovenia. Neither belongs to the European Union.

There are banks in all international arrival airports. That's the recommended place to acquire Euros or Swiss francs. You don't need them before you get there.

Credit card transactions are always in the local currency, and ATMs usually accept American cards and spit out Euros or Swiss francs. Your account will be charged in your currency at a bank exchange rate that is probably better than any other. Banks and train stations usually have exchanges. In rural train stations, the ticket seller may do the changing. Sometimes it's necessary to go to one teller to make the exchange, and then to a cashier to get the money. Banks often have a double door system that admits people one at a time. Sometimes you have to push a button.

Most American credit cards have toll-free numbers to call in each European country in case the card is lost. It's probably good to keep these numbers separate from the card.

PASSPORTS AND STUFF

Border guards between countries in the European Union are fast disappearing. (Switzerland isn't in the Union.)

When there are guards (also at airports) there are two checks: a passport check, to identify the person; and a customs check to identify the "stuff." At most small border crossings in the Alps, the same official checks both. But there will still be two checks. The country you're leaving will check you out. Then, after you've crossed the border, the country you're entering will check you in. The two checks may be some kilometers apart. Usually, the customs folk are more interested in what natives may be bringing back than what visitors are carrying. With the coming of the European Union, there is less hassle, even about insurance, since it's assumed that everyone must be legal. Should a border guard note a non-European license plate, he'll very likely decide to check insurance papers. On some remote unstaffed crossings, a little sign may say something to the effect of, "If you have something to declare, stop in the next town."

Remember that you and your bike are passing through, not staying, so Americans don't need visas, but you must have a valid driver's license, and preferably an international one (available from auto clubs in the U.S.) as well as a passport.

A thin wallet on a string around your neck is handy for passports and official papers. Hiking, camping, and bicycle shops in America, and motorcycle shops in Europe sell inexpensive ones. A passport in your luggage is almost useless.

Photocopies of passport, driver's license, traveler's check numbers, vehicle registration, and airplane ticket (the big long ticket number is important should the ticket be lost) can be stashed in various bags.

SO WHAT ARE WE GOING TO CALL IT?

We call it Germany. Italians call it Germania or Tedesco! French call it Allemagne. But the Germans call it Deutschland.

We call it Lake Geneva. Germans call it Genfer See. The folks who live there call it Lac Leman.

We call it Venice. So do the French. The Germans call it Venedig. Italians call it Venezia. When you're there, Vienna is Wien (say vean).

Most of us call it the Matterhorn. But half of it is in Italy where it's Monte Cervino.

Most signs will be local. So will most maps. So, it's the intent here to use local names. The exception: herein it's Germany and Austria and Italy, not Deutschland and Osterreich and Italia, even though that's what local signs will say (except in Italy, where signs pointing to Austria will say Austria). The international code is used everywhere in the Alps, and here: (D) is Deutschland, Germany; (A) is Osterreich, Austria; (CH) is Die Schweiz, Switzerland; (I) is Italia, Italy; (F) is France; (FL) is Liechtenstein; (SLO) is Slovenia; and Spanish vehicles have an (E) for Espana. Accordingly, Swiss bikes and cars are identified by a "CH" sticker, presumably for *Confederation Helvetia.*

Germans put two dots over some vowels. They are called "umlauts" and are supposed to help in pronunciation. For example, there are supposed to be two dots over the "u" in Zürich and also over the "u" in München. Some texts leave out the dots but add an "e", so it's Zuerich and Muenchen. That all seems confusing. Here, there will be no dots and no "e"s.

Sometimes Germans use a letter that looks something like a capital "B" (β) instead of a double "s" at the end of a word like "pass." Here, it will always be double "s".

And, Germans have the habit of tacking modifiers onto a word without spacing, so that a menu item might read "Grandmothersrecipeforsteakontoast," or a highway sign, OBERALPPASS. Here it will be "grandmothers recipe for steak on toast," and "Oberalp Pass."

BESONDER UBERWACHUNG UND VERSICHERUNG UND UMLEITUNG, OR, "SPECIAL WATCHING AND INSURANCE AND DETOUR"

Some German words don't slide easily from the English tongue. The French and Italian equivalents almost make good sense. But a couple of German words like those above are not in most handy "where is a good restaurant?" guides.

BESONDER UBERWACHUNG is on signs around Austria under a picture of a motorcycle. Motorcyclists will be especially watched! Other signs at Austrian borders advise that Austrian police use radar "in the whole land." Radar traps exist, especially in Austria. Typically, there is an unmarked radar in some area with a speed limit, like a village of a couple of houses, and the police wait farther along the road at the edge of the village and pull hapless drivers or riders over, waving them in with a red "ping pong" paddle. Friendly as Austrians are, their police will extract fines on the spot in cash for speeding. Most police in Europe do the same.

Police waved a bunch of motorcyclists into a big parking lot on the edge of Interlaken, in Switzerland. Seems there'd been a radar back in the town where the speed limit is automatically 50 kilometers per hour (about 30 mph.) Each biker was fined on the spot, one modestly for a mere four kilometers over the speed limit, others several hundred Swiss francs. The police accepted Visa and Mastercard!

Recently, Austria has put signs along the road that show a motorcyclist with an angel above, and words to the effect of "give your guardian angel a chance." Switzerland has had signs picturing a rider with the words "look out." Most auto drivers assume it is the rider who is supposed to look out! Both countries keep the motorcycles pictured up to date.

Helmets are mandatory in the Alps. Some countries require headlights at all times.

The international sign showing a motorcycle (usually ancient) in profile in a red circle means "motorcycles forbidden." The key is the little white sign underneath it, reading something like "between 2230 and 0600." There's often a second white sign that reads something like "except for bikes with business in the area."

Germany has a lot of low speed limit signs, even on autobahns. The key is the little white sign underneath that says BEI NASSE, "when wet."

Versicherung, insurance, is mandatory. Proof of liability insurance is required before a vehicle license plate is issued in Europe. And it's expensive, like thousands of dollars a year. Many motorcyclists turn in their license plate for the winter to save money. Rental bikes should already be insured. Insurance should be included with any bike purchased in Europe. Bikes brought from America must have proof of European insurance before they're allowed out of customs.

Americans living or stationed in Europe can get motorcycle insurance like car insurance. But few U.S. carriers will or can sell it to American motorcyclists traveling for pleasure. European insurance companies complain of bad luck with American bikers. Proof of insurance is a green piece of paper called a green card. That's what police and border agents will want to see. It should be in hand (or pocket) before operating on any European road.

European liability (and optional collision/comprehensive) insurance can be purchased for U.S.-registered vehicles from several sources. Most companies that specialize in shipping bikes to Europe will arrange for the insurance needed (see the Appendix "So, How About a Bike?").

European automobile clubs are inclined to be more motorcycle friendly than those in America. Some think its worth joining a European club, like ADAC in Germany. Check with your American club about reciprocal services abroad.

Fun mountain roads are labor-intensive, and the labor usually can only be done in summer, when the roads are open and the ice is gone. Detours are a possibility, labeled *deviazione* in Italian and *Umleitung* in German. Sometimes a portable traffic signal allows traffic past the repair area one way at a time. It's common, though not legal, for bikes to go to the front of any line waiting for the green, with the obligation, of course, to take off fast when the light turns green so as not to delay others. A tardy response to the green will elicit some angry responses from other drivers with whom the road may have to be shared. On popular bike roads, the light may collect quite an array of motorcycles, and the green light is almost like the start of a race. It does make sense to get ahead of any trucks or buses.

WHERE ARE THEY FROM?

Everybody plays the game of guessing where their fellow travelers are from. License plates help. Cognoscenti can tell which town a long French license plate comes from. Some insist that shoes and socks (or lack thereof) are telltale. Chances are that any American will be identified as such without saying a word, especially while eating. Only right-handed Americans hold a fork in the right hand. Only Americans ever put the other hand below the table. Right-handed Europeans hold the knife in the right hand and the fork in the left. So, it's hard for an American to hide. In Europe, there have been plenty of wars, with bombings and occupations and refugees and invasions, unpleasant invasions of tourists as well as soldiers. Everybody has had plenty of opportunity to develop prejudices as well as preferences. In the long run, you might as well be identified as American as anything else.

Europeans all know of U.S. speed limits, and presume no American can go over 55. Keeping up with local traffic can be helpful as well as entertaining. British and Dutch drivers usually stand out because they have orange license plates. Both are usually very cautious in the mountains—the Dutch because they have no mountains to practice on, and the poor British because the driver is seated on the wrong side of the car and can't see the road ahead. At least both speak good English. (How far can you go speaking Dutch?) Locals are almost always more aggressive drivers than visitors.

A couple of American customs need modification in the Alps. The forefinger raised when ordering means two, like "two beers" (it is the second finger). The thumb raised means one beer. And the thumb and forefinger touching, the okay sign in America, is not okay in the Alps. The middle finger? Let's hope it's three beers.

NEWS
In America, many newsstands carry *The European,* a British paper of continental news. It is a good way to find out what's happening in the Alps, including weather, road conditions, and status of Alpine passes. In Europe, most newsstands have three American newspapers, the *Herald Tribune, USA Today,* and the *Wall St. Journal,* all printed at multiple sites in Europe.

ROAD SIGNS AND DRIVERS
Alpine signs almost always point toward towns and passes. Route numbers are obscure. It's best to know which town you're going to.

City limit signs are automatic speed limit signs, and villages and towns are where speed laws are usually enforced. Conversely, the end of a city, the city sign with a slash through it, means "resume highway speed."

Direction arrows often point *at* the road, which may not necessarily be the direction of travel. For instance, an arrow on the left side of the road pointing right most likely does not mean turn right. It means that "this is the road."

Schematic signs of anticipated intersections don't necessarily mean "now." There are often signs diagramming how roads will intersect in the next town.

You usually can't go around the block. If you miss a corner in a city, there probably will be another sign to the destination. If all else fails in a city or town, head back for the middle and start again. All towns have signs to the middle: STADTMITTE, in German, CENTRO, in Italian. French have a wonderful sign: TOUTES DIRECTIONS, meaning "you can get anywhere going this way." The yellow diamond sign used in Europe means "this road has the right of way over all entering or cross traffic." A slash mark through any sign means the end of it, whatever it was. A slash across a white circle means the end of whatever was being regulated, like the speed.

European drivers are usually very good and alert. Drivers' licenses are expensive and hard to get, and motorcycle licenses almost always require expensive schools and long periods of probation. European drivers will expect you to be competent and alert, too. If you are, they will usually accommodate you. Just remember, they consider the road to be a commodity in short supply. Anybody on it should be using it. Don't block the road. Some rules of the road and right of way are different than in America, and it sure helps to know them (for example, no turn on red in Europe, and no passing on the right on a freeway).

National attitudes about driving vary. Italians especially are inclined to think, "if it works, why not?" French riders are very aggressive about passing against oncoming traffic, sure that the other vehicles will make room. Observe. Then do what suits you. Just don't dawdle in the traveled way.

In all European towns and cities it's quite customary for motorcycles to park on the sidewalk, making sure to leave room for pedestrians.

French highways are numbered and well marked. "N" numbers are national roads and "D" numbers are department roads. These numbers are reliable (except in cities) and are used in the text here.

IN A HURRY

You can get from one part of the Alps to another in a hurry by taking a freeway (an autostrada) across Italy. The Alps arc around northern Italy from the French Riviera to Austria. So Italy is in the middle. Its autostradas are like a chord that connects ends of an arc. They may not be as romantic as riding the roads of the Alps, but you can get from one end of the Alps to the other in a few hours on the autostradas of the Po Valley. (They're toll. Push a button and take a ticket when you enter. The toll is computed from the ticket when you leave).

The train is another way to make time, maybe while you sleep. You and your bike go on the train: the bike, well-strapped down on a double deck vehicle carrier, you in a chair car or sleeper. For instance, a train loads in Munich in the afternoon and the next morning you and the bike are in the south of France. Going to or from Germany, it's the DeutscheBahn Autozug. Check the web pages.

Skid marks on mountain roads are evidence that not all drivers have been perfect. Sometimes the marks head in unsatisfactory directions.

TOURIST INFO

Each Alpine country has a tourist office in the U.S. Be warned, they are more into hiking than motorcycling.

Austrian National Tourist Office: Box 1142; New York, NY 10108-1142; 212 944-6880.

German National Tourist Office: 122 East 42nd Street, 52nd floor; New York, NY 10168-0072; 212 661-7200.

Italian Government Tourist Office: 630 Fifth Avenue, Suite 1565; New York, NY 10111; 212 245-4961.

Slovenian Tourist Office: 122 East 42nd Street, Suite 3006; 212 682-5896.

Switzerland Tourism: 608 Fifth Avenue; New York, NY 10020; 212 757-5944, www.myswitzerland.com.

Hotels

Hotel addresses here use the alphabetic country code before the postal code: A for Austria, F for France, I for Italy, CH for Switzerland, FL for Liechtenstein, D for Germany, and E for Spain. The telephone and fax numeric country codes are: Austria 43; France 33; Italy 39; Switzerland 41; Liechtenstein 41; Germany 49; Spain 34. Calling within any country use a zero before the area code just as you would use a one (1) in the U.S.

Here are a few Alpine hotels that are unique. Each in its own way will surely please.

Chapter 1. In the center of Andermatt, Switzerland. Reachable from Munchen, Zurich, and Milano. Alpen Hotel Schluessel, Andermatt, Canton Uri. The mountain village of Andermatt is quaintly rustic, with magnificent pass roads in each direction. Practically the only newer building in town is the Hotel Schluessel, built over a grocery store in the middle of the village. Rooms and baths are roomy and modern. All rooms have balconies. No lobby. Small bar and breakfast room on the top floor. Featherbeds. No restaurant.

Chapter 6. In the Rhone Alps village of Chichilane, France. South of Grenoble. Chateau de Passieres. Just off the road to the Col de Menee, on the east side of the Vercors Massif, at the entrance to the small village with the musical name, Chichiliane, is the 14th century Chateau de Passieres. It has a massive door counter-balanced with weights on pulleys. Stone turrets have circular stone stairs and stone floors worn down through centuries, and a "parlor" chock full of historic bric a brac. Modest rooms are mostly in newer construction. The bath for one room is in a turret with a four foot high door. Fine French food. Outdoor pool. Used by American and German motorcycle tour groups. The host is the entertaining bartender and his wife is the cook. French beds.

Chapter 11. In the Engadine valley of Switzerland, in the resort called Pontresina, an easy ride from Munchen, Zurich or Milano. Hotel Allegra, Pontresina, Canton Graubunden. Excitingly new and very modern with lots of glass, the hotel is on the main street of otherwise quaint Pontresina, a famous resort, just a couple of kilometers from St. Moritz, at the north base of the Bernina Pass. Elegant Hotel Allegra has been built with exciting attention to detail. Its management has been know to offer an "American motorcycle discount." Featherbeds. No restaurant.

Chapter 12. In Italy near where the Stelvio (Stilfserjoch) and Ofen and Reschen Passes meet, in the village called Mals easily available from Munchen and Zurich. Possible from Milano. Hotel Garberhof, Mals, Sud Tirol, overlooking a vast ring of mountains and a beautiful valley, the Garberhof boasts spacious rooms and gardens and generous meals served on heavy linen. A lovely indoor pool overlooks valley and mountains. Family run for generations. Pasta and featherbeds.

Chapter 13. In Italy at the north end of Lago di Garda, a day's ride from Munchen or Milano. Best Western Hotel Europa, Riva del Garda. Surrounded by Alpine mountains, Riva is a middle-ages town at the north tip of the lake. The interiors of several centuries-old buildings on the town square have been remodeled to accommodate modern hotel rooms. The town square is for pedestrians only, so an important asset of Hotel Europa is fenced parking accessible from a back street. Step out the front door into a thriving pedestrian zone full of restaurants and shops and gelaterias on the lake shore. Reasonable Italian cuisine and Italian beds. Air conditioned.

Chapter 14. In a small Italian village, in the center of the Dolomites, a day's ride from Munchen or Milano. Hotel Evaldo, Arabba, Dolomiti, Italy. Vertical massifs and mountain passes all around. Family run Hotel Evaldo has grown in a few years from a modest hotel to a wonderful resort with multiple facilities. Large garage usually full of motorcycles, individually decorated rooms, elaborate dinners, indoor pool, jacuzzi, steam room and sauna. Pasta with waiters in black tie, and featherbeds.

The indoor pool, the Hallenbad, at MoHo Hotel Glocknerhof, at the north entrance of the Grossglockner Hochalpenstrasse.

Chapter 18. In Austria, on the south end of the Grossglockner Hoch-alpenstrasse, a day's ride from Munchen and a couple of hours from Salzburg. Alpen Hotel Glocknerhof, a MoHo, Heiligenblut, Karnten, Austria. Small village Heiligenblut is nestled on the south edge of the great Grossglockner Hochalpenstrasse in the Hohe Tauern National Park.. The hotel hangs on the mountain at the entry to the village. Fine rooms, great views, nice dinner served on heavy linen with multiple courses, and a indoor pool (in German, a Hallenbad) overlooking mountains and valleys. Featherbeds, of course. (Check for a complementary pass over the Grossglockner Hochalpenstrasse).

ANDERMATT

Note, the country code for Switzerland is 41 and the area code for Andermatt is also 41. Calling from abroad, you dial 41 twice. If you're calling from within Switzerland, dial one 41 with a zero (0) before it.

Alpenhotel Schlussel (Andermatt, 41 888 7088, www.hotelschluessel.com)

Hotel 3 Konige & Post (Andermatt, 41 887 0001, www.3koenige.ch)

Hotel Monopol-Metropol (Andermatt, 41 887 1575, www.monopol-andermatt.ch)

Hotel Olivone and Post (Ticino, 41 91 872 1366)

Hotel Posthaus (Urigen, 41 879 1153, www.hotel-posthaus.ch)

Hotel Rhodannenberg (Glarus, 41 55 650 1600, www.rhodannenberg.ch)

Hotel Steingletscher (Meiringen, 41 33 975 1222, www.sustenpass.ch)

Sport Hotel Sonne (Andermatt, 41 887 1226, www.sporthotelsonne.com)

Tourist Office (Andermatt, 41 887 454, www.andermatt.ch)

THE BERNER OBERLAND

Best Western Hotel Freienhof (Thun, 41 33 277 5050, www.freienhof.ch)

City Hotel (Interlaken, 41 33 822 1022, www.city-hotel.ch)

Hotel Blumlisalp (Beatenberg, 41 33 841 4111, www.hotel-bluemlisalp.ch)

Hotel Goldey (Interlaken, 41 33 822 4445, www.goldey.ch)

Hotel Jungfrau (Lauterbrunnen, 41 33 855 3434, www.hoteljungfrau.ch)

Hotel Krebs (Interlaken, 41 33 822 7161, www.krebshotel.ch)

Hotel Rischli (Sorenberg, 41 42 488 1240, www.hotel-rischli.ch)

Hotel Schutzen (Lauterbrunnen, 41 33 855 2032, www.hotelschuetzen.com)

Motel Restaurant Brunig (Brunig; 41 33 971 1133)

Sternen Hotel am See (Beckenried, 41 620 6161, www.sternen-beckenried.ch)

Strand Hotel (Iseltwald, 41 33 845 1313)

Strand Hotel Seeblick (Faulen See, 41 33 854 2321, www.hotel-seeblick.at)

That's the Oberalp Pass starting up right in the village of Andermatt, with a new traffic circle sporting the Andermatt Bear, and the blue awning of the Monopol-Metropol Hotel. The yellow Swiss bus is coming into the village from the Schollennen Gorge. Behind the camera are the St. Gotthard and Furka Passes.

LEYSIN/VILLARS

E and G Hotels (Villars, 41 24 495 1111, www.rooms.ch)
Eurotel (Villars, 41 24 495 31313, www.eurotel-victoria.ch)
Hotel La Paix (Leysin, 41 24 494 1375, www.hotelapaix.ch)
Hotel Mont Riant (Leysin Feydey, 41 24 494 2701, www.mont-riant.ch)
Hotel Steigenberger (Gstaad-Saanen, 41 33 748 6464,
    www.gstaad-saanen.steigenberger.ch)

MONT BLANC REGION

Aux Mille Etoiles (Les Marecottes, 41 27 761 1666, www.mille-etoiles.ch)
La Mainaz (Gex, 41 50 41 3110, www.la-mainaz.com)
La Porte d'Octodure (Martigny Croix, 41 27 722 7121,
    www.porte-octodure.ch)
Hotel l'Autanic (Bourg St. Maurice, 41 33 04 79 07 0170,
    hotel.autanic@wanadoo.fr)
Hotel Le Plein Soliel (Le Rosiere, 33 04 79 06 8043, le-plein-soleil.net)
Hotel Miramonti (Cogne, 39 01 65 74 030, www.miramonticogne.com)
Relais du Foyer (Chatillon, 01 66 51 1251, www.relaisdufoyer.it)

LAC D'ANNECY

Alp Hotel (la Clusaz, 45 002 4006, info@clusaz.com)
Hotel Alpazur (Lanslebourg-Mont-Cenis, 47 905 9369,
     www.hotel-alpazur.net)
Hotel Bergerie (Bonneval-sur-Arc, 47 905 9497, www.hotel-bergerie.com)
Hotel Beau Site (Talloires, 45 060 7104)
Hotel la Charpenterie (Talloires, 45 060 7047, www.la-charpenterie.com)
Hotel le Lac (Talloires, 45 060 7108, www.hotel-le-lac.com)
Hotel Sapins (la Clusaz, 45 002 4012, info@clusaz.com)
Hotel la Villa des Fleurs (Talloires, 33 04 50 60 7114,
     www.hotel-lavilladesfleurs74.com)
Le Cottage (Talloires, 45 060 7110, www.cottagebise.com)

GRENOBLE HIGHS

Best Western Grand Hotel de Paris (Villard de Lans, 33 04 76 1006,
     www.ghp-vercors.com)
Chateau de Passieres (Chichilianne, 47 634 4548,
     www.chateau-de-passieres.fr.cx)
Hotel La Buffe (Autrans, 33 04 76 94 7070, www.la-buffe.fr)
Hotel Chalet (Gresse-en-Vercors, 47 634 3208, lechalet.free.fr)
Hotel Ibis (Gieres, 47 644 0044)
Mont Barral (Treschenu les Nonieres, 33 04 75 21 1222,
     www.hotelmontbarral-vercors.com)

THE GRAY ALPS

Chateau Renard (St. Veran Haute Alpes, 49 245 8543,
     www.hotel-chateaurenard.com)
Hotel Les Barnieres (Guillestre, 49 245 0507,
     www.hotel-lesbarnieres.com)
Hotel les Bartavelles (Embrun, 33 04 92 43 2069, www.bartavelles.com)
Hotel le Catinat Fleuri (Guillestre, 49 245 0762, www.catinat-fleuri.com)
Hotel Monte Nebin (Sampeyre, 01 75 97 7122, www.hotelmontenebin.it)
Relais du Galibier (Valloire, 47 959 0045, www.relais-galibier.com)

SOME HIGH STUFF

Alp Hotel (la Sauze, 33 04 92 81 05 04,
     en.federal-hotel.com/hotel-information_alp-hotel_74735.htm)
Azteca (Barcelonnette, 33 04 92 81 46 36, www.azteca-hotel.fr)
Hotel Le Chalet Suisse (Peone, 33 04 93 02 50 09,
     www.chalet-suisse.com)
Prieure de Molanes (Pra Loup, 33 04 92 84 11 43,
     www.prieure-praloup.com)
Le Soleil des Neiges (la Sauze, 33 04 92 81 05 01, www.soleildesneiges.fr)

Tonic Hotel (Digne-les-Bains, 33 04 92 32 20 31,
   perso.orange.fr/tonic.hotel.digne)

EN PROVENCE

Les Florets (Gigondas, 33 04 90 65 85 01, www.hotel-lesflorets.com)
Mas de Vence (Vence, 33 04 93 58 06 16,
   www.azurline.com/masvence1h.htm)
Tonic Hotel (see "Some High Stuff" above)

LAGO MAGGIORE

Hotel Carmine (Locarno-Muralto, 41 091 735 30 60,
   www.carminehotel.ch)
Hotel Consolina (San Nazzaro, 41 091 794 23 35, www.consolina.ch)
Ramada Hotel Arcadia (Locarno, 41 91 756 18 18,
   www.ramada.de/hotels/hotels_index_eng.php?hotel_code=15743)

ST. MORITZ

Hotel Allegra (Pontresina, 41 044 804 44 44, www.hotel-allegra.ch)
Hotel Garberhof (Mals, 39 0473 83 13 99, www.garberhof.com)
Hotel Hauser (St. Moritz-Dorf, 41 081 837 50 50, www.hotelhauser.ch)
Hotel Le Prese (Le Prese, 41 81 844 0333, www.hotelleprese.com)
Hotel Stelvio (Santa Maria, 41 81 858 53 58, www.stelvio-hotel.ch)
Hotel Stilfser Joch (Passo dello Stelvio), (Stelvio, 39 0342 903162)
Hotel Vittoria (Monte Spluga, 39 0343 54250)
Post Hotel Engiadina (Zuoz, 41 81 854 10 21, www.hotelengiadina.ch)

SUD TIROL

Albergo la Mela d'Oro (Sanzeno, 39 04 634 34384)
Gasthof Plorr (Ritten, 39 04 71 602 118)
Hotel Augusta (Merano, 39 04 73 222 324)
Hotel Belvedere (Molveno, 39 04 61 586 933, www.belvederemolveno.it)
Hotel Dolomitenblick (Klobenstein, 39 04 71 356 367,
   www.dolomitenblick.com)
Hotel Kabis (Villnoss, 39 04 72 840 126, www.hotel-kabis.com)
Hotel Stroblhof (St. Leonhard, 39 04 73 010 100, www.stroblhof.com)
Kurhotel Palace (Merano, 39 04 73 271 000, www.palace.it)

RIVA AND LAGO DI GARDA

Grand Hotel Riva (Riva del Garda, 39 04 64 521 800,
   www.grandhotelriva.it)
Hotel Bellevista (Riva del Garda, 39 04 64 554 271,
   www.hotelresidencebellavista.it)
Hotel Centrale (Riva del Garda, 39 04 64 552 344,
   www.welcometogardalake.com/centrale)

Hotel Europa (Riva del Garda, 39 04 64 555 433,
www.hoteleuropariva.it)

Hotel Montana (Monte Bondone, 39 04 61 948 200,
www.hotelmontana.it)

Hotel Panorama, (Pregasina, 39 04 64 520 344,
toniatti1@hotelpanoramapregasina.191.it)

Hotel Paradiso (Tremosine Pieve, 39 03 65 953 012,
www.terrazzadelbrivido.it)

Hotel San Giacomo (Brentonica, 39 04 64 391 560,
www.hotelsgiacomo.it)

Hotel Sole (Riva del Garda, 39 04 64 552 686,
www.hotelsole.net/index2.html)

Hotel Villa Miravalle (Riva del Garda, 39 04 64 552 335,
www.hotelvillamiravalle.com)

Rifugio Bocca Navene (I-37018 Malcesine, 39 04 57 501 794)

THE DOLOMITES

Hotel Col Alto (Corvara, 39 04 71 831 100, www.colalto.it)

Hotel Edith (Palmschoss, 39 04 72 521 307, www.hotel-edith.it)

Hotel Evaldo (Arabba, 39 04 36 79 109, www.hotelevaldo.com)

Hotel Kabis (St. Peter, Villnoss, 39 04 72 840 126, www.hotel-kabis.com)

Hotel Kreuzberg Pass (Sexten, 39 04 74 710 328,
www.passomontecroce.com)

Hotel Olympia (Arabba, 39 04 36 79 135, www.arabba.com)

Hotel Posta Zirm (Corvara, 39 04 71 836 175, www.postazirm.com)

Hotel de la Poste (Cortina d'Ampezzo, 0436 4271,
www.hotels.cortina.it/delaposte)

Pension La Fontana (Corvara, 39 04 71 836 000, www.lafontana.com)

Restaurant Gerard (Selva Gardena, 39 04 71 795 274,
www.chalet-gerard.com)

Tandlerstuben (St. Jakob, 43 48 73 63 550, www.tandlerstuben.at)

LIECHTENSTEIN

Hotel Adler (Damuls Bregenzerwald, 43 55 10 2200,
www.adler-damuels.at)

Hotel Landgasthof Schatzmann (Triesen, 423 399 12 12,
www.schatzmann.li)

Hotel Santis (Unterwasser, 71 999 28 11)

Hotel Warther Hof (Warth, 43 5583 3504, www.wartherhof.com)

Montana (Malbun, 43 5583 24 600, www.montanaoberlech.at)

Nurnberger's Hotel Martha Buhler (Triesenberg, 75 237 3777)

Rizlina Berg Gasthaus; FL-9497 Triesenberg Liechtenstein; 75 262 0224

Stump's Alpenrose Hotel (Wildhaus, 41 071 998 52 52,
   www.stumps-alpenrose.ch)
Tourist Office (Vaduz, 423 239 63 00, www.tourismus.li)

AUSTRIAN TIROL
Hotel Antonie (Gries in Sellrain, 43 5236 203271, www.hotel-antonie.at)
Hotel Boglerhof (Alpbach, 43 5336 52270, www.boeglerhof.at)
Hotel Capella (Neustift, 43 5226 2515, www.hotel-cappella.com)
Hotel Ferienschlossl (Haimingerberg Tirol, 5266 87178,
   ferienschloessl.hotel@telecom.at)
Hotel Linserhof (Imst, 54 12664 1516)
Hotel Muttererhof (Mutters, 43 5125 48491,
   www.hotel-muttererhof.at.tt)
Hotel Post Kassl (Oetz, 43 5252 6303, www.posthotel-kassl.at)
Hotel Post; A-6458 Vent; 5254 8119; e-mail info@vent-hotel-post.com
Hotel Post Steeg (Steeg, 43 5633 5306, www.poststeeg.at)
Kaiserhof (Berwang, 43 5674 8285, www.kaiserhof.at)
Zur Gemutlichkeit (Bschlabs, 43 5635 259, www.gemuetlichkeit.at)

DEUTSCHE ALPENSTRASSE
Brauneck (Lenggries, 80 42 2021, www.brauneck-bergbahn.de)
Lenggrieser Hof (Lenggries, 49 08042 50560, www.lenggrieser-hof.de)
Waldgasthof Buchenhain (Buchenhain, 49 8974 48840,
   www.hotelbuchenhain.de)

AUSTRIA EAST OF THE TIROL
Gailtaler Hof (Kotschach-Mauthen, 43 4715 318, www.gailtalerhof.com)
Hotel Gasthof Ursprung (Konigsleiten Wald Pinzgau, 43 06564 8253,
   www.kingshill.at/maine.html)
Hotel Glocknerhof (Heiligenblut, 43 04824 2244, www.glocknerhof.info)
Hotel Iselsbergerhof (Iselsberg, 43 4852 64112, www.iselsbergerhof.at)
Landhaus Jausern (Saalbach, 43 6541 7341, www.jausern.com)
Sporthotel Stock (Finkenberg, 43 5285 6775, www.sporthotel-stock.com)

SALZBURG LAND
Edelweiss Spitz Gasthof (Fusch am Grossglockner, 43 6545 6131)
Gasthof Brauwirt (Lengfelden, 43 6624 52163, braeuwirt@net4you.co.at)
Hochberghaus (Grunau im Alm Tal, 43 7616 8477,
   www.hochberghaus.at)
Hotel Gasthof Gmachl (Bergheim, 43 662 4521 240, www.gmachl.at)
Hotel Solaria (Obertauern, 43 6456 7250, www.hotel-solaria.at)
Motorradhotel Hubertushof (Aflenz-Kurort, 43 3861 3131)

KARNTEN LAND AND STEIERMARK

Burg Hotel (Deutschlandsberg, 43 3462 56560, www.burghotel-dl.at)
Hotel Post Hauptplatz (Villach, 43 4226 1010, www.romantik-hotel.com)
Hotel Pulverer (Bad kleinkirchheim, 43 4240 744, www.pulverer.at)
Schlosshotel Seewirt (Turracherhohe, 43 4275 8234,
    www.schlosshotel-seewirt.com)

CORSICA

Ferries

Corsica Ferries: (www.corsicaferries.com)
    in Bastia (F), 33 495 32 9595
    in Nice (F), 492 004376
    in Munchen (D), 89 389 991
    in Zurich (CH), 1 364 1600
S.N.C.M./Ferryterranee: (www.sncm.fr)
    in Nice (F) 493 136699
    in Paris (F) 139 447206
    on Corsica (F) Bastia; 495 545599
Navarma/Moby Lines: (www.simplonpc.co.uk/MobyPCs.html)
    on Corsica (F) 495 348494
Happy Lines: (I) 018 756 4530
    on Corsica (F) 495 552552

Hotels

Grand Hotel du Monte d'Oro (Vizzavona, 33 495 472106)
Hotel Belvedere (Porto, 33 495 161201, www.hotel-le-belvedere.com)
Hotel Dolce Notte (St. Florent, 33 495 370665,
    www.hotel-dolce-notte.com)
Hotel Restaurant Les Flots Bleus (Porto, 33 495 261126,
    www.hotel-lesflotsbleus.com)
Hotel Shegara (Porto Vecchio, 33 495 700431, www.shegara.fr)
Hotel Solemare (Bonifacio, 33 495 730106, www.hotel-solemare.com)
Hotel U Dragulinu (Favona, 33 495 732030, www.hoteludragulinu.com)
La Marine (Sagone, 33 495 280003, www.hotellamarinesagone.com)
Scopa Rossa (Evisa, 33 495 262022, www.hotelscoparossa.com)

PYRENEES AND PICOS

Hotels

The Paradores (www.parador.es)

Alps Pass Bagging List

How many of the 322 on this list can you bag?

To help you keep track of the passes you've bagged, here's a list based on their height in meters, in "descending" order, along with the country and trip in this book where you can find them. (Most are in the index, in alphabetical order along with all the other good places in the Alps.)

All the passes of the high Alps are on this list. That is, the ones that are roads. Some passes with names are little more than foot trails. They aren't on this list. A couple here have short unpaved sections, all noted in the text, but all can be enjoyed on road bikes. Highest is always best, just because it exists. The best rides are starred. Opinions as to elevations may vary. A meter here, a meter there, might change the rankings listed here. But the elevations seem to be from reliable sources.

The intention is to list every significant paved Alpine pass. There are a lot of passes at about 1,000 meters or less that aren't significant.

Just a few kilometers up and out of Bourg St. Maurice, the south slopes of the Cormet de Roseland seem to have entered a never-never land.

1 ★★2,862 La Bonette (F) Trip 26
2 ★★2,769 Col de lIseran (F) Trip 17
3 ★★2,758 Passo dello Stelvio (Stilfser Joch) (I) Trip 39
4 ★★2,744 Col Agnel (del Agnello) (F-I) Trip 24
5 ★2,678 Col du Restefond (F) Trip 26
6 ★★2,645 Col du Galibier (F) Trip 23
7 ★★2,621 Passo di Gavia (I) Trip 40
8 ★2,575 Grossglockner Hoch Tor (A) Trip 67
9 ★★2,509 Timmels Joch (I-A) Trip 41
10 2,501 Umbrail Pass (I-CH) Trip 39
11 ★2,478 Nufenen Pass (CH) Trip 2
12 ★2,469 Col du Grand St. Bernard (CH-I) Trip 13
13 ★2,431 Furka Pass (CH) Trips 1 & 2
14 ★2,428 Grossglockner Fuscher Tor (A) Trip 67
15 2,408 Port dEnvalira Trip 84
16 ★2,383 Fluela Pass (CH) Trip 38
17 ★★2,361 Col dIzoard (F) Trip 23
18 ★★2,351 Col de Lombarde (I-F) Trip 24
19 ★2,328 Bernina Pass (CH) Trip 39
20 ★2,327 Col de la Cayolle (F) Trip 25
21 2,320 Drei Zinnen (Tre Cime di Lavaredo) (I) Trip 56 (not a pass)
22 2,315 Forcola di Livigno (I) Trip 40
23 ★★2,312 Albula Pass (CH) Trip 38
24 2,291 Passo di Foscagno (I) Trip 40
25 ★2,284 Julier Pass (CH) Trip 36
26 2,284 Col de Sampeyre (I) Trip 24
27 2,251 Col de Sanetsch (CH) Trip 12
28 ★2,244 Passo di Sella (I) Trips 50 & 52
29 ★2,240 Col dAllos (F) Trip 25 & 27
30 ★2,239 Passo Pordoi (I) Trips 50 & 52
31 ★2,233 Passo di Giau (I) Trip 51
32 ★2,224 Susten Pass (CH) Trip 1
33 ★2,214 Penser Joch (Passo di Pennes) (I) Trip 43
34 2,210 Passo dEira (I) Trip 40
35 ★2,192 Passo di Valparola (I) Trips 50 & 52
36 ★2,188 Col du Petit St. Bernard (I-F) Trip 13
37 ★2,165 Grimsel Pass (CH) Trip 1
38 2,174 Col de Finestre (I) Trip 23
39 2,149 Ofen Pass (CH) Trip 39
40 ★2,121 Passo di Gardena (Grodner Joch) (I) Trips 50 & 52
41 ★★2,113 Splugen Pass (Spluga) (CH-I) Trip 37
42 ★★2,115 Col du Tourmalet (F) Trip 87

43 2,111 Col de Vars (F) Trip 24
44 2,108 St. Gotthard (San Gottardo) (CH) Trips 2, 3 & 31
45 ★2,105 Passo di Falzarego (I) Trips 50 & 52
46 ★2,094 Jaufen Pass (Passo di Monte Giovo) (I) Trip 43
47 ★2,087 Col de Champs (F) Trip 25
48 2,083 Col du Mt. Cenis (F-I) Trip 23
49 2,072 Port de la Bonaigua (E) Trip 86
50 2,068 Col de la Croix de Fer (F) Trip 17
51 2,065 Passo del San Bernardino (CH) Trip 32
52 2,058 Col du Lautaret (F) Trip 23
53 2,057 Passo di Fedaia (Marmolada) (I) Trips 51 & 52
54 ★2,052 Staller Sattel (I-A) Trips 57 & 66
55 ★2,047 Passo Manghen (I) Trip 54
56 2,044 Oberalp Pass (CH) Trip 3
57 2,042 Eisen Tal Hohe (Nockalmstrasse) (A) Trip 70
58 ★2,036 Bieler Hohe (Silvretta Strasse) (A) Trip 60
59 2,033 Sestriere (I) Trip 23
60 2,033 Passo di Valles (I) Trips 52 & 53
61 ★2,017 Kuhtai (A) Trip 62
62 ★2,006 Brueil (I) Trip 14 (not a pass)
63 ★2,006 Simplon Pass (Sempione) (CH) Trips 12 & 33
64 ★2,002 Wurz Joch (Passo di Erbe) (I) Trip 54
65 1,996 Col de Larche (Maddelena) (I-F) Trip 24
66 ★1,992 Passo di San Marco (I) Trip 48
67 1,989 Col de Sarenne (F) Trip 20
68 ★1,984 Col de la Madeleine (F) Trips 17 & 18
69 ★1,971 Colle San Carlo (I) Trip 13
70 1,955 Passo di Rolle (I) Trips 52 & 53
71 1,951 Col du Glandon (F) Trips 17 & 18
72 1,948 Klausen Pass (CH) Trip 4
73 ★★1,943 Passo di Croce Domini (I) Trip 48
74 ★★1,922 Cormet de Roselend (F) Trip 13
75 1,920 Heiligenbach (Nockalmstrasse) (A) Trip 70
76 1,920 Col du Puymorena (F) Trip 84
77 1,918 Passo di San Pellegrino (I) Trips 52 & 53
78 1,914 Lukmanier Pass (Lucomagno) (CH) Trip 3
79 1,909 Mount Ventoux (F) Trip 30 (not a pass)
80 ★1,896 Passo di Mortirolo (I) Trip 40
81 ★1,894 Hahntenn Joch (A) Trip 62
82 ★★1,894 Passo di Tremalzo (I) Trip 46
83 1,883 Passo Tonale (I) Trip 49
84 1,875 Passo di Campolongo (I) Trip 50 & 52

 85   1,860 lAlpe dHuez (F) Trip 20 (not a pass)
 86   1,850 Col de Montgenevre (F-I) Trip 23
 87 ★1,828 Passo di Vivione (I) Trip 48
 88   1,815 Maloja Pass (CH) Trip 37
 89   1,805 Passo Tre Croce (I) Trip 56
 90   1,805 Passo di Lavaze (I) Trips 52 & 54
 91   1,800 Collada de Toses (E) Trip 84
 92   1,794 Port del Portelet (F-E) Trip 87
 93   1,793 Arlberg Pass (A) Trip 60
 94   1,790 Sella Ciampigotto (I) Trip 57
 95   1,788 Solker Tauern Pass (A) Trip 69
 96   1,783 Turracher Hohe (A) Trip 70
 97 ★1,778 Col de la Croix (CH) Trip 10
 98   1,775 Monte Grappa (I) Trip 55 (not a pass)
 99   1,775 Arosa (CH) Trip 38 (not a pass)
100   1,773 Flexen Pass (A) Trip 60
101   1,773 Passo Forcella Staulanza (I) Trips 50 & 53
102   1,761 Furka Joch (A) Trip 60
103   1,760 Col de Joux Verte (F) Trip 15
104   1,760 Sella di Razza (I) Trip 57
105   1,760 Col de lEschelle (F-I) Trip 23
106   1,759 Furkel Sattel (I) Trip 56
107   1,745 Passo di Costalunga (Karer) (I) Trips 52 & 54
108   1,739 Radstadter Tauern Pass (A) Trip 69
109   1,731 Col de Quilliane (F) Trip 85
110   1,725 Collada del Canto (E) Trip 86
111 ★1,712 Col du Joux Plane (F) Trip 15
112   1,709 Col dAubisque (F) Trip 87
113 ★1,703 Col du Pre (F) Trip 13
114   1,700 Dr. Josef Mehrl Hutte (A) Trip 70
115   1,699 Cret de Chatillon (F) Trip 19
116   1,688 Passo Nigra (Niger Pass) (I) Trip 54
117 ★1,685 Haiming Joch (Silzer Sattel) (A) Trip 62
118   1,682 Passo Campo Carlo Magno (I) Trip 49
119   1,679 Hochtannberg Pass (A) Trip 60
120   1,678 Col de la Couillole (F) Trip 26
121   1,668 Col Valberg (F) Trip 26
122   1,668 Weinebene (A) Trip 72
123   1,664 Col du Noyer (F) Trip 21
124   1,656 Col du Lein (CH) Trip 13
125   1,650 Chamrousse (F) Trip 20
126   1,645 Col de St. Pantaleon (I) Trip 14

127 1,644 Col de Noyer (F) Trip 21
128 1,644 Klippitztorl (A) Trip 71
129 ★1,643 Glaubenberg Pass (CH) Trip 6
130 1,641 Katchberg Pass (A) Trip 70
131 ★1,640 Col di Joux (I) Trip 14
132 1,638 Col du Mollard (F) Trip 17
133 1,636 Passo di Monte Croce (Kreuzberg) (I) Trip 56
134 1,633 Col des Saisies (F) Trip 13
135 1,631 Wolfgang Pass (CH) Trip 38
136 1,616 Passo di Brocon (I) Trip 53
137 1,613 Col de la Colombiere (F) Trip 15
138 ★1,611 Glaubenbuelen Pass (CH) Trip 6
139 1,611 Vrsic Pass (SLO) Trip 74
140 1,609 Puerto San Glorio (E) Trip 88
141 1,608 Gurnigel Pass (CH) Trip 7
142 1,604 Col de Turini (F) Trip 28
143 ★1,601 Passo Duran (I) Trips 52 & 53
144 1,599 Malbun (FL) Trip 58 (not a pass)
145 1,578 Col du Telegraphe (F) Trip 23
146 1,569 Col de Peyresourde (F) Trip 87
147 1,561 Hochrindl (A) Trip 70
148 1,558 Piller Hohe (A) Trip 61
149 1,557 Nassfeld Pass (I-A) Trips 57 & 66
150 1,552 Passo Carson di Lanza (I) Trip 57
151 ★1,550 Pragel Pass (CH) Trip 4
152 1,547 Gaberl Sattel (A) Trip 72
153 1,547 Lenzerheide (CH) Trip 38
154 1,546 Col du Pillon (CH) Trip 10
155 1,543 Hirschegger Sattel (A) Trip 72
156 1,542 Forcella di Lavardet (I) Trip 57
157 1,537 Monte Bondone (I) Trip 54
158 ★1,536 Rossfeldringstrasse (D) Trip 64
159 1,531 Grand Colombier (F) Trip 16
160 1,530 Passo di Cibiana (I) Trip 53
161 1,529 Passo Cimabanche (I) Trip 56
162 1,526 Col de la Forclaz (CH) Trip 13
163 ★1,526 Kartischer Sattel (A) Trip 66
164 1,520 Puerta de San Isidro (E) Trip 89
165 1,518 Gampen Joch (Palade) (I) Trips 43 & 45
166 1,509 Jaun Pass (CH) Trip 9
167 1,507 Gerlos Pass (A) Trip 65
168 1,504 Reschen Pass (Passo Resia) (A-I) Trips 42 & 61

169 1,502 Col du Chasseral (CH) Trip 11
170 1,500 Post Alm (A) Trip 66
171 1,500 Col St. Martin (F) Trip 27
172 1,491 Mattarone (I) Trip 34
173 1,490 Puerto de Tarna (E) Trip 89
174 1,487 Faschina Joch (A) Trip 60
175 1,486 Col des Aravis (F) Trip 15
176 1,486 Champex (CH) Trip 13
177 1,480 Col Rigat (F) Trip 85
178 ★1,477 Col de Vergio (F) Trip 76
179 1,476 Passo del Zovo (I) Trip 56
180 1,474 Col du Soulor (F) Trip 87
181 1,467 Col de la Croix Fry (F) Trip 15
182 1,461 Col des Montets (F) Trip 13
183 ★1,458 Acherli Pass (CH) Trip 6
184 ★1,457 Col de Menee (F) Trip 22
185 1,449 Passo Redebus (I) Trip 54
186 1,447 Col de Marchairuz (CH) Trip 11
187 1,445 Col des Mosses (CH) Trip 10
188 1,441 Col du Festre (F) Trip 21
189 1,437 Panider Sattel (Passo di Pinei) (I) Trip 54
190 1,434 Col du Coq (F) Trip 19
191 1,433 Cavallo di Novezza (I) Trip 47
192 1,431 Col de la St. Michel (F) Trip 27
193 1,430 Reidberg Pass (D) Trip 61
194 1,425 Passo del Pura (I) Trip 57
195 1,425 Passo San Valentino (I) Trip 47
196 1,411 Col des Planches (CH) Trip 13
197 1,406 Ibergeregg (CH) Trip 4
198 1,402 Passo di Vezzena (I) Trip 55
199 1,400 Flattnitz (A) Trip 70
200 1,399 Petersberg (I) Trip 54
201 1,395 Passo Alpi de Neggia (CH) Trip 35
202 1,378 Passo di Cereda (I) Trips 52 & 53
203 1,374 Brenner Pass (A-I) Trip 61
204 1,371 Col dOrnon (F) Trip 18
205 1,369 Pas de Morgins (CH-F) Trip 15
206 1,367 Col de Rousset (f) Trip 22
207 1,367 Loibl Pass (A-SLO) Trip 75
208 1,363 Mendel Pass (Passo di Mendola) (I) Trip 43
209 1,362 Plocken Pass (I-A) Trips 57 & 66
210 1,360 Hebalpe (A) Trip 72

211 1,357 Dientener Sattel (A) Trip 67
212 1,349 Soboth (A) Trip 75
213 1,346 Col de Maure (F) Trip 27
214 1,345 Col de Louis (F) Trip 85
215 1,343 Passo di Sommo (I) Trip 55
216 1,342 Col de lAllimas (F) Trip 22
217 1,336 Berwang (Namlos) (A) Trip 62
218 1,333 Col St. Jean (F) Trip 27
219 1,320 Col de la Faucille (F) Trip 16
220 1,320 Collada del Portillon (F-E) Trip 86
221 ★1,318 Col de Grimone (F) Trip 22
222 1,311 Col de Sorba (F) Trip 81
223 1,304 Madonna di Colletto (I) Trip 24
224 1,301 Col de Pontis (F) Trip 27
225 1,298 Passo della Mauria (I) Trip 57
226 1,294 Passo di Presolana (I) Trip 48
227 ★1,293 Col de lAiguillon (CH) Trip 11
228 1,291 Filzen Sattel (A) Trip 67
229 1,289 Col de Verde (F) Trip 81
230 1,286 Cima di Sappada (I) Trip 57
231 1,283 Vue des Alpes (CH) Trip 11
232 1,280 Puerto di Ponton (D) Trips 88 & 89
233 1,279 Weissenstein (CH) Trip 11
234 1,279 Saanenmoser (CH) Trip 9
235 1,278 Schwagalp (CH) Trip 59
236 1,278 Rottenmanner Hohentauern (A) Trip 73
237 1,273 Pass Thurn (A) Trip 65
238 1,268 Col de Haute Beaume (F) Trip 22
239 1,262 Col Luitel (F) Trip 20
240 1,257 Col di Zambla (I) Trip 48
241 1,253 Aflenzer Seeberg (A) Trip 73
242 1,249 Riepl (A) Trip 75
243 1,248 Col Bayard (F) Trip 21
244 1,246 Seetaler Sattel (A) Trip 69
245 1,237 Col du Corbier (F) Trip 15
246 1,232 Prabichl Pass (A) Trip 73
247 1,230 Col de Corobin (F) Trip 27
248 1,229 Col de la Givrine (CH) Trip 16
249 1,227 Col du Mont Crosin (CH) Trip 11
250 1,222 Col de St. Alexis (F) Trip 22
251 1,220 Col de la Croix-Perrin Jaume (F) Trip 22
252 1,219 Diex Sattle (A) Trip 71

253 ★1,218 Col de Bavella (F) Trip 81
254 ★1,215 Seeburg Sattel (A) Trip 75
255 1,212 Col de lHomme Mort (F) Trip 30
256 1,209 Fern Pass (A) Trip 62
257 ★1,208 Col de Grimone (F) Trip 22
258 1,204 Iselsberg (A) Trips 66
259 1,201 Cirque de Vaumale (F) Trip 29
260 1,190 Sattelegg (CH) Trip 4
261 1,190 Passo Sella Nevea (I) Trip 74
262 1,180 Oberjoch (D-A) Trip 63
263 1,180 Col de Cabre (F) Trip 22
264 1,180 Col du Mollendruz (CH) Trip 11
265 1,176 Passo dellAprica (I) Trips 40 & 49
266 1,174 Col de Plainpalais (F) Trip 19
267 1,169 Passo Santa Barbara (I) Trip 47
268 1,169 Pack Sattel (A) Trip 72
269 1,167 Schallenberg (CH) Trip 6
270 ★1,163 Col de Vizzavona (F) Trip 80
271 1,163 Col des Gets (F) Trip 15
272 1,154 Col de lArzelier (F) Trip 22
273 1,152 Col des Etroits (CH) Trip 11
274 1,150 Col de la Forclaz (F) Trip 13
275 1,150 Passo de Predil (I-SLO) Trip 74
276 1,142 Col dEspreaux (F) Trip 21
277 1,139 Col du Cucheron (F) Trip 19
278 1,135 Ramsau (A) Trip 69
279 1,134 Col du Granier (F) Trip 19
280 1,134 Passo di Telegrafo (I) Trip 47
281 1,126 Holzleitner Sattel (A) Trip 62
282 1,120 Col de Toutes Aures (F) Trip 27
283 1,118 Ammer Sattel (A-D) Trip 62
284 1,110 Col Lebraut (F) Trip 27
285 1,110 Windische Hohe (A) Trip 74
286 1,100 Col de Proncel (F) Trip 22
287 1,097 Sudelfeld (D) Trip 64
288 1,094 Col de Sevi (F) Trip 78
289 1,093 Gaichtberg Pass (A) Trip 63
290 1,090 Wildhaus (CH) Trip 59
291 1,077 Kreuzberg Sattel (A) Trip 74
292 1,073 Wurzen Pass (A-SLO) Trip 74
293 1,068 Col de Macuegne (F) Trip 30
294 1,068 Schaid Sattel (A) Trip 75

295 1,066 Sella di Cereschiatis (I) Trip 57
296 1,065 Soboth (A) Trip 75
297 1,060 Col de Richemond (F) Trip 16
298 1,060 Col de Clavel (F) Trip 29
299 1,056 Filzmoos (A) Trip 69
300 1,054 Col de Luens (F) Trip 29
301 1,040 Col de Foureyssasse (F) Trip 21
302 1,039 Vol du Villar (F) Trip 21
303 1,039 Gurzenberg (A) Trip 71
304 1,032 Col dAyen (F) Trip 29
305 1,015 Lahn Sattel (A) Trip 73
306 1,010 Forcella di Luis (I) Trip 57
307 1,008 Brunig Pass (CH) Trip 6
308 1,002 Col de Braus Trip 28
309 995 Col de St. Eustache (F) Trip 79
310 992 Potschen Hohe (A) Trip 73
311 982 Gailberg Sattel (A) Trips 66 & 74
312 969 Pass Gschutt (A) Trip 73
313 963 Passo Zovello (I) Trip 57
314 963 Col de Vence (F) Trip 29
315 954 Pyhrn Pass (A) Trip 73
316 950 Etzel (CH) Trip 4
317 941 Achen Pass (A-D) Trip 65
318 940 Passo Durone (I) Trip 49
319 902 Col de Tamie (F) Trip 17
320 858 Kesselberg (D) Trip 64
321 849 Ursprung Pass (D-A) Trip 64
322 703 Passo di San Boldo (I) Trip 53

Special Little Roads

There are many special little roads that might have been put there just for motorcyclists to play on. It has taken me many enjoyable years to discover them; this book is my tribute to the joy they have given me. For your convenience, they are arranged according to the regions they occupy. But some of these roads are so exceptional, their potential for enjoyment so great, that they deserve to be singled out and given special consideration by any motorcyclist.

All the roads I'll mention here are described elsewhere in the book, in their appropriate geographical context. Most of them don't go anywhere in particular, certainly nowhere of commercial importance. They are not necessarily high or awesome, although some are both. Most of them have stretches that are only one lane wide. They are all paved. Some of them are short and some long. Some remain obscure even though they're close to major tourist areas or routes.

SPECIAL LITTLE ROADS IN SWITZERLAND

1. Pragel Pass between the towns of Glarus and Schwyz (part of Andermatt Trip 4).

2. Glaubenbuelen Pass between the towns of Schupfheim and Giswil (part of The Berner Oberland Trip 6).

3. Glaubenberg Pass between the towns of Entlebuch and Sarnen (also part of The Berner Oberland Trip 6).

4. Acherli Pass between Sarnen and Dallenwil, Trip 6

SPECIAL LITTLE ROADS IN FRANCE

1. Cormet de Roselend and Col du Pre between the towns of Bourg St. Maurice and Beaufort (part of Trip 13, Mont Blanc region).

2. Col de Joux Plane between the towns of Morzine and Samoens (part of Trip 15, Lac d'Annecy region).

3. Col Agnel between Guillestre in France and Sampeyre in Italy (part of Trip 23, The Gray Alps).

SPECIAL LITTLE ROADS IN ITALY

1. Colle San Carlo between the towns of Morgex and La Thuile (part of Trip 13, Mont Blanc region).

2. Passo di Croce Domini between the towns of Bagolino and Breno (part of Trip 46, Riva and Lago di Garda).

3. Passo di Vivione between the towns of Forno Allione and Shilpario (part of Trip 46, Riva and Lago di Garda).

4. Wurz Joch (Passo di Erbe) between the towns of St. Martin and Bressanone (Brixen) (part of Trip 43, Sud Tirol, and Trip 52, The Dolomites).

5. Passo Manghen between the towns of Cavalese and Borgo (part of Trip 51, The Dolomites).

6. Col di Sampeyre between Sampeyre and Donero (part of Trip 23, The Southern Alps).

7. Passo Duran between Villa and Agordo (part of Trip 51, Southern Dolomites).

SPECIAL LITTLE ROADS IN AUSTRIA

1. Furka Joch between the towns of Rankweil and Damuls (part of Trip 58, Liechtenstein, Santis, and the Arlberg).

2. Hahntenn Joch between the towns of Imst and Elmen (part of Trip 60, Austrian Tirol).

3. Haiming Joch between the village of Haiming and Ochsengarten (part of Trip 60, Austrian Tirol).

4. Zillertaler Hohenstrasse between the towns of Ried and Ramsberg (part of Trip 63, Austria East of the Tirol).

A SPECIAL LITTLE ROAD IN CORSICA

Over Col de Bigorno, from St. Florent through Muralto and down to Ponte Leccia (Trip 76).

A SPECIAL LITTLE ROAD IN SPAIN

Mirador del Fito, from Arriondas to the Atlantic Coast (Trip 89).

IF YOU HAVE ONLY A LITTLE TIME

It's better to ride a little in the Alps than not at all. So if you just have a few days, which country, which roads, should you aim for? Where will you have the most fun and see the most in just a few days? A week?

First Andermatt, Switzerland. It's covered right at the beginning of this book. The mountains are spectacular, the roads exciting, facilities plentiful, and there's no big city traffic to worry about. You can get to the area quickly by autobahn, and then leave the autobahn and traffic behind. There are several full days of riding around Andermatt.

Second, the Dolomites in northern Italy. They're covered in the section of the same name. Like those around Andermatt, the mountains are special and the roads are right up in them. Facilities are plentiful, and there is no big city traffic. You can get there quickly from the Brennero Autostrada. Several more full days of riding.

Just remember the warning in the front of this book. Alpinitis is contagious.

Other European Goals

Are all the great roads in the Alps? Aren't there any others?

Of course. But truly, all suffer in comparison to the Alps. Try the roads anywhere else, as many have. They may seem pretty good. Sometimes the scenery is almost as good. Then come back to the Alps. There's no getting around it. The roads of the Alps are the best. Nothing compares. Except Corsica.

Other areas tested, in no particular order:

NORWAY

A real challenge. There is a lot of it, about 2,400 kilometers from Oslo to the North Cape. And there's almost nobody there. Cruise posters illustrate how lovely the fjords are. They don't show how tedious and occasional the roads are. There is a lot of water. But facilities are few, modest, and very expensive. One-lane roads with trucks and buses going both ways cling to the edges of the fjords. An overlay of skid marks is a constant reminder of what may be around endless blind corners. From the fjords, the roads climb up into a tundra-like crossing to the next fjord. And Norway is a long haul from the core of Europe.

It's possible to cut some of the travel time to and from Norway by using ferries from Newcastle in the north of England or from the Netherlands, to Bergen; or from Kiel, in north Germany to Oslo. All of the ferry connections take about 18 hours. However, it's also possible to fast ferry in 2-1/2 hours from Hirtshals, Denmark, to Kristiansand, on Norway's south coast, where Beach's Motorcycle Adventures (see their listing in An Organized Tour?) offers motor-cycle tours or independent bike rentals throughout Norway. For about the price of a night in a modest hotel (less than any hotel in Norway), it's possible to get a tiny cabin on the ferry and eliminate a bunch of flat road time to boot. It is heady to ride all night in daylight. There can be a bit of a high about 1 a.m.

SARDINIA (SARDEGNA)

Visible from the south of Corsica, Sardinia is not nearly as rugged, and doesn't make the cut.

ISLE OF MAN

Since the first years of the 20th century, the first week of June has been motorcycle week on the Isle of Man. The adjective for it is Manx, for cats and for Nortons. The island is in the Irish Sea, west of England, north of Wales, and east of Ireland. The collection of enthusiasts from all over the world is a joy to be part of. The major TT races are the first weekend of June, with practice during the prior week. Practice can be as much fun as the racing. The course is all public roads about the island, totaling about 30 miles. It's open to the public except during practice hours and during races. The course is open to all on the first Sunday in June. It's come to be known as Mad Sunday, as too many amateurs overestimate their skills. The atmosphere is motorcycle-friendly.

Accommodations are working-class British, as is the food. The island has some nice roads to explore besides the course. Access is by ferry from Heysham on the Lancashire coast of England, north of Liverpool, with a weekly run from Dublin. Both take about five hours. Reservations for the ferry are essential, and can be obtained from the Isle of Man Steam Packet Company in Douglas, 1624 661661; res@steam-packet.com. Accommodation information is available from the Isle of Man Tourist Board, 01624 686766; or at their web site: www.isle-of-man.com. They do indeed speak English there, but they drive on the left, even on the TT course.

NURBURGRING

The historic and famous Nurburgring is often available to riders. It's much longer than most tracks, the north ring being about 14 kilometers, and it sweeps and wiggles through the low Eifel Mountains up near the border of Belgium, about 40 kilometers west of Koblenz. (It's easy for the English speaker to confuse the Nurburgring up north with the Bayrisch city, Nurnberg, where the war crimes trials were held after World War II.)

Many Americans have participated in the driving school held over a period of several days each summer on the Nurburgring by the BMW Clubs of Europe. Contact Werner Briel in Mulheim am der Ruhr; 020 335 8020; SchultenHL@t-online.de. The school concentrates on learning the multitudinous curves of the 'Ring. A reasonable beginning competence is presumed. It's a good place to make European contacts.

So, How About a Bike?

There are several ways to have a bike in the Alps. Each depends on two factors: time and money. Usually, a little of one will save a bit of the other.

- borrow or rent
- buy
- ship it from home
- keep a bike there

BORROW OR RENT ONE

It surely would be nice to have a friend in Europe to borrow a bike from. Lacking that, you can rent one.

Bikes are available for rent from many sources. Most of the tour operators who are known in the United States rent bikes to riders who attend their tours. However, several tour operators will also rent motorcycles to riders who are not on tour with them.

BMW rents (and sells and services) from its Niederlassungs (that's an Anglicised plural of Niederlassungen), its company-owned subsidiaries located in several major cities, including Munchen. The BMW "factory," the museum and office tower are near the Olympic Center on Peutel Ring in Munchen. BMW Niederlassung Munchen is north of that on Frankfurter Ring. (Both are easily accessible by U-Bahn, subway.) 89 35 35 180. The Niederlassungs have several rental plans and several kinds of bikes available. They accept credit cards.

Several rental sources advertise in America.

Moto-Mader, Obentfelden, Switzerland (near Zurich)

Moto-Center Thun, Thun, Switzerland, between Bern and Interlaken

Bosenberg Motorcycle Excursions in Bad Kreuznach, Germany; 067 16-7580; bosenberg@compuserve.com.

Knopf Motorcycle Touring in Heidelberg, Germany; 62 217-8213; knopftours@aol.com Knopf will meet arrivals at the Frankfurt airport.

Motor Center Thun, Switzerland; 33 439-5959; www.moto-center.ch.

Moto Touring, Milano, Italy; 02 2720 1556; www.mototouring.com.

Court Fisher of BMW Motorcycle Owners of America makes a continuous and experienced study of the motorcycle scene in Europe. Details about shipping, renting, insuring, and buying are constantly changing and he reports the shifts in the *BMW Owners News.* He is most congenial about sharing his hard-learned information from his home in Princeton, N.J., 609 924-1773.

Members of Harley Owners Group can make arrangements to rent a Harley in Europe through H.O.G. in Milwaukee.

Bikes can also be rented from a Honda dealer in Switzerland: Grisoni; CH-7302 Landquart; 81 322-7288. Landquart is in Graubunden, east of Zurich.

Ad-Mo-Tours; P.O. Box 1803, Wrightwood, CA 92397; 800 944 2356; www.admo-tours.com. Admo cooperates with many rental sites throughout Europe.

Any rental should be ready to ride; serviced, good tires, insured.

BUY ONE THERE

Some factors beyond the control of individuals, and even dealers and manufacturers, bear on the choice, and they vary from year to year and season to season.

The rate of exchange is crucial, along with the rules and cost of shipping. In some years American currencies are high and that makes everything in Europe, including motorcycles, seem like a bargain. In such circumstances, shipping a bike from America won't make much sense since they're cheaper in Europe than America and almost all bikes are available for sale. Then the opposite happens. American currency sinks in relative value and everything is cheaper in America. It then may make sense to ship your bike from America.

Then there's the matter of U.S. specifications. Only the manufacturer can certify to them, and it's practically impossible to get a non-U.S.-spec bike into the U.S. Of course, if the goal is to leave the bike in Europe, then U.S. specs are not so important, unless U.S. registration is desired.

BMW no longer has a program for European delivery of U.S. specification bikes.

Dealers all over Europe are selling new and used bikes. Magazines and papers are full of ads, just like in America. Investing some time and patience can result in a good deal. Europeans do have strict vehicle inspection, called TUV in German, that limits modifications and maintains safety and pollution controls. They also have a significant value-added tax. A dealer selling to a non-resident alien should be able to take care of everything including insurance, and possibly, the refund of the value-added tax upon proof of export.

SHIP A BIKE FROM HOME

Shipping from America can be a good deal, but it's an ever-changing game. What worked well one time may not the next. Shipping by sea, short of taking a bike as baggage, takes time and planning. Usually the bike must be crated or containerized, and then it must be forklift handled to the dock, and the process reversed at the other end. Docks are often inconveniently located. Rats can eat the plastic! Freighters may not be on an exact schedule, so time at both ends is required.

So air freight is almost always the choice. On some airlines, bikes must be crated to be flown. It is fun to get off the airplane in Europe, go around to the freight terminal, go through customs, and ride away from the airport. Agents for carriers are hungry for business, and are willing to talk both price and crating. Sometimes containers can hold several bikes for the price of one. Prices are related to cubic space needed.

The airline and agent that worked wonders one time may not the next. Call a variety of airline freight agents. One of them may be a biker. If you're planning on bringing the bike back to the U.S., arrange both ways at the same time.

Michael Mandell in New York and Warren Motorcycle Transport in Florida specialize in arranging the shipping of motorcycles by air.

Mandell; 800 245-8726

Warren; 800 443-7519

To get your bike out of customs in Europe, you will need proof of European insurance (see "Good Stuff to Know"), and the customs agent will want to be assured that the bike is just passing through, not being imported. If the bike is legal in America, then it's legal for an American to operate it on holiday in Europe.

If the bike is ever sold to a European, then it will have to be imported with all the taxes and inspections Europeans require.

KEEP A BIKE IN EUROPE

Sometimes it's harder to find a good air freight deal back from Europe to America. Many Americans are so hooked that they keep bikes in Europe from one holiday to the next. Some rent garages. Some leave them in bonded warehouses. Some leave bikes with cooperative dealers. Then the only problem is how to keep the thing registered in America, while avoiding permanently importing it to Europe.

An Organized Tour?

Most every road is better shared. It's possible to meet new lifelong motorcycle friends on an organized tour. Other smart, creative, attractive, motorcycle crazies like you. If time is limited, the tour folk will take care of the details and leave the riding to you. They just may have some good ideas about where to go and how to get there. And they've had practice helping if something should not go as planned.

Tours are a good bet for anyone with limited time and/or Euro-riding experience. You meet the nicest people . . . .

Recently, an American couple riding a very narrow and rarely traveled Italian pass (Vivione, Trip 37) sideswiped a protruding rock. It split the transmission housing. For anyone traveling independently, that might have been the end of the trip. Their next worry would have been how to get themselves and the busted bike down out of the boondocks. Then, how to get the bike fixed. Then what to do while it's getting fixed. In this case, the couple was on a Beach trip.

Many makes and styles of bikes are inclined to ride together in Europe. Explore the Alps with a tour group and you'll make lifelong friends (photo by Stacy Silverwood).

The Beach luggage van carries a cellphone. A phone call was made, the bike stashed beside the road, and the couple continued to the next hotel aboard other tour members' bikes. Later, after delivering all the luggage, the Beach van took off for the little pass and retrieved the bike. Next day, the couple continued their trip on a different bike.

Here are several tour operators who specialize in trips through the Alps. They'll even carry the hair dryer.

AYRES ADVENTURES
P.O. Box 864018
Plano, TX 75086-4018
United States
877 275-8238
www.ayresadventures.com

BEACH'S MOTORCYCLE ADVENTURES, LTD.
2763 West River Parkway
Grand Island, NY 14072-2053
United States
716 773-4960
www.bmca.com

BOSENBERG MOTORCYCLE EXCURSIONS
Mainzer Strasse 54
D-6550 Bad Kreuznach
Germany
49 671-67312
www.bosenberg.com

EDELWEISS BIKE TRAVEL
Steinreichweg 1
A-6414 Mieming
Austria
43 526-45690
US 800 877-2784
www.edelweissbiketravel.com

EUROPEAN ADVENTURES
2 The Circle, Bryn Newydd
Prestatyn, Clwyd LL19 9EU
Wales
44 745 85-3455
www.europeanadventures.co.uk

JED HALPERN'S S.A.P. TOUR
(Swiss Alps and Passes Tour)
Route du Simplon 35A; CH-1907 Saxon
Switzerland
41 79 225-1988
www.saptour.com

MHS MOTORRADTOUREN GMBH
Donnersbergerstrasse 32
D-80634 Munich
Germany
49 89 168-4888

MUENCHNER FREIHEIT
Postfach 44 01 48
D-8000 Munich 44
Germany
49 89 39-5768
www.muenchnerfreiheit.de

TEAM AVENTURA
Karlsebene 2
D-8924 Steingaden
Germany
49 8 862-6161
www.teamaventura.ch

VON THIELMANN TOURS
P.O. Box 87764
San Diego, CA 92138
United States
619 463-7788 or 619 234-1558
vonthielmanntour@cs.com

WORLD MOTORCYCLE TOURS
7106 NW 108th Avenue
Tamarac, FL 33321
800 443-7519 or 954 726-0494
bikeship@icanect.net

AD-MO-TOURS
Box 1803
Wrightwood, CA 92397
800 944 2356
www.admo-tours.com

Glossary

aiguille French word for needle, applied especially to peaks in the Mt. Blanc massif, as Aiguille du Midi

albergo Italian word for inn or small hotel

Allemagne The French word for Germany

Alpenglow The almost flourescent pink glow of snow covered peaks at sunrise and sunset.

Alpenstrasse German, a road in the Alps, plural is Alpenstrassen

Alpinist A mountain climber in the Alps; alpinist is a mountain climber in general

Alpinitis A Hermannism meaning infected by the Alps

alt, alte German word for old

aperto Italian word for open

Apfel German word for apple

aubergine French word for eggplant

Ausfahrt German word for freeway exit (a pedestrian exit is ausgang)

Ausstellung German word for exhibition

Autobahn German word for freeway; plural is autobahnen

Autoroute French word for freeway

Autostrada Italian word for freeway, plural is autostrade

aux French preposition, "to the;" hotel Aux Mille Etoiles, Les Marecottes (CH)

bain French word for bath

basilica A special name for a large church; not a cathedral

Bayern German word for Bavaria

Bayrisch Adj. German word for Bavarian

bei German word, preposition for at or near; Trimbach bei Olten

Berghaus German for house on a mountain; Berghaus Gurnigel (CH)

Bergstrasse German for mountain road; Bergstrasse Ferrenau (A)

Berner German word for Bernese, adjective of Bern (CH)

Bernese Adjective & noun pertaining to Bern

besonder German word for special

bis German word, preposition, until

bleu French word for blue

bolognese Italian adjective for the town Bologna, often applied to a meat sauce on pasta

bourg French word for village

Brot German word for bread

Brucke German word for bridge

Bundesstrasse German for federal road, i.e., not a freeway

cambio Italian word for change, exchange

campanile Bell tower

cannelloni A kind of pasta

cappuccino Italian coffee with steamed milk

carne Italian word for meat, flesh

centro Italian word for center, downtown

certosa Italian word for charterhouse; Hotel Certosa (I) near Merano, called Karthaus in German

chiuso Italian word for closed, shut, locked

cognoscente A connoisseur, one in the know

col French word for pass, as a mountain pass

corso Italian word for course, large street; *in corso* is Italian for in progress

creme de la creme The very choicest

Cyrillic Slavic alphabet, Russian

Danemark German word for Denmark; Coupe Danemark, hot fudge sundae

del Italian "of the" masculine before a consonant

della Italian "of the" feminine before consonant, singular

demi French word for half

der German word for article "the," masculine

des French preposition, "of the"

Deutsch German word for German; adjective, requires declension; Deutsche Alpenstrasse

Deutschland (D) German word for Germany

deviazione Italian word for detour

di Italian word, preposition "of," "by," "with"

d' French preposition, "of," before a vowel

Dolomiten German word for Dolomites

Dolomiti Italian word for Dolomites

Dorf German word for village

drei German word for three

Edelweiss German name for Alpine flower

einfach German word for simple

Eisenbahn German word for railroad; name of a restaurant known as motor-cycle meeting place (CH)

Eisenwaren German word for hardware

Eis German word for ice, also ice cream

entrecot French for sirloin steak

etoile French word for star, plural is etoiles

Euro Prefix for European

Fahrrad German word for bicycle

ferme French word for closed

formaggio Italian word for cheese; often Parmesan

forno Italian word for furnace, oven; al forno means baked

franc French and Swiss unit of money

frei German word for free, vacant; Zimmer Frei, room for rent

Furstentum German word for principality; Furstentum Liechtenstein (FL)

Furst German word for prince

Gasthaus German word for inn

Gasthof German word for inn

gelateria Italian word for ice cream parlor

gelato Italian word for ice cream

gemutlich German word for comfortable

Gemutlichkeit German word for coziness

Germania Italian name for Germany

glace French word for ice, ice cream

grosse German adjective, big

Hauser German word for houses, plural of Haus

haut, haute French adjective for high

Heidi German woman's name; fictional Alpine story for children

heiss German word for hot

Hochalpenstrasse German for high Alpine road

Hochberghaus German for high mountain house

hoch German word for high

Hof German word for court, courtyard, yard, as in Gasthof

Hohe German word for height

Hohenstrasse German for high road

Hutte German word for hut, a mountain refuge

insalata Italian word for salad

Italia (I) Italian word for Italy

Joch German word for yoke, often applied to a pass

joli French word for pretty

Kaiser Schmarrn Sweet Austrian dessert

Kalte German word for cold (coldness)

Kaserne German word for barracks

Kirche German word for church

Konige German word for kings

Konigschloss German word for royal castle, palace

Kurort German word for health resort, also see Aflenz Kurort

lac French word for lake

lago Italian word for lake

lavoro Italian word for work, labor

le, les French word for "the," singular and plural

linguini Pasta

magno Italian word for great; see Campo Carlo Magno

malhereusement French word for unhappily

marmottes Mountain animal; Les Marmottes, a restaurant in La Thuile (I)

massif A principle mountain

militaire French word for military; see Route Militaire

mille French word for thousand, see Les Mille Etoiles

Mitte German word for middle, center, Stadtmitte means downtown

Montessori Italian educator

Motorrad German word for motorcycle; German motorcycle bi-monthly; plural is Motorrader

Moto Sport Schweiz Swiss motorcycle weekly

Munchs German motorcycle brand

Nasse German word for wet

nazionale Italian word for national

neu German word for new

Novembre Italian for November

ober German word for upper

Osterreich German name for Austria

ost German word for east

ouvert French word for open

parco Italian word for park

parmesan Italian variety of cheese

passo Italian word for pass

Perrier Bottled water from France

Pinzgau Region (A) South of Salzburg

pomodoro Italian word for tomato

ponte Italian word for bridge

pre Prefix denoting priority

Prix French word for prize

Puch Austrian motorcycle

Rader Plural of Rad, German word for wheel

rifugio Italian mountain refuge

ristorante Italian word for restaurant

Rivella A bottled soft drink in Switzerland

Romansch The language of Graubunden (CH)

sacrario Italian word for sanctuary, cemetery

Sattel German word for saddle or pass

Schlucht German word for gorge

Schweinshax'n Typical Austrian and Bavarian cut of pork

Schweiz German word for Switzerland

See German word for lake

Semmelknodel An Austrian and Bavarian dumpling

Sinalco Soft drink in Switzerland

Sonne German word for sun

Spezi Soft drink in Austria and Bavaria

Spitze German word for top, tip, point; Edelweiss Spitze

Stadt German word for city

Stau See German word for reservoir created by a dam

Stau German word for traffic jam

Strasse German word for road or street

sud German word for south

Suisse French name for Switzerland

Svizzera Italian name for Switzerland

Tal German word for valley

telepherique French word for cable car

terme Italian word for hot spring

Tiroler German for pertaining to Tirol

Toffel Strudel An Austrian dessert

Toffler Swiss German for motorcyclist

Toff Swiss German word for motorcycle

Tofftreffpunkt Swiss German for a motorcycle meeting place

Tor German word for gate

toutes French word for all; toutes directions means all directions

trattoria An Italian word for restaurant

tre Italian word for three

Uberwachung German word for oversee, supervise; Besonder Uberwachung
  means special supervision

Umleitung German word for detour

und German word for and

val Italian, short for valle (valley)

valle Italian for valley

Verkehrsburo German for travel bureau

Versicherung German word for insurance

viale Italian word for avenue

vietato Italian word for forbidden

vorder German word for front

vous French word for you

vue French word for view

Wald German word for forest

WC Common sign for toilet (Water Closet)

wechseln German word for change, exchange

weiss German word for white

Wienerschnitzel Cutlet (meat) Viennese style

Wurst German word for sausage

Zimmer German word for room; Zimmer Frei means room for rent

Index

About the Author

John Hermann bought his first bike in 1960. He's had a couple of other brands and eighteen BMWs. Three of the eighteen are still in the garage. In 2006, he received a trophy from BMW of North America, recognizing his million miles on BMWs. About a third of those million miles have been in Europe, mostly in the Alps.

In the 1960s, he made a couple of car trips in the Alps that persuaded him that Alpine roads were for biking. So in 1970, he took delivery of a new BMW in Munich, only to discover that Alpine roads required more skills and planning than he'd anticipated. So he tried it with Beach's Motorcycle Adventures in 1975, and was hooked. Even though he rode the new R90S from dawn to dark, he couldn't cover all the roads he had planned. The riders he met with Beach's became life time friends, and many came back to ride the Alps together year after year.

Most years since that 1975 adventure, he has been back twice a year, riding into every nook and cranny of the Alps as well as exploring roads in other parts of Europe. He found the riding and motorcycle culture that exists in Europe and especially in the Alps intoxicating.

It's never too cold for a Coupe Danemark atop Edelweiss Spitze, Grossglockner.

It gets better each time, as the roads and the views and the local food and fun hotels and people become increasingly familiar. Always, he's been lucky enough to share these wonders with like-minded friends.

About fifteen years ago, he noted a story in a German magazine about Corsica. So he and his friends checked it out, and found it exotically beautiful, full of mountains and motorcycle roads. Then it was the Pyrenees, and on out to the Picos on the north coast of Spain. Hence, their inclusion in this book.

Home is a couple of blocks from the Pacific Ocean in Coronado, California, with nearby mountains and canyons for year-round riding. Coronado's sort of an island just 18 miles from Mexico and a bridge away from San Diego.

Hermann is member number 13 of BMWMOA and BMWRA. In 2001, he was designated a "Friend of the Marque" by BMW. He's a founding member of his local BMW club. He's been known to surf and snorkel and play the piano, and for 18 years he sang with the San Diego Opera (always commuting to re-hearsals and performances by bike). The opera company once designated him an "Outstanding Resident Artist."

He's been trustee of his church in San Diego and of Meals on Wheels of Greater San Diego. Twice he's participated in the riding school at the Nurburgring in Germany. In California, he's been to riding schools at Willow Springs and Laguna Seca.

One of his greatest pleasures in recent years has been this book. "How lucky can you get," he asks, "getting to check all those wonderful roads with good friends, then getting to write about them for more good friends.?"